THE FILMS OF
DAVID
LYNCH

JOHN ALEXANDER

CHARLES LETTS · *Letts* of London® · FOUNDED 1796

First published in 1993
by Charles Letts & Co. Limited
Letts of London House,
Parkgate Road,
London SW11 4NQ

Text copyright © John Alexander 1993
Illustrations: Magritte, p.x © Boymans van Beuningen,
Netherlands; Dune, p. 74
© Universal Pictures; The Elephant Man, p.56 © Movie
Acquisition Corporation Organisation, Pinewood Studios; Blue
Velvet, p. 90 and front cover © Dino de Laurentiis
Communications

ISBN 1 85238 360 7

A CIP catalogue record for this book is available from the
British Library

Printed and bound in Great Britain

Cover photograph: Blue Velvet, Isabella Rossellini

Contents

Acknowledgements

Thanks to Maria Ekenhed, Penny Simpson, Isabel Sturrup, Cortina Butler, Marie-Louise Rinman, Henrik Orrje, Lennart Warring, Louise O'Konor and Anne Jerslev. Thanks to David Lynch for the films.

Note

With the exception of *Eraserhead*, David Lynch's feature films have been shot in Panavision (2.35:1 ratio). Television and video screenings have been reduced to the 1.33:1 ratio, which means that the viewer sees just over half of the intended film. Special wide-screen VHS-video editions of *Blue Velvet* and *Wild at Heart* have been released in the UK, supplementary to the standard 1.33:1 issue. *Wild at Heart* is a case in point, as the wide-screen format is composed to the advantage of the convertible front-seat shots, the motel bedroom shots and the open highway shots. The 1.33 issue 'pan and scan' makes these carefully-considered compositions redundant. Similarly, *Blue Velvet*, *Dune* and *The Elephant Man* contain much side-line detail which disappears in the standard VHS-video releases or television screenings.

Introduction

Dark Romances

The film credits of *Eraserhead* describe her as 'the beautiful girl across the hall'. In the middle of the night she knocks on the door of Henry Spencer. She has come to seduce him. She and Henry embrace on top of the bed which dominates Henry's dark, claustrophobic room. Together they sink slowly into a pool of liquid in the middle of the mattress and disappear. Her black hair floats on the surface of the white pool.

In *Blue Velvet* a young man watches a woman disrobe from behind the jalousied wardrobe door. She discovers him and forces him to have sex with her at knife point, cutting his cheek open with the point of the blade.

In the Lynch world desire induces suffering; pleasure releases demons of the spirit from which there is no respite. Lula in *Wild at Heart*, Laura in *Twin Peaks*, Dorothy in *Blue Velvet*, fall victim to sexual psychopaths and must pay a fearful price. John Merrick, the deformed 'elephant man', experiences a moment of tenderness with a kindly actress, but is also humiliated by a twisted soul who initiates him into the shadow side of love, perverse desire. For Lynch desire is the key which unlocks a door into the darker regions of the human spirit.

Fear has many guises in the Lynch film – the psychopath, sexuality, chaos, disorder, even the body itself, instil fear, contrasted with an idyll of the contented family and the harmony of a small town.

'In a large city I realised there was a large amount of fear. Coming from the Northwest, it kind of hits you like a train,' says Lynch.[1]

Otherwise, he claims, his childhood was like a 1950s magazine advertisement with a 'well-dressed woman bringing a pie out of the oven... a couple smiling, walking together up to their house with a picket fence.' 'We are children of the city,' said French director

Jean-Jacques Beneix describing the new wave of filmmakers of the 1980s. Lynch 'is a small-town American boy'.[2]

Lynch says his films both reveal and hide his fears, but he avoids self-analysis and intellectualising. 'It's better not to know so much, in a way, about what things mean or how they might be interpreted, or you'll be too afraid to let it keep happening.'

Psychology, says Lynch, 'destroys the mystery, this kind of magical quality. It can be reduced to certain neuroses or certain things, and since it is now named and defined, it's lost its mystery and the potential for a vast, infinite experience.'[3]

The overhanging threat in the Lynch world is loss of control, upheaval, chaos. The 'worst possible' scenarios of David Lynch describe the hapless protagonist at the mercy of forces he is powerless to contain or resist. Henry Spencer in *Eraserhead* is left with a deformed monstrosity that holds him captive in his own room. John Merrick (*The Elephant Man*) swoons away at Victoria station. Having endured a lifetime of brutal subjugation, he is suddenly without Master. Fate abandons him, then delivers him into the benign hands of Dr Treves.

In *Dune*, the seemingly all-powerful House of Atreides collapses overnight as a result of a single act of betrayal. In *Blue Velvet*, Jeffrey shrewdly manipulates his investigations into a secret and hidden world, finally to stand powerless before a man without conscience. Lula (*Wild at Heart*) careers down a make-believe yellow brick road, but Sailor Ripley is steered from one predicament to another with the hapless disarray of Hans Christian Andersen's *Little Tin Soldier*.

The 'wounded hero' of Lynch's world is the victim of events determined by a perversely macabre fate. Lynch's stories are tales of initiation, where 'innocents' traverse darkness to emerge on the other side, traumatised, purged and, finally, absolved.

For the viewer, the Lynch film is similarly an initiatory experience, exposed to his taste for crime, his erotic obsessions, his savagery 'on a level not counterfeit and illusory, but interior.'[4]

Influences

David Lynch was born in Missoula, Montana in 1946, where his father worked as a research scientist for the Department of Agriculture. He grew up in Idaho, Washington State and Virginia. He shared a studio with

Jack Fisk (who would become a cinema art director) in his high school days, and studied painting at the Corcoran School of Art in Washington DC.

After a year at the Boston Museum School he left for a three-year trip to Europe, but returned after fifteen days. 'I didn't take to Europe. I was all the time thinking, this is where I'm going to be painting. And there was no inspiration there at all for the kind of work I wanted to do.'[5] He returned to the US and took up jobs at an art store and frame shop before entering the Pennsylvania Academy of Fine Arts in Philadelphia in 1965.

Inspired by such painters as Francis Bacon and Edward Hopper, Lynch graduated two years later with a collection of large dark paintings, which 'needed just to move a little bit'.[6] He completed his first film, a one-minute long animated tape loop which was entered in a contest for experimental painting and sculpture at the Academy. 'Not so much a film as a moving painting, a loop which could repeat itself endlessly... the figures caught fire, got headaches, their bodies and stomachs grew, and they all got sick.'[7] The six figures of the film consisted of three sculptured surfaces based on plaster-casts of Lynch's head (executed by art college colleague Jack Fisk) and three animated film figures. Their movements were accompanied by the sound of a wailing siren.

A wealthy patron, H. Barton Wasserman, financed Lynch's next project which would be a similar combination of animation on a repeating loop with a sculptured screen. The film was ruined but Lynch had sufficient funds to finance The Alphabet, completed in 1968, a four-minute long film combining animation and live action. He used a similar combination of techniques to make The Grandmother (1970) which was financed by the American Film Institute.

Lynch worked at a variety of jobs while filming his first feature film, Eraserhead, which was completed in 1976. Its foreboding and surrealistic quality attracted discriminating audiences of the art house circuit, and finally the attention of commercial cinema. With the support of Mel Brooks he made The Elephant Man (1980) based on accounts recording the life of the deformed Joseph Merrick in London in the late 1800s. Dune, one of the largest science fiction film projects undertaken, with a budget of $45 million, was completed by Lynch in 1984 – a critical and commercial fiasco. He made Blue Velvet in 1986 and Wild at Heart, which won the Cannes Film Festival Palme d'Or, in 1990.

David Lynch became a household name when the television series *Twin Peaks* was screened throughout the world in 1990 and 1991. His most recent film, *Twin Peaks: Fire Walk With Me*, was released in 1992.

He photographs, paints, makes commercials and videos, produces records, composes song lyrics, writes *The Angriest Dog in the World* comic strip for *The LA Reader*, and produces television programmes together with Mark Frost, the most recent of which is the TV situation comedy, *On The Air*, a parody of old radio shows based on the ficticious 'Lester Guy Show', set in the USA, 1957.

Unlike many of his contemporaries amongst the American new wave of filmmakers, David Lynch is not a director who has climbed up through the ranks of the commercial film industry, nor is he the film school graduate who perceives life in terms of what he's seen on a cinema screen – David Lynch is the art school student who made his paintings move.

Lynch's quirky visual style and apparent disregard for narrative makes him something of an anachronism in the mainstream of the commercial cinema. The preoccupation of the Hollywood cinema is story-telling, and since the silent films of D. W. Griffith and Cecil B. de Mille, the efficiently told narrative has been paramount in American film production. This has not always been the case in Europe where the avant-garde, expressionism and surrealism, have, in the wake of other art movements, rejected the 'iron script' and filmed pictures first and stories second.

David Lynch – art student and animator – does not share the same preoccupation with stories as such, with the conventions of a dilemma, an intrigue and its resolution. For Lynch narrative conventions are simply a means to an end, and the end is creating an atmosphere, a resonance, of 'making the phenomenon strange', whether that phenomenon is ordering coffee and pie in a small town diner, cockroaches in underwear, or watching a strangely dressed man mime a Roy Orbison song, while executing acts of incongruous violence.

Scorsese, Coppola, Woody Allen and others, make essentially American films, even outside the restrictive grip of the studio system, but often from the perspective of immigrant ethnic groups, and how they adapt to America. Lynch, a self-confessed 'all-American boy', uses quintessentially American settings and characters (there are no socially integrated foreigners in a Lynch film – not even on the Planet Arrakis), yet seen through a lens distorted by an outsider's perspective – the eye of the estranged artist.

Lynch's portrayals of America have more in common with the America filmed by Europeans such as Werner Herzog, Wim Wenders, John Schlesinger or Nicolas Roeg, than the America we see in the films of Martin Scorsese, Francis Coppola, Steven Spielberg, Oliver Stone et al. *The Elephant Man*, filmed in Great Britain, is a triumph of authenticity – Lynch has succeeded in creating a world, not only credible, but it seems, a world in which he is 'at home'. Alternatively, never has America looked so foreign, so strange, sinister and exotic, as in his first feature film, *Eraserhead*.

Aside from Lynch's personal influences – a childhood in the Northwest, life in Philadelphia, and the entanglements of his personal relationships, his films reveal artistic influences ranging from the surrealists to the American Romantic movement and the *film noir* of the 1940s and 1950s.

Surrealism

A painting by René Magritte entitled *Réproduction Interdit* (1937) shows a man in a dark suit, with his back to the viewer, facing a mirror. The mirror also shows the man's back to the viewer, rather than reflecting his face. It is a paradoxical image, suggesting an inverted narcissism, of the kind with which Lynch's cinema is imbued. In films such as *Eraserhead* and *Blue Velvet*, Lynch shows himself, but only his back view, and always neatly dressed in a dark suit. Like Magritte, who walked daily to his nearby studio in suit and bowler hat, Lynch's methodical lifestyle extends to dress, and the strict control over the expression of artistic creativity. And like Magritte, his work is what the surrealists describe as 'a loosening of the horizon's belt through an increased fertility of the senses... the abandonment of accepted perspectives...'[8]

In a programme made for the BBC's *Arena* in 1987, Lynch presented what he described as, 'films made by some of the greatest artists this century – the surrealists. They discovered that the cinema was the perfect medium for them because it allows the subconscious to speak. If surrealism is the subconscious speaking... I could say I was somewhat surrealistic.'[9]

In the *Surrealist Manifesto* published in 1924, André Breton wrote:

> 'Surrealism is based on the belief in the superior reality of certain forms of association heretofore

neglected, in the omnipotence of the dream, and in the disinterested play of thought. It leads to the permanent destruction of all other psychic mechanisms and to its substitution for them in the solution of the principal problems of life...
'The mind of the dreaming man is fully satisfied with whatever happens to it. The agonising question of possibility does not arise. Kill, plunder, move quickly, love as much as you wish. And if you die, are you not sure of being roused from the dead? Let yourself be led. Events will not tolerate deferment. You have no name. Everything is inestimably easy.'

David Lynch, 'the Hieronymus Bosch of middle America', cites Jean Cocteau, Man Ray, Hans Richter and other surrealistic filmmakers as his mentors in the art of creating strange pictures. However, in an interview from 1990, he maintains: 'I still haven't seen a lot of Buñuel... I don't even know that much about surrealism. I guess it's just my take on what's floating by.'[10]

Lynch's 'take on what's floating by', like the surrealists, draws from dreams and the imagery of the subconscious. Not surprisingly his own favourite film sequences are either dream sequences, or have a dreamlike quality: the dancing dwarf sequence, ('the best piece of film I've ever made'), the opening sequence to *Blue Velvet*, the dream sequences in *The Elephant Man* and *Dune*; *Eraserhead*, one long dream sequence; and the flashback and fantasy sequences in *Wild at Heart*. *Twin Peaks: Fire Walk With Me* is redeemed by a dream sequence, which has the resonance and intrigue of a painting by René Magritte. Laura Palmer receives a photographic image of a room with an open door, from the young David Lynch lookalike. She places the picture on her bedroom wall and as she sleeps, walks into the image and through the open door. It leads into a labyrinth of corridors and curtains, and her dream swiftly becomes a nightmare, without the overt bravado and manipulative 'scare tactics' of, for example, Wes Craven's *Nightmare on Elm Street* (1984).

The dreamer structures the random imagery of the dream into a kind of narrative; similarly, the viewer structures the images of a film, if order doesn't exist, into a cognisant form. Structure provides the possibility of comprehending a meaning. 'Meanings,' wrote Carl Jung, 'make things bearable.'

American Gothic

As well as the man's back, reflected in the mirror in Magritte's *Reproduction Interdit* there is a copy of Edgar Allan Poe's *The Adventures of Arthur Gordon Pym*. The story concerns a young man who endures a series of terrifying experiences, and thereby undergoes an initiation – a descent into hell from which he emerges transformed.[11] It is the theme which pervades Lynch's films.

Just as the British horror film draws from the tradition of English Gothic literature,[12] there is a parallel between the films of David Lynch and the Romantic movement of American literature.

The surrealists, and André Breton in particular, generally spurned the novel as a form, yet singled out the English Gothic novelists (as well as, understandably, the writings of Lewis Carroll and Edward Lear) for praise. It can be argued that the Gothic novel, like the Lynch film, is more concerned with atmosphere and mood, than the conventions of narrative structure.

The Gothic movement of the late eighteenth century heralded 'a new preoccupation with death, solitude and the visual/emotional appeal of ruins...'[13]

The Gothic novels, which preceded these writers by a century, have been a constant source of inspiration to filmmakers – Shelley's *The Vampire*, Mary Wollstonecraft Shelley's *Frankenstein*, and later the work of the Irish writers, Bram Stoker and Sheridan le Fanu. Old houses and chateaus, social outsiders bearing dark secrets, unresolved intrigues, the decay and delapidation of antiquated structures, (social structures, architectural structures, psychological structures), identify the Gothic novel – night, cemeteries, winter, gloom, death and decay. Apparitions, giants, dwarves, hunchbacks and freaks have a place in the Gothic tradition.

These are elements notable in the literature of American Romanticism, and in particular in the writings of Edgar Allan Poe, Emily Dickinson, Whitman, Melville and Emerson.

The other element of Gothic and American Romanticism is that of the unattainable 'other'. In *American Romantic Psychology*, Martin Bickman writes: '...In the works of Edgar Allan Poe and Emily Dickinson, a figure of the opposite sex, surrounded by an aura of the mysterious and numinous, holds out the promise of harmonious unity, of initiation into the higher secrets, a promise usually accompanied, though, by the possibilities of dissolution and death.'[14]

The mid 1980s marked a period in which the US cinema delved into the murkier realms of the human condition, and not since the *film noir* period of the 1940s and 50s had so many commercial film releases contained the themes attributed to American Romanticism. In 1986, when *Blue Velvet* was released, came *Something Wild* (Jonathan Demme), *River's Edge* (Tim Hunter, later a director of several episodes of *Twin Peaks*), *Blood Simple* (Joel and Ethan Coen), and other films in which death, in the guise of the feminine, predominate.

Lynch's portrayal of the feminine, whether as the 'unobtainable other' or as a figure of death, has a correspondence in the writings of Poe, and the tradition in American literature in which Poe is a central figure. In addition, Lynch's films, like the stories of Edgar Allan Poe, reveal a fascination with the process of decay and corruption.

Underlying the Romantic movement is a yearning for the past and a nostalgia for past values. It is a yearning borne of anxieties over the impermanence of things; a deeply rooted mistrust of the present and contempt for the future; ambiguous hallmarks of Lynch's film world.

Film noir

Gothic elements are apparent in Lynch's earlier films: *Eraserhead* and *The Elephant Man,* and *Dune.* Dark corridors, gloomy hallways, and despondent women in black, framed in windows and doorways. The Caladan sequence of *Dune* depicts a raging sea, a stormy night, and a gloomy castle on a cliff-top, the Atreides household. The Duke's concubine, Jessica, walks through the wooden portals shrouded in a black cape, across a cobble-stoned courtyard. The Duke sits in his ill-lit study, a bulldog at his side, his features illuminated by intermittent flashes of lightning. The time and place pertain to another galaxy, but the mood is Victorian Gothic, from the pages of Bram Stoker, George MacDonald or the Reverend Maturino.

In *Blue Velvet* Lynch begins a disquieting journey into *noir* territory. *Blue Velvet* captures the mood of the small town *noir* films of the 1950s — *film noir* of the 1940s encapsulated the fears and anxieties of the big city — with the later *noir* films, nowhere was safe — the psychopath could be the next door neighbour, a friendly face on the local train (*Strangers on a Train*, 1951), the town's sheriff (*Touch of Evil*, 1958), a visiting preacher (*The Night of the Hunter*, 1955), or a forgotten face from the past (*Cape Fear*, 1962). It was an underlying fear that British director, Alfred Hitchcock, tuned into in his early years in the US, which found expression in *Shadow of a Doubt* (1943), where the 'favourite uncle' is revealed to be a psychopath.

The 1950s are a rich source of inspiration for Lynch; his contemporary films (not least *Twin Peaks*) are imbued with an idealised pastiche of a 50s 'look' – clothes, cars, roadhouse diners, and apron-dressed smiling women. The era is represented by a spate of Hollywood films, in both *film noir* and the increasingly popular science fiction film – expressing fear of infiltration. The threat could be communist (*Pickup on South Street*, 1953), alien (*Invasion of the Body Snatchers*, 1956), radioactive fallout (*The Incredible Shrinking Man*, 1957) or the vindictive woman, (*Born to be Bad,* 1950), any of which could threaten the ideal of the nuclear family.

Film noir describes a style rather than a genre – the kind of film that delves into the darker side of society and human nature. Hollywood *film noir* found its public in the 1940s and 50s, and *noir* elements can be found in films as diverse as Hitchcock's *Rebecca* (1940), Welles' *Citizen Kane* (1941) and Frank Capra's *It's a Wonderful Life* (1946) – *Blue Velvet* is its 'evil twin' according to *Time*'s film critic, Richard Corliss. Directors, many of them European exiles, integrated the visual style of German expressionism and the narrative style of the American 'hard-boiled' novel, creating a low-budget film form which contravened many of the accepted requirements of the Hollywood film.

The *noir* film embraces the 'black' side of the human condition – the destructive feminine, the *femme fatale*; the destructive masculine, the psychopath; and brooding melancholy. Carl Jung borrowed an alchemical term to describe the condition of depression and melancholy – the 'blackness' of the human spirit: *nigredo*. 'To slip into the blackness of the psyche is to regress from order to disorder, or from structuring into destructuring, or from adaptedness to unadaptedness,' writes Jungian analyst, John Weir Perry.[15]

In *Laura* (Otto Preminger, 1944), Mark McPherson is the unruffled, yet compassionate detective investigating the murder of the much-loved Laura. Just as *Twin Peaks* is dominated by the photographic portrait of Laura Palmer, the film *Laura* is dominated by a painting of the eponymous heroine. The detective finds her 'secret diary' and is finally compelled to reconcile the real life of the young woman with her flawless image.

Another near namesake, Laurie Palmer, is a beautiful girl beaten to death by a psychopathic killer in the Robert Wise film, *Born to Kill* (1947). The *Twin Peaks* television series is a catalogue of references to these and other *noir* films, integrating their plot lines into the series sub-plots: Walter Neff, an insurance agent (Fred MacMurray in *Double Indemnity*, 1944); James Hurley playing a naive Joe Gillis character to a Norma Desmond spider woman named Evelyn Marsh, with lines lifted from the pages of the *Sunset Boulevard* screenplay (Billy Wilder, 1950). Anna May Wong, in the 1933 Sherlock Holmes film, *A Study in Scarlet*, plays the part of Mrs Pyke, a beautiful Chinese woman, whose husband fakes his own death in order to wreak his revenge upon unsuspecting victims. Mrs Pyke, like Jocelyn Packard (Joan Chen) is, despite her innocent countenance, duplicitous and culpable, and goes towards her premature demise with calm fatalism.

Dorothy Vallens (Isabella Rossellini), *Blue Velvet*'s nightclub singer seductress with a secret past and a sentimental signature song, succeeds such legendary *noir* women as *Gilda* (Charles Vidor, 1946) and Kitty Collins (Ava Gardner in *The Killers* – Siodmak, 1946). In Lynch's debut feature film, *Eraserhead*, the character entitled 'the beautiful woman across the hall', appears as an alluring manifestation of the *femme fatale*, enticing Henry to the bed and drowning him in a pool of slime.

Perdita, in *Wild at Heart*, is a stylised Lily Carver figure from *Kiss Me Deadly* (1955), with the nonchalance and ready contempt of a Gloria Grahame character of the 1940s. As her name suggests, perdition, damnation and loss of soul are what she has in store for the film's protagonist, Sailor Ripley.

The cinema's *femme fatale* has precedents in Romantic literature and pre-Raphaelite art – in Keats' *La Belle Dame Sans Merci*, and the alluring and deadly maidens of J. W. Waterhouse paintings. She is a recurring figure in Lynch's films – 'fatale' to the men she allures, as she is ultimately to herself.

A David Lynch film

David Lynch and the dollar-motivated Hollywood movie can be seen as two different avenues of interest which, against all probability, have met up somewhere in the middle. *Blue Velvet* and *Wild at Heart* proved that original can be profitable.

Many of Lynch's films transgress the conventions of the Hollywood film, yet remain attuned to its commercial demands. Lynch's ironic use of cliché, his emphasis on motif, mood and texture as opposed to a lineal narrative, are also tendencies in, say, the films of Jim Jarmusch and the recent films of Woody Allen. But unlike these directors, Lynch's audience extends beyond the art-house cinema circuit. The commercial failure of *Dune* notwithstanding, Lynch's films, since and including *The Elephant Man*, have been marketed within the parameters of commercial mainstream cinema.

Eraserhead excluded, Lynch's films balance precariously between the popular and the elitist, treading the fine line of commercial appeal and art-house critical acceptance. Just as Hitchcock's films appeal to the broad general market (good stories well told) and, following the acclaim of the French *nouvelle vague*, the film 'literate' (innovative, experimental in extending the film medium into untried territory), the same broad generalisation can be made of Lynch. Like Hitchcock, he has also made the transition to media personality, in front of the camera as well as behind it. Lynch has appeared in most of his films, and created a plot-bearing character, for better or worse, in the *Twin Peaks* film and television series.

Unlike Hitchcock, Lynch is not associated with a particular genre. A Hitchcock film is synonymous with the thriller, and his few exceptions Hitchcock later considered errors of judgement. The Lynch catalogue, brief though it now may be, covers all genres, and the Lynch name is synonymous more with a particular style – namely, the bizarre – than a category.

Lynch is both representative of our post-modern times – a 'shopper' picking out medial images, narratives and characters from cultures popular and elitist; and a filmmaker adapting to the demands of the commercial cinema – where the innovative and the new is modified to the needs of the market.

Cliché

'Two clichés make us laugh but a hundred clichés move us,' wrote Umberto Eco, describing the cumulative effect of clichés in *Casablanca*.[16]

Commercial cinema employs clichés as recognisable signals to facilitate the correct understanding of a narrative. The familiarity of the cliché assists the viewer, making commonplace the untrodden territory of a new story, amplifying audience identification. Lynch's films, and in particular his self-penned personal films (*Eraserhead* and *Blue Velvet*), subvert and parody cliché. His films are a game with clichés, and just as Umberto Eco describes the cineastes who join in the game as they watch a film like *Casablanca*, cinema *aficionados* are likewise moved by the array of the familiar and the identifiable in the Lynch film. For the uninitiated, a Lynch film is accessible by virtue of the recognisable elements flourishing wildly within his visual landscapes. The unprecedented success of *Twin Peaks* as viable commercial television functions primarily on this level, 'because we sense dimly that the clichés are talking among themselves, celebrating a reunion... the extreme of banality allows us to catch a glimpse of the Sublime.'[17]

In *The Wake of the Imagination*, Richard Kearney describes 'A Critique of the Rule of Cliché' whereby 'postmodern society is increasingly portrayed as an artificial world woven together out of repeatable clichés and bereft of any real experience of historical praxis or coherence.'[18]

According to the contemporary French philosopher, Gilles Deleuze, clichés are 'floating and anonymous images which circulate in the external world, but also penetrate each person and constitute his internal world, so much so that each one of us possesses no more than the psychic clichés by means of which he thinks and feels, becoming himself a cliché amongst others in the world which surrounds him. Physical clichés of sight and sound and psychic clichés feed off each other. In order for people to survive such a world it is necessary that this miserable world has infiltrated into their innermost consciousness, so that inside is like the outside.'[19]

In several exchanges in *Blue Velvet*, Sandy and Jeffrey, fresh-faced innocents of middle suburbia, deliver the line 'life is strange'. Uttered once such a line would constitute a line of cliché dialogue – with each repetition the line becomes parody. Are Sandy and Jeffrey actually proclaiming that 'life is strange', or drawing attention to their characters as stereotypes that observe the banal and proclaim it 'strange'?

For just as 'cliché' is 'stereotype' – the duplication of an original – it is also, by implication, the duplication of an 'archetype'. Lynch's conscious manipulation of cliché, as we shall explore in the opposing elements of *Blue Velvet*, elevates the banal to the mythological.

Lynch describes *Wild at Heart* as 'a violent comedy'.

'Some scenes are a game with clichés,' he says. '*Wild at Heart* has a lot in common with B-film violence. I love these honest film-films which don't have any purpose other than being a film.'[20]

The games with cliché, in particular in *Wild at Heart* and *Twin Peaks*, exemplify Lynch's humour, if it can be called such, which in part may explain the failure of *Dune*. Lynch's fidelity to the literary source extended to its earnest, humour-free literary style – Frank Herbert's seriousness of purpose, appropriate within the context of the novel, proves a restrictive framework, unsuitable for Lynch's play with pastiche and cliché.

Lynch's humour is a combination of cynicism and naivety: the happy endings of *Wild at Heart* and *Blue Velvet* (even *Dune*) are so overstated as to caricature the traditional happy ending – they are derisive appendages of mock narrative closure.

The contrived 'happy ending' of *Wild at Heart* ('I couldn't buy the ending of the book,' says Lynch)[21] is at once complying with the mainstream cinema's convention of an ending most gratifying to the largest possible audience, but at the same time, a pastiche of such exaggerated proportion as to lack credibility. The happy ending is intrinsic to the nature of the popular film, and it is the cinema's 'happy ending' that has become the most potent cliché of all.

Literary purists object to Lynch's treatment of both *Wild at Heart* and *Dune*, where the 'happy ending' transgresses the supposed necessity of cinematic closure, by perverting a narrative convention as if either to ridicule such a convention, or at least parody it.

In *Blue Velvet*, once harmony has been restored, a robin sings on the branch of a tree outside a suburban home, in answer to Sandy's earlier wish that everything will be all right 'when the robins come back'. Closer examination reveals that the 'singing robin' is a mechanical device which the characters regard in wide-eyed delight, pretending that it's real. Is Lynch mocking the audience, the narrative convention of the 'happy ending', or simply revelling in the game of toying with clichés?

In the opening of the same film, the garishly red roses and yellow tulips against the perfect white of the picket fence and the vivid green of the freshly cut lawn, are a pastiche of the stereotypical attributes of suburban happiness, the banal made strange with intent. Lynch's extreme imagery signifies a dissatisfaction with the cinema's constant recourse to clichéd images. When, in the same opening sequence, a fireman on a passing fire-engine, looks directly to the camera, smiles and waves, the effect is comic, but are we meant to laugh? That beneath this suburban idyll, the forces of chaos are lying in wait, ready to engulf our smug self-satisfaction? Or is Lynch laughing at himself, that he is mockingly lured into his own pastiche image of the suburban American dream?

Motif

A motif is 'any significant repeated element in a film'.[22] Motif may be an object, a colour, a place, a person, a sound. A lighting pattern or camera angle may be 'motif' if it is repeated meaningfully throughout the narrative.

Lynch's first animated film (tentatively entitled 'Six Figures Get Sick'), is a ten-second loop accompanied by the sound of a wailing siren, which depicts stick figures vomiting, catching fire and burning up. Vomit and fire are two motifs in *Wild at Heart*. The flame motif in particular is interwoven throughout the narrative, subtly signifying shifts in the relationship between the principal characters, Sailor and Lula.

The film begins with the sound and image of a striking match, followed by an engulfing fire. This image recurs at key points in the narrative, ostensibly as a flashback to the death of Lula's father, but the image also represents the nature of the relationship between Sailor and Lula. Other more specific uses of the fire motif follow: Sailor lights up a single cigarette with a single match, proclaiming his individuality; on the drive to New Orleans Sailor and Lula light up – two matches, two cigarettes – a couple. As they lie together in a motel room the significance of the motif is clarified: apart from the symbolic value of the image (inflamed passion, burning love), a pertinent plot point is established with Lula's accompanying line of dialogue: 'Daddy poured kerosene over himself then LIT A MATCH.' She is mistaken, it transpires. 'Daddy' didn't light it. Following an intense round of lovemaking in the New Orleans hotel, a single match lighting a single shared cigarette is enough to suggest the culmination of unity. Their lovemaking prior to leaving New Orleans is followed by a succession of dissolves from a match to the flame, the road, lovemaking once more, and again the road. There is an intensity to this couple's flight unmatched by the profusion of the cinema's Bonnie and Clyde style of road journey. 'Maybe you got too close to a fire. Maybe you're gonna burn,' is Lula's mother's warning that keeps coming back to Sailor.

Lula and Sailor betray each other – they sell out to Bobby Peru; Lula by responding to his sexual advances, Sailor by agreeing to a planned hold-up. He lies on the motel bed and lights a single cigarette with a single match. They both nurse their secrets, they both nurse their guilt – there is no contact, no 'fire' between them. Only a close-up of an extinguished cigarette and its ashen remains. No passion.

Reference to *The Wizard of Oz* is another underlying motif in the film. Lula plays Dorothy and Lula's mother, Marietta, appears as the Wicked Witch of the East. The Good Witch, Glinda, appears 'deus ex machina' to redeem Sailor in his moment of despondency.

A tube of bright red lipstick helps define Marietta's descent into madness, beginning with her intense red mouth, then, at intervals throughout the story, her red wrist, red mirror, and finally, her entire face painted in garish red lipstick.

David Lynch's films abound with aural motifs: the industrial sounds accompanying images of steam and vapour in *The Elephant Man*; the striking match in *Wild at Heart*, a splashing drop of water in *Dune*, the wurlitzer music in *Eraserhead*, the title song in *Blue Velvet*.

Lynch's collaboration with sound technician Alan Splet began with *The Grandmother*, and between them they have created some of the most imaginative soundtracks in contemporary American cinema. Lynch's predeliction for the sounds of industry creates a relentless narrative drive in both *Eraserhead* and *The Elephant Man*, creating an atmosphere of alienation. Combined with the mood and imagery of the film, the grinding noise of machinery evokes the human spirit estranged in a fabricated environment – a sense of not belonging.

Likewise, the song as motif, an established narrative component in the American *film noir* of the 1940s, features in *Eraserhead, Twin Peaks*, and serves as a foundation in both *Blue Velvet* (named after the song), and *Wild at Heart*, where Sailor's shift of feeling is defined by his singing Elvis Presley's 'Love Me' at the outset, imbued with sexual inuendo and self-depreciation, and concluding with a pledge to conjugal unity, 'Love Me Tender'.

In addition to these specific motifs, there are certain themes which recur in many of Lynch's films. The elements to which Lynch persistently returns provide a key to understanding the esoteric themes his films embrace.

The Lynchian protagonist is a social outsider striving for acceptance against impossible odds; characters with little or no control over their fate – Henry Spencer (John Nance in *Eraserhead*), stuck with a monstrously deformed infant and isolated within an industrial landscape, a machine operator who dresses in a suit and tie; John Merrick (John Hurt in *The Elephant Man*) who, in spite of his deformity, wants only to dress up in a suit and tie and sleep 'like a normal person'; even Paul Atreides (Kyle MacLachlan in *Dune*), who has perfect control over his body and mind, becomes a prisoner of his own myth; Jeffrey Beaumont (Kyle MacLachlan in *Blue Velvet*) transgresses the unwritten laws of suburban conformity and enters a netherworld of violence and sexuality over which he has no control, and does not even comprehend; Sailor Ripley's (Nicolas Cage in *Wild at Heart*) search for a normal life is constantly thwarted by 'Moira', the goddess of fate and, according to the Greeks, the oldest power in the universe, at her most vindictive in the form of Lula's mother. Dale Cooper (Kyle MacLachlan in *Twin Peaks*) is the archetypal Lynch protagonist – a fresh-faced innocent in a dark suit and dark tie, the bearer of dark secrets, estranged from yet enamoured of an alien environment, and pitted against the forces of destiny. It's hardly surprising that the same face should represent intrinsically the same character; Arrakis, Lumberton, Twin Peaks are different geographies within the same space of the Lynchian universe in which the displaced seeker discovers that knowledge is a dangerous thing.

Lynch's antagonists are most often psychopaths: 'I think it's the scariest thing,' says Lynch, 'to know someone, or suspect someone, that has a very intelligent mind – really nothing is wrong with them in any way – but who is possessed by evil and who has dedicated themselves to doing evil.'[23]

John Merrick's tormentor, Bytes (Freddie Jones in *The Elephant Man*) is a character fabricated by Lynch, and developed further in *Dune*; the Baron Vladimir Harkonnen is far removed from author Frank Herbert's character. In his Lynchian guise the Baron is a bloated psychopath, bereft of the political cunning of the novel's character, so grossly overweight that an anti-gravity mechanism is necessary for his mobility, so enamoured with his own pustulant flesh that his physician admires and embellishes his festering boils rather than attempting to cure them, and so exaggerated his homosexual appetites that the sexual abuse of young boys culminates in the Baron's cannibalising of them.

The psychopathy of Frank Booth (Dennis Hopper in *Blue Velvet*) is rather more complex. Whereas Bytes wants his 'treasure', Merrick, and the Baron wants the treasure of Dune, the spice, it is never entirely clear what Frank Booth wants. Is it sexual gratification with Dorothy Vallens? Gratification through drugs, money, power? Similar questions can be asked of the characters in *Wild at Heart* – Santos and Bobby Peru, and in particular of 'Bob' – the wandering evil spirit seeking souls to possess amongst the inhabitants of Twin Peaks. Lynch provides no answers as to the motives of such characters: 'I've never exactly figured out what the fascination is – but I think we want to understand it, so we can conquer it,' he says.[24]

The homosexuality in the Lynch antagonist, whether overt or latent, is just one more facet of the threat these characters pose to family structure and the established social order.

Lynch's maternal characters are either nurturing or destructive, manifestations of the archetype Jung terms 'the Great Mother' (also the term used by Frank Herbert in *Dune* as the principal deity of the Bene Gesserit). *Eraserhead, The Elephant Man, Dune, Blue Velvet* and *Twin Peaks* either begin or end with a close-up of a woman's face, smiling compassionately.

Manifestations of the nurturing mother include Mrs Kendal, John Merrick's mother in *The Elephant Man*, and Irulan and Jessica in *Dune* – both these films begin with a woman's face superimposed against the cosmos.

'On the negative side,' writes Carl Jung, 'the mother archetype may connote anything secret, hidden, dark; the abyss, the world of the dead, anything that devours, seduces and poisons, that is terrifying and inescapable like fate.'[25] Mary X's mother in *Eraserhead*, and Lula's mother in *Wild at Heart*, attempt to seduce their daughter's boyfriend – in both films they unleash their wrath upon the unsuspecting protagonist – Henry is left holding the 'baby'; Sailor has psychopathic killers on his trail. The Reverend Mother Gaius Helen Mohiam in *Dune* both seduces and torments Paul Atreides with the role of 'messiah'. She is as much 'Moira', the feminine embodiment of fate, to Paul as Lula's mother is to Sailor.

Lynch's other feminine archetype is the victim: Dorothy Vallens in *Blue Velvet*; Laura Palmer, Ronette Pulaski, Teresa Banks and many young women besides in both the television and cinema versions of *Twin Peaks*; even Lula in *Wild at Heart* becomes a victim of her own sensuality, loathsomely seduced by the psychotic Bobby

Peru, and raped by an uncle at the age of fourteen.

Relatively uncomplicated women seem to hold little interest for Lynch – the character of Chani in *Dune*, a pivotal figure of the novel, is glanced over briskly in the film, and Sandy in *Blue Velvet* functions primarily as the 'blonde' contrast to the 'dark' Dorothy.

Among the many 'object' motifs in Lynch's films, as distinct from characters, one in particular warrants consideration, the velvet curtain. *Eraserhead*'s 'lady in the radiator' appears from and retreats into a velvet stage curtain. At the end of her song she disappears into darkness leaving a bewildered Henry standing on an empty stage staring blankly at the velvet curtain. The curtain is a significant plot device in *The Elephant Man* – not velvet, but a drape concealing the deformed body of John Merrick, through which his silhouette is visible. The drape is a veil, the final stage before Merrick is disrobed entirely, when he is revealed in the plain light of day, both for an attending day nurse and the viewer.

As the title of the film suggests, the velvet curtain motif is replete with meanings in *Blue Velvet*, which begins with the image of drifting blue velvet curtains. The 'blue lady' sings a song entitled 'Blue Velvet' in front of a blue velvet curtain, dressed in a blue velvet dress. The opening credits come up in front of a gently billowing stage curtain which suggests matters undisclosed – things hidden, dark secrets. The psychopathic Frank Booth clutches at a piece of blue velvet material from Dorothy Vallens' dress, weeps into it as she sings, clutches at it and, later, sobs wildly into it as he violates her.

In *Wild at Heart*, a parody of the 'blue lady' character, an earthy negress in a blue sequin dress sings 'Up in Flames' (lyrics by David Lynch) in front of blue velvet curtains for the psychopathic Santos and his cohorts. Before the film's culminating sequence, a screen title declaring the time passed before Sailor's release from prison, is shown over the gold-framed photograph of a smiling young Lula in front of a red velvet curtain. A gold-framed photograph of a smiling young girl is in itself a motif subject to further scrutiny – velvet drapes permeate Lynch's films like stage curtains before a performance.

Perhaps the most significant of all the velvet curtain motifs is that in *Twin Peaks*, where red velvet drapes form a labyrinth in which all manner of secrets, psychopaths, dreams and nightmares are both hidden and revealed. The surging red material forms channels of an anonymous mind, like ventricles of the brain, leading us into unknown areas of a dark and sinister imagination.

Plot

The Hollywood cinema favours the story-teller, so Lynch's presence in the commercial mainstream is slightly incongruous. Lynch's originality owes more to the way he tells stories, rather than the stories he tells. He is a visualist first, and story-teller second.

His two original feature film screenplays, *Eraserhead* and *Blue Velvet*, revel in mood and atmosphere; his screenplay adaptations (self-penned, or in collaboration) reveal a reliance bordering on the naive on the plot structure of his source material. *Wild at Heart*, 'film-film' notwithstanding, is benignly faithful to the plot structure of Barry Gifford's novel, down to the seemingly Lynchian lines of dialogue, with the notable exception of the ending.

Lynch's attempt at a faithful adaptation of *Dune* proved a burden too great for the limitations of film screenplay conventions, its literary style imposing uneasy restrictions upon Lynch's cinematic excesses. *Wild at Heart* reads like a filmscript; *Dune*, like so much of literary science fiction, lends itself to film interpretation rather than adaptation.

Lynch's priorities, he affirms, are atmosphere and mood. Plot points and narrative structure are impositions to meet the demands of the commercial cinema. Lynch uses story lines as vehicles around which to structure particular moods and themes. Fear pervades the Lynch film, born of character types capable of the most perverse and inexplicable acts of violence. The uneasy mood of the Lynch film is accentuated by the corruption of the human body, the discordant balance between opposites, and perverse sexuality. Sex and violence in Lynch's films border on the obscene, but are not pornographic – the obscenity relates to the limits of degradation to which the human spirit can succumb. For the viewer, the question is not about titillation or arousal, but about the means by which we can extricate ourselves from the depravity projected before us.

The Hollywood film aims to deliver a narrative as efficiently and economically as the film medium allows (through script, camera, editing, sound). Lynch uses isolated sequences within the narrative which have no direct bearing on plot development, disrupting the syntactic flow with casual abandon, but which form integral narrative segments.

The car accident in *Wild at Heart* disrupts Sailor's and Lula's hitherto uneventful journey, and serves as a premonition of the dark sequence of events to follow. In itself, the episode seems bizarre and out of context. A car wreck, several bodies, and a young girl who dies of visually explicit head injuries, doesn't relate to Sailor and Lula's 'story', but suggests a mood. The film assumes a darker tone after the incident, and prepares us for a later false lead. In the final sequence, when Lula drives to meet Sailor, she encounters a similar meaningless and bloody road accident – like a harbinger of doom and their fateful meeting.

Gilles Deleuze suggests the characteristics of the new cinema include: 'the dispersive situation, the deliberately weak links, the voyage form, the consciousness of clichés, the condemnation of the plot. It is the crisis of both the action-image and the American Dream.'[26]

Eraserhead 'is not a true narrative, but an intense mood piece,' wrote one critic. 'It defies a coherent plot description, in fact, it defies description of any kind,' wrote another.[27]

Eraserhead's absurd scenarios of man-made chickens oozing putrescent liquid; a deformed lady from behind the radiator, singing, dancing and crushing umbilical cords with her shoes; brain substance transmuted into rubber for the tips of pencils, collude to torment a central character who is left holding a mutated infant.

Plot disparity is less extreme in other films, but Lynch's cinema is at its most provocative with the absurdist scenarios that enhance the mood of a narrative, without relating directly to it. The ill-lit face miming 'In Dreams', a severed ear in a field, warring ants beneath a newly trimmed suburban lawn are a few examples of the visual idiosyncrasies of *Blue Velvet*.

Behind the velvet curtain

The billowing blue velvet curtain in *Blue Velvet*'s opening credits creates a mood of intrigue and subterfuge. Curtains conceal things, both for the viewer inside looking out, and the observer outside looking in. They represent a shifting surface behind which may be found a performance, as in a theatre; or a performer, as in a nightclub. Curtains cover windows, doors and spaces. The velvet curtain is the seductive surface of artifice.

'I like the idea that everything has a surface which hides much more underneath,' says Lynch. 'Someone can look very well and have a whole bunch of diseases cooking: there are all sorts of dark twisted things lurking down there. I go down in that darkness and see what's there.'[28]

The velvet surface is luxurious yet deceptive, its sheen changing tone according to the light. For Lynch, velvet is a perversely sensual fabric: blue velvet aids Frank Booth's masturbation fantasies; red velvet is the fabric of nightclubs, luxury brothels and the Red Chamber of the Ghostwood lodge in *Twin Peaks*.

Lynch's preoccupation with surfaces implies a risk of dealing only with surfaces, namely, the superficial, surface without depth. The television series, *Twin Peaks*, guides the viewer through a multi-layered text of surfaces, with isolated moments of clarity. By contrast the film version, *Twin Peaks: Fire Walk With Me*, emerges as a text of well-worn surfaces, with only glimpses of what lies beyond the superficial.

The intrigue of a surface lies in what it conceals. When Lynch delves beneath the top layers and drags up whatever he finds in his own subconscious, he is also tapping into the murky depths of the collective subconscious – the cumulative reservoir of 'things hidden' which is coloured by the global consciousness of American television and Hollywood cinema.

What's underneath? What's inside? What's on the other side of the door? Only in the American *noir* films of Fritz Lang do doors feature as significantly as an icon of intrigue as in the Lynch film; half-opened doors, slightly opened doors, doors ajar and closed doors.

Dorothy listens helplessly to her crying son behind a closed door in *Blue Velvet*; she furtively opens a chained door as she casts her eye upon Jeffrey for the first time; the slatted wardrobe door in her apartment conceals Jeffrey, but not his vulnerability. In *Eraserhead*, behind the door to number 26 waits Henry's seductress who will drown him in his own bed; she spies on Henry predaciously from behind her door, and Henry looks through the keyhole of his door to watch her claim another male victim. And behind the door of a bleached white stone shack in a small Texas town waits Perdita, Sailor Ripley's perdition in *Wild at Heart*.

In *Twin Peaks: Fire Walk With Me*, Laura cautiously opens the door to her own bedroom, inch by inch, until she reveals 'Bob' in all his psychopathic glory. Later, the painting of a half-open door hanging in her bedroom comes to life as she sleeps, taking her ethereal body through the doorway and into a labyrinth of red velvet curtains. Velvet curtains again! If not a door – a velvet curtain. What's on the other side?

David Lynch is not the only film director beset with red drapes. Red scenography dominates Ingmar Bergman's colour films; *Cries and Whispers* (1972) and *Fanny and Alexander* are awash with blood red curtains, walls, table cloths and decor, as if to recreate a blood-lined womb – a placenta from which Bergman draws his creativity. His work is fed by an unsevered umbilical cord – the memories of his childhood, unresolved issues with his parents that stretch back to a precognitive state. For Lynch, the colour red is cerebral, like the blood feeding the ventricles of the brain. In the Lynch film autopsies and violence open up the cranium in search of what lies beneath the bone; is that brain substance 'us', our identity, our individuality?

Wild at Heart begins with a fight in which Bob Ray Lemon's brains stain a white marble floor, and ends with Bobby Peru's brains being blown out of his head with two barrels of a sawn-off shotgun, splattering the beige wall of a small town food store. A beautiful young girl, wandering dazed after a car accident, inserts a finger into her cut-open cranium and complains about 'this sticky stuff in my head....', then dies. A bullet between the eyes penetrates the brain of Johnnie Farragut as he stares down the gun barrel before him.

The velvet curtain is David Lynch's metaphor for surface. We look behind the velvet curtain seeking meaning in the Lynch film, but there is no guarantee we will find it. What we do find takes us beneath our own 'surfaces', both of the mind and the flesh. Especially the flesh.

Decay

Behind Dr Treves' hospital screens is the grotesquely deformed body of John Merrick, the Elephant Man. The corruption and deformity of the human body are central to both *Eraserhead* and *The Elephant Man*, and permeate Lynch's film world, like the malaise he implies but never defines. In *Dune* it is the grotesquely disfigured character of Baron Harkonnen. In *Blue Velvet* the psychopathy of Frank Booth is emphasised by his predeliction for inhaled stimulation. A severed human ear is the 'disruptive event' which initiates the story. Dorothy accuses Jeffrey of putting his 'disease in me'.

In *Wild at Heart* two characters with the name Bob have their heads split open. Lula recollects her abortion – a crimson embryo cast into a stainless steel waste depository; a new embryo takes hold of her womb and she vomits – meanwhile, back at home, her mother rages in madness, and she also vomits.

In *Eraserhead*, Henry Spencer cuts open the ailing monstrosity, and pierces its pulsing organs with a pair of scissors. Rather than perish, it oozes putrescent substance, stretches its umbilical cord-like neck and terrorises Henry with its pustulate face.

Lynch's preoccupations concern the 'abject'[29], rather than the object – the 'otherness' discarded from the body. Julia Kristeva in *Powers of Horror* writes that 'abjection, which modernity has learned to repress, dodge or fake' becomes 'a substitute for the role formerly played by the sacred...'[30]

'The abject is perverse,' she says, 'because it neither gives up nor assumes a prohibition, a rule, or a law; but turns them aside, misleads, corrupts; uses them, takes advantage of them, the better to deny them.'[31]

As a child Lynch describes 'a force, a wild pain and decay accompanying everything.' Wild 'because it's not able to be controlled. A small world like a painting or a film gives you the illusion that you're... in control. The smaller the world, the more safe you feel and in control.'[32]

Decay is the ultimate loss of control – the abject is the triumph of the body over mind – flesh deteriorates, wastes must be expelled. A young girl vomits blood in *The Alphabet*, which is transformed into letters; in *The Grandmother*, out of a young boy's bedwetting is born a grandmother, who, in her brief sojourn, becomes a ten-year-old kid's guide through life and death.

From *The Grandmother* to *Blue Velvet, Wild at Heart* and *Twin Peaks*, males urinating facilitate pivotal episodes in plot development. In *Blue Velvet*, Jeffrey expelling a substantial quantity of Heineken lager results in him missing a given signal and being trapped in the wardrobe of Dorothy Vallens' apartment. Bobby Peru's insistence on using the toilet in Lula's motel room, in *Wild at Heart*, leads to her 'seduction', and in *Twin Peaks*, Agent Cooper's predeliction for the joys of urinating in the great outdoors provides an untimely absence and the abduction of Major Briggs into a realm where Cooper himself will confront the ultimate 'otherness'.

Lynch's autopsy sequences (*Twin Peaks* and *Twin Peaks: Fire Walk With Me*) are exercises in the abject, as are birth sequences (*The Grandmother, Eraserhead, The Elephant Man, Dune*), and Lula's abortion in *Wild at Heart*. '... the idea of birth was a mysterious and fantastic thing,' says Lynch, 'involving again, like sex, just pure meat and blood and hair. And then at the

same time this feeling of life, this spiritual thing.'[33]
Lynch's preoccupation with the 'abject' deals with the
constitution of the physical form, both inside and outside
– between the self and the other.[34]

'He put his disease in me,' repeats Dorothy in *Blue
Velvet*, a disease which is never named, and which
Lynch declines to define. 'Just the word disease used in
that way – it's so beautiful just to leave it abstract. Once
it becomes specific it's no longer true to a lot of people.
Where if it's abstract there could be some truth to it for
everybody.'[35]

Lynch reveals himself a sensualist in the word's
intended meaning – relating to the sensory perceptions
and placing trust in what can be seen, heard, touched,
smelled, tasted. The abstract is suspect – even the
dreams of the David Lynch film are firmly rooted in
tangibles. But if sensualism is the issue, decay is only
one side of the sensory perceptions. The polarity
between 'thanatos' and 'eros' – death and pleasure – is
one of an array of contrasts in which the viewer can
undertake the task which Lynch claims he dare not;
namely, the search for meanings.

Contrast

Lynch's recurring contrast lies between the perfect body
and the imperfect body, between wholeness and decay.
The perfect body is formally dressed in a dark suit and
tie, utterly concealing man's bestial nature. The perfect
body is never exhibited unclothed, and is only under the
most discreet of circumstances subject to the 'abject'
(Jeffrey urinating, Cooper urinating, and 'the boy' of
The Grandmother urinating). The perfect body houses
the rational man who expresses reason, but rarely
feelings. He is controlled and subject to the lack of
control, misdeeds and emotional imbalance of those
around him.

The imperfect body is deformed, unsuited to clothing,
'broken' – either with disease or deformity, and stripped
of clothing to reveal and emphasise its imperfections.
The imperfect body bleeds, pustulates and rots before
our eyes. Within the imperfect body dwells the irrational
man; unpredictable and imbued with feeling. The
following perfect/imperfect pairings illustrate this
contrast:

> Henry Spencer – 'infant' (*Eraserhead*)
> Frederick Treves – John Merrick (*The Elephant
> Man*)

Paul Atreides – Vladimir Harkonnen (*Dune*)

Jeffrey Beaumont – Frank Booth (also Don, Dorothy's husband whose ears are severed from his head) (*Blue Velvet*)

Sailor Ripley – Bobby Peru (*Wild at Heart*)

Dale Cooper – 'Bob' (also 'Mike', the one-armed man) (*Twin Peaks*)

The Boy – The Grandmother (*The Grandmother*)

The over-simplified and clearly labelled division of 'good' and 'evil' is a contrast Lynch justifies as part and parcel of film narrative: 'Everybody's got many threads of (Good and Evil) running through them. But I think in a film, white gets a little whiter, and black gets a little bit blacker, for the sake of the story. That's part of the beauty of it, that contrast...'[36]

This kind of contrast can be attributed to a Lynchian manipulation of cliché; conflict is central to film form, but Lynch consciously manipulates contrasts – to the level of cliché, predetermining an outcome (good triumphs over evil), but perverting it. Lynch's 'happy endings' are rarely happy.

The formal closure of *Blue Velvet* fulfils the promise of singing robins, but it is a fake robin; the formal closure of *Wild at Heart* re-unites Lula with Sailor, who finally gets to sing 'Love Me Tender', but the implied ending leaves Lula's deranged mother still anxious to be rid of Sailor, and Santos still with a contract to eliminate him.

'Psychomachia', a struggle between opposites, is the primary source of conflict in Lynch's feature films, where 'good becomes bad' and 'bad becomes good' – characters transform into the express opposite of their original personality.

The psychomachia is 'a drama externalising conflicts between certain interior human traits, desires and capabilities... Plots turning on good guys (selfless, decent to others) versus bad guys (selfish, cruel to others) may be crude psychomachias... Some films turn on pairs or doubles. Hitchcock frequently employs this device, one character in *Strangers on a Train* (1951) being the evil form of an opposing character, or in *Shadow of a Doubt* (1943) the naive form, each pair constituting the potential of any one human being.'[37]

'I see films more and more as separate from whatever kind of reality there is anywhere else,' says David Lynch. 'They are more like fairy tales or dreams... they should obey certain rules. And one of them is Contrast... I like murder mysteries. They get me completely because they are mysteries and deal with life and death.'[38]

Lynch contrasts psychological types with each other: innocence against guilt, reason against the psychopathic, compassionate against ruthless. Hence:

Jeffrey Beaumont – Frank Booth (*Blue Velvet*)
Sailor Ripley – Marcello Santos (*Wild at Heart*)
Dale Cooper – 'Bob' (*Twin Peaks*)
Frederick Treves – Bytes (*The Elephant Man*)
Dorothy Vallens – Sandy Williams (*Blue Velvet*)
Lula – Perdita (*Wild at Heart*)

Similarly, there are contrasts between places: the degeneracy and hostility of those who inhabit Deer Meadows in contrast to the wholesome and goodnatured residents of Twin Peaks. The suburban calm of Lumberton in *Blue Velvet* harbours unspeakable horrors. John Merrick, the Elephant Man, is caught in the dichotomy of the doctor, Treves, representing compassion on the one side, and the malevolent sideshow proprietor, Bytes, representing the forces of barbarism on the other. In *Dune* the conflict is clearly labelled between House Atreides (order) and House Harkonnen (chaos).

In the film world of David Lynch, order is unremittingly vulnerable – the forces of chaos lurk beneath the surface, ready to exploit any frailty. Beneath the well-trimmed suburban front lawn, ants and beetles tear each other apart with venomous intensity. A gold-framed photograph of a high school girl sophomore conceals a life of drug abuse, promiscuity and self-depredation.

It is a dichotomy that pervades the human personality as much as surfaces and the order of things: the conflict is between 'self' and 'shadow', and opposites struggle for supremacy; decent becomes obscene, ugly becomes beautiful, wrong becomes right.

'Enantiodromia' is a term Jung uses (borrowed from Heraclitus *ca* 500BC) to describe a process extended so far as to become its opposite. The word means 'running counter to' and implies that everything that exists turns into its opposite. 'From the living comes death and from the dead life, from the young old age and from the old youth; from waking, sleep, and from sleep, waking; the stream of generation and decay never stands still.'[39]

'The more extreme a position is, the more easily may we expect an enantiodromia, a conversion of something into its opposite. The best is the most threatened with some devilish perversion just because it has done the most to suppress evil.'[40]

In *Twin Peaks* the deranged character called Bob, a

spirit of evil that possesses the father of victim, Laura Palmer, finally inhabits the form of the 'incorruptible' special agent, Dale Cooper.

Thus, from a psychological perspective, Cooper's conversion from the purely 'righteous' to the purely 'evil' (harbouring the spirit of the psychopathic 'Bob') was inevitable because of his unblemished 'purity'.

In *Blue Velvet*, Jeffrey's 'enantiodromia' takes him from blue-eyed naivity to the pain of knowledge and experience; while Sailor Ripley's conversion at the end of *Wild at Heart* is as dramatic as the conversion of St Paul – Jung's chosen example of enantiodromia.

Lynch's most pertinent contrast is the conflict between the masculine and the feminine. Male and female are simply two sides of the duality which makes up our world. But like all dualities they flow into one another, continually transgressing their own boundaries. There is good in evil, and evil in good. There is no wholly masculine man, no purely feminine woman.

Sex

Behind Lynch's velvet curtains a woman waits – in *Eraserhead* she is deformed and smiling, telling us that in heaven 'everything is all right'; in *Blue Velvet* she sings, slightly off-key, but the message is allure, desire, 'know me if you dare'. If we dare, we discover she is being raped and brutalised by a demented psychopath. In *Twin Peaks*, a smiling beautiful seventeen-year-old whispers the name of her murderer in someone's ear. Terrible secrets. Dark secrets.

From *Eraserhead* onwards the sublimation, perversion and expression of sexual desire has been integral to Lynch's films – the nightmare of Henry Spencer (*Eraserhead*) is generated by the fear of sexual relations; the understated 'horror' for John Merrick (*The Elephant Man*) is that his appearance prevents him fulfilling his desires; in *Dune*, Paul, by an accident of birth, is the only male allowed entry into the hitherto exclusively feminine domain of psychic powers; in *Blue Velvet*, Jeffrey enters an arcane world of voyeurism and perverse sexuality; and even in *Wild at Heart* the intense passion of Lula and Sailor finally leads to them betraying each other, and isolation.

'Lynch is one of the cinema's great sensualists,' writes critic, Clas von Sydow. 'But this is the sexual nervousness of a Catholic schoolboy who perceives sex as both pleasure and threat.'[41]

It is a nervousness founded in the apprehension of the 'other' – the unknowable feminine. Yet the urge to know leads the Lynchian protagonist into hiding in a wardrobe at night, content just to watch.

She is a particular kind of woman – the woman on the other side of town, rather than the girl next door. 'Independence is her goal, but her nature is fundamentally and irredeemably sexual... The insistence on combining (aggressiveness and sensuality) in a consequently dangerous woman is the central obsession...' writes Janey Place describing the women of *film noir*.[42]

Richard Dyer maintains that 'women in *film noir* are above all else unknowable... *Film noir* thus starkly divides the world into that which is unknown and unknowable (female) and... that which is known (male).'[43]

The same can be said of Lynch's films regardless of the setting – the world of Caladan is similarly divided into known and unknown (male and female), with Paul a lone male perpetrator into the unknown feminine; likewise, Jeffrey Beaumont, a male vigilante at the knife point of an 'unknowable woman', and Sailor Ripley, for all his sexual intensity, is only truly united with Lula when he accepts Lula's pantheon of gods in the same way she has always accepted his – he allows Lula's Good Witch Glinda from *The Wizard of Oz* to touch his heart.

But underlying Lynch's portrayal of sexuality is fear – it is the driving force in *Eraserhead* and *Blue Velvet*, and even the comparatively wholesome sexuality of Sailor and Lula conceals dark undercurrents, as Bobby Peru's mock seduction of Lula illustrates.

'Sex,' says Lynch, 'was like a world so mysterious to me, I really couldn't believe there was this fantastic texture to life that I was getting to do... it has all these different levels, from lust and fearful, violent sex to the real spiritual thing at the other end. It's the key to some fantastic mystery of life.'[44]

The mystery is fuelled by secrets, a conspiracy of unspoken subterfuge – specifically sexual secrets: Laura Palmer's secret diary is secret because it details sexual escapades unknown to family and friends, a life incongruous with her pristine image. But she is only one of many of *Twin Peaks*' female victims – victims of the secrets they harbour.

'Part of the thing about secrets is that they have a certain kind of mystery to me. A dark secret... I don't want to see something so clearly that it would destroy an imaginary picture... secrets and mysteries... provide a beautiful little corridor where you can float out and many, many wonderful things can happen.'[45] Lynch conceals his own character behind a veil of subterfuge and uncertainty, protecting his work from what he sees as the demystifying process of analysis – a deliberate cloak of vagaries and abstractions, self-conscious diffusion in order not to be brought into the realm of specifics. Lynch avoids particulars as they may destroy the artifice of banality. He is a filmmaker who makes romance of decay, creates irony out of horror and transforms cliché into poetry.

The Alphabet (1968)

Synopsis: *A pale-faced young girl, about eight years old, lies half prone in a bed as a voice sings out the alphabet. The letters illuminate the bedroom's sombre walls. At the end of the alphabet the girl doubles up and vomits blood in violent spasms.*

Lynch's early student works provide an insight into themes of his later feature films. *The Alphabet*, which combines several animation techniques and is just four minutes long, is a study in creativity and 'abjection' which Lynch would explore further in *Eraserhead*.

The setting is a bedroom, portrayed in a starkly hyperrealistic scenography, and the film culminates with the violation of 'the bed', a recurring anxiety in later films, not least *The Grandmother*. In *Eraserhead*, Henry Spencer sinks into a quagmire in the middle of his mattress as he embraces his lover; John Merrick's bedroom in *The Elephant Man* is the scene of his 'violation' as he is made the humiliated victim of the hospital porter's evil sport; *Blue Velvet* is structured around the violation of the bedroom of nightclub singer, Dorothy Vallens; in *Wild at Heart*, exchanges of intimacy, both physical and verbal, are acted out in motel bedrooms across the southern United States; and *Twin Peaks: Fire Walk With Me* is the study of a young girl's nightly violation in the assumed sanctity of her own bedroom.

The little girl of *The Alphabet* lies in her bed, white-faced in the style of a Japanese Noh-player, and listens attentively as she hears children singing the letters of the alphabet. Her white smock and pallid complexion suggest she is bed-ridden, incapable of participating in the life beyond the walls of her darkened room. While a male voice acclaims the joys of the alphabet (lyrics by David Lynch), a 'growth' appears beside a curious plant next to her bed. The 'growth' transforms vaguely into the form of a genderless human infant while the plant sprouts forth letters which fall upon the infant, levelling it to a mess of bloody slime. The little girl and her bedclothes are splattered with red measles-like dots. She grabs at each letter as it appears; the capital letter 'A' gives birth to little 'a's, and so on through the alphabet, as a woman sings the alphabet song.

When all the letters have appeared (and been sung) tendrils bind her up, and as she writhes trying to escape, she vomits blood across the sheets.

Lynch's film could be dismissed as a student work imbued with the excesses of an artist seeking 'form', but precisely because it *is* the work of an artist seeking 'form', the film provides us with an early glimpse into Lynch's film world which evolves in *Eraserhead*, *Blue Velvet* and beyond.

'There are things in *The Alphabet* that keep coming back,' says Lynch. 'And *The Grandmother* too. Maybe you do keep doing the same things over and over.'[1]

The 'plant', for example, comes to play more significant roles in *The Grandmother* and *Eraserhead*, but never more explicitly than in *The Alphabet*, where it stands there issuing forth letters; letters which make words; words which form knowledge. The letters of the alphabet are cast out at the little girl, there for the taking. Her final 'abjection', as she vomits blood over the bed, emphasises the gap between the knowledge of the outside world, and the 'abject', the material inside her body.

Philip Strick, in the *Monthly Film Bulletin*, describes the film as 'an urgent message of pity, disgust and shame at the physical processes of conception, birth and adolescence.'[2] At the same time it is just these processes which Lynch sees as the material for inspiration. Material cast out from the body must be rationalised by the mind; 'This is part of me – this needs to be examined and evaluated.'

The Alphabet describes the process of imagination and healing – a striving for articulation and creative expression, a theme he returns to in his later films.

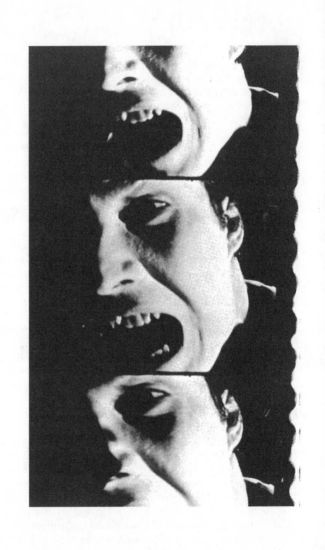

The
Grandmother
(1970)

Synopsis: *A boy, about eight years old, neatly dressed in contrast to the slovenly appearance of his parents, is beaten by his father for bedwetting. The boy takes refuge in his room. He plants a seed in his bed which grows into an enormous tree. The tree gives birth to his grandmother, who becomes his companion.*

She becomes ill and the boy's frantic cries for help go unheeded by his parents. The old lady and the boy wander through a graveyard, and the grandmother disappears. The boy returns to the isolation of his room.

The Grandmother continues Lynch's development from a young painter of 'dark, sombre pictures' into a maker of 'film painting', animation, pixilation and 'straightforward' film drama. The film, made with a $7,200 grant from the American Film Institute, follows on from *The Alphabet*'s themes of creativity, abjection and childhood estrangement. It is thirty-four minutes long and combines 'live-action' and animation. The story describes the dilemma of a bright but anxious young boy in a repressive household.

We are introduced to the family at the dinner table; mother, father and the young boy. The mother and father are unruly, dressed in a slovenly way, seemingly bereft of any social graces, and communicate with grunts, squeaks and primitive tonal utterances – articulation is superfluous in the primal world.

The boy wears a suit and tie, has brylcreemed hair and is mainly silent. Subject to the haranguing and abuse of his parents, he is the subdued witness to the barbarism of his household – a lone vestige of intelligence stranded amongst authoritarian primates. But his intelligence is betrayed by his body. He wets the bed and incurs the wrath of his father.

The boy's yellow patch that stains the bed is linked schematically to the animated yellow sun in the blue sky – whether Lynch is simply playing with the interaction of shape and colour, or drawing a parallel between the sun's sustaining energy and body fluids as a source of fecundity, is open to interpretation. The juxtaposition of these images recurs several times in the film.

The boy finds a bag of seeds in the hallway (marked 'seeds'), and places one on his bed, covers it in soil and waters it. A cactus-like monstrosity grows towards the ceiling, while the tendril-like roots grow beneath the bed. The base of the plant splits apart into a gaping orifice, and the plant gives birth to a dark and shapeless form. The delivery is a long, protracted process amplified by the suggestive and repellent sounds of Alan Splet's elaborate sound design.

Estrangement, procreation, anxiety, disease – the main themes of *The Grandmother* – are explored in *Eraserhead*, where the disparate imagery of the former merges into a homogenous whole. *Eraserhead*'s protagonist, Henry Spencer, finally identifies himself with the monstrous infant of which he is the assumed father. The 'monster' takes over his identity. The polarity between the two principal characters in *The Grandmother* works in another way. Henry's 'infant' is a hindrance to his daily routine, the boy's 'grandmother' is a catalyst; a source of consolation and companionship in his isolation, and a compassionate contrast to his vindictive father.

When the grandmother emerges, covered in secretion and slime, the boy runs to fetch some flowers and presents them to her, and an empathy is divined between them both. Whereas the boy's parents communicate with discordant squawks and jeers, Grandmother converses in light amiable whistling tones.

At dinner time the mother and father heap abuse upon the boy and he takes refuge in his room, finding harmony in the presence of the grandmother who rocks in a rocking chair as the boy sleeps.

He wakes up the next morning having wet the bed once more (yellow sun on blue sky), and in a violent animated dream sequence the boy slaughters his parents, returning to a 'live' sequence where he and the grandmother smile and touch each other. Later the boy sleeps, and the grandmother falls ill.

Illness precedes catastrophe in the David Lynch film; the little girl in *The Alphabet* gets measles; the illness of the *Eraserhead* 'baby' precedes Henry's 'losing his head'; and John Merrick's life, as portrayed in *The Elephant Man*, is a struggle against the malignant disease that finally kills him at the age of twenty-eight. In Lynch's later films, disease persists as a precedent to disaster: the doctor embellishing the Baron's festering diseases in *Dune* precedes the demise of the Duke; Dorothy's obsession in *Blue Velvet*, with the disease which Jeffrey has 'put inside her', leads to the denouement between Jeffrey and Frank Booth; Lula's illness in *Wild at Heart* precedes both catastrophe (Sailor's incarceration) and the birth of her son.

When the boy seeks help from his parents for the ailing grandmother they respond with derision, leaving him more isolated than ever. For all his efforts, the grandmother's condition deteriorates and finally she fades away. The boy leaves the confines of the house and wanders through a field; he meets the grandmother in a cemetery, and after a brief farewell she disappears. The boy returns to his room, to his bed, and sleeps.

The grandmother's brief sojourn in the boy's friendless life is graphically portrayed from the very explicit 'birth' from the soil around the planted tree, to her 'departure' at the cemetery. The film reiterates Lynch's fundamental preoccupation with, as interviewer David Breskin termed it, 'how we start and how we finish as the biggest subject on [Lynch's] table.'[3]

Another Lynch preoccupation at work in *The Grandmother*, to which he returns in subsequent films, is the creative process – particularly creativity born of despair and isolation. Lynch describes the alchemical process transforming *nigredo* – the 'blackness' of the human spirit – into the kind of 'gold' the boy requires – compassion, kindness and a sympathetic ear.

He also describes the rich fantasy world of childhood, and how a rejected young boy creates a companion of his own. When the grandmother dies, his 'fantasy' dies. The common sense of maturity imposes itself on the freewheeling imagination of childhood. Reason becomes the blight of the unfettered imaginative mind.

Although it's unlikely that in 1970 Lynch would have seen any of the animated films of the Czech film maker, Jan Svankmeyer, the brooding resignation of the two artists' work makes for an interesting comparison. They both make use of a variety of animation techniques, also they draw on the literary influences of Kafka and Poe, Svankmeyer quite consciously, Lynch less so. Svankmeyer's *The Pit, The Pendulum and Hope* (Kyvaldo, Jama a Nadeje, Czechoslovakia 1983) is a fifteen-minute long film (told entirely with a subjective camera) in homage to the same Poe stories that have helped shape Lynch's visual sense of the macabre.

A young boy accompanied by a grandmother returns in several episodes of *Twin Peaks*. In *Twin Peaks: Fire*

Walk With Me, this young boy hops about wearing a mask, performs magic tricks and whispers dark secrets. 'Someone is reading your secret diary,' he tells Laura Palmer. The grandmother gives Laura a painting and at night she and the boy together lure Laura into the dream world of the red chamber. Perhaps the end of *The Grandmother* is not so much concerned with the grandmother's death, but with her retreat into the limbo world where she awaits the time when the young boy may need to summon her again.

The downbeat ending of *The Grandmother* makes it still possibly Lynch's most pessimistic film. His next film moves into an even darker realm, and although the ending is more hopeful, to get to it the viewer must undertake a dark journey into an intensely personal nightmare.

Eraserhead
(1976)

*'In Heaven everything is fine
You've got your good things and I've got mine.'*

the lady from behind the radiator

Synopsis: *Henry Spencer sleeps and dreams – a curious umbilical cord-shaped entity floats from his mouth. He awakens to a darkened room, with a single window which opens to a solid brick wall. A 'man inside a planet' releases brake levers, and we emerge from darkness through a jagged orifice, into the glaring light of day. Henry visits a girl acquaintance, Mary, and her family for dinner. The domestic atmosphere is stifling and Henry represses a rising anxiety. The girl's mother informs Henry that he is father to her daughter's unborn child. Henry is obliged to fulfil his paternal duties. The baby is born, a monstrous mutation, and Mary and the child move into Henry's single room. On the first night Mary flees in despair, leaving Henry literally holding the baby.*

Henry attempts to relate to the mutant monstrous infant. His introspective withdrawal in the face of an increasingly displeasing reality emphasises Henry's subconscious state. An empty theatre stage Henry had previously seen behind the radiator now features a young woman with a deformed face performing a curiously sadistic dance routine. The monstrous 'child' becomes increasingly capricious, develops an undiagnosable ailment, recovers, and continues its spiteful malevolence towards Henry.

Henry watches the stage – his head leaves his shoulders, flies through an open window, and crashes to the concrete below. A boy picks it up and takes it to a workshop where a pencil-machine operator uses Henry's brain substance to make pencil erasers.

Henry is back in his room and takes a pair of scissors to the infant mutant's vital organs. The infant turns into a monster and attacks Henry – the light bulb explodes.

**John
Nance**

'The man inside the planet' pulls on the brake levers,
and Henry is embraced by *'the lady in the radiator'.*

Eraserhead isn't necessarily a film to make sense of, in
the way that it isn't necessary to make sense of an
unsettling dream. All the same, like the unravelling of an
unsettling dream, there is an intrinsic logic to the
claustrophobic world *Eraserhead* portrays. Henry's
nightmarish ordeal transpires to have been a protracted
anxiety dream; his subconscious fears of becoming
involved with the opposite sex create a 'worst possible'
scenario of Kafkaesque proportions.

This 'worst possible' scenario suggests that Henry
Spencer's encounter with a girl from the neighbourhood
will lead to the girl's mother accusing Henry of being
father to her daughter's unborn child. When the girl
gives birth to a grotesque and spiteful monstrosity, one
night in Henry's single room apartment is enough to
drive her to a hasty exit, and to leave Henry 'holding the
baby'. And this is not a baby to occupy the pages of the
family photograph album.

A recurring 'dream within the dream' shows Henry
staring into the spaces between the radiator. Behind it is
concealed the stage of a rundown theatre. First it's
empty, and as Henry's precarious relationship develops,
he watches a deformed and smiling woman perform a
curious parody of a tap-dancing routine. 'Umbilical
cords' rain onto the stage which she crushes under her
dancing shoes in malicious pleasure. Finally, when the
burdens of paternity force Henry into his own private
world, the woman appears on stage and sings: 'In
heaven everything is fine.'

'Umbilical cords'[1] appear in Henry's bed in the
middle of the night, expelled from Mary as she sleeps.
Henry, horrified, casts them against the apartment wall.
They burst and ooze a white liquid putrescence, as they
did beneath the dancing shoes of the lady behind the
radiator. These are 'umbilical cords' with tadpole-
shaped heads, resembling spermatozoa; an impossible
hybrid, which belies a curious logic in view of the sexual
paranoia the film conveys.

The spermatozoon is the first stage of the procreative
process, the severance of the umbilical cord concludes
it. If, in this hybrid and detached state, the result is
grotesque and repelling, this too is a logical synthesis of
reproduction and birth. *Eraserhead* is the story of a man
who wants no part of it.

Some dark moments

Eraserhead is the one David Lynch feature film over which he had complete artistic control. Apart from writing and directing the picture, additional credits include editing, production design, scenography, special effects, and, in collaboration with Alan Splet, sound design.

The collaboration with the production team was a fruitful one, the beginning of associations which have continued throughout Lynch's filmmaking career. In *Eraserhead* Lynch and Splet's efforts culminated in a soundtrack that was as innovative as it would be influential on their work with sound in the productions to come.

John Nance, the withdrawn Henry Spencer, has subsequently found roles in most of David Lynch's productions, not least as Pete Martell in *Twin Peaks*. Lynch describes Nance as 'a zero-motivated actor... content to stay at home, not even watching television, just sitting, thinking in his chair, wearing his little slippers,'[2] attributes for which he was ceaselessly thankful, as the film production stretched out over a six-year period. According to David Lynch, the main problem was maintaining 'Henry's singular hairstyle over such a long period. 'It just stayed up in the air – it was so tall that the first night none of us could believe we could ever film something like this.' Nance recollects periods of months, sometimes years, between takes, which were later matched up in the cutting room.[3]

Eraserhead was initially financed by a $10,000 grant from the American Film Institute (who had financed *The Grandmother*), and Lynch received financial assistance from many quarters, including actress Sissy Spacek. In the six-year production period, Lynch's jobs included building sheds, delivering newspapers and installing hot water heaters. 'It's a very satisfying thing to direct water successfully,' he says.[4]

'There were some dark moments.' says Lynch. 'At one time I was thinking about building a small eight-inch Henry and stop-motioning him through some small cardboard sets to fill in the blanks. Just to get it finished.'

Lynch describes the 22-page script as 'a kind of free-form poem', and the film is rich with the kind of poetic imagery that renders analysis superfluous. Nonetheless, beneath the images lies a story – a story of transformation, and creativity. *Eraserhead* is a portrait of the artist creating art out of madness.

The trials of Henry Spencer and David Lynch

Behind Henry's floating head is a single planet and a few stars. We approach the planet, exploring its texture, its furrows; it is grimy, earthy, with a texture of rich soil. Henry Spencer is about to be brought 'down to earth' and from out of his ethereal dream state. We are in a room, and a man stares through a window. His naked flesh is burned and seared – most of the window panes are broken.

The man, a kind of cosmic station master, an instrument of fate, pulls on a lever as though opening a railway line signal to let a train out. A scream, like a steam train issuing forth, echoes in the incessant industrial rumble. It is a signal that announces the beginning of a process – an allegorical birth. The umbilical cord (or sperm) falls into a pool of water within a rocky crag. It sinks deeper and deeper and finally we emerge through the jagged orifice and into the blinding white light of day. A seed is sown, something is born.

Henry is outside and looking over his shoulder. He walks straight ahead and into the black shadows of an industrial landscape. We don't know where he's coming from, but we watch him enter a realm of shadows. It is an imposing exterior location, one of the few exteriors in the film, which, according to photographer Frederick Elmes, was chosen 'because of the scale: what appears to be a very natural looking piece of architecture until you walk up underneath it and you become this little ant. It seemed to be the perfect place for Henry to live – that was really his world.'[5]

He walks through a bleak industrial landscape – over mounds of earth, past derelict buildings, carrying a paper bag under his arm. He steps into a muddy puddle, and gets his foot wet, while the incessant throbbing sounds of industry pound away in the background.

'There's not one particular kind of sound that I like but if I had to pick a category it would be factory sounds', says Lynch. 'I like the power of them and it makes a picture in my mind... I like the idea of factories and factory life probably because I don't know that much about them. I can just imagine a world and it leads to a bigger place where many strange and beautiful things can happen.'[6]

As Henry stands in the dark ill-lit corridor, opening the door to his apartment, a door across the hall opens and an exotic-looking woman described as 'the beautiful girl across the hall', asks; 'Are you Henry?' Henry says yes, and the woman tells him that a girl named Mary telephoned – her parents have invited him to dinner.

Henry's apartment is a dim, sombre and claustrophobic affair and the inadequate lighting casts dark shadows on the wall. Henry empties his paper bag, puts on a 78 rpm of old-fashioned cinema wurlitzer music and examines his wet foot. He places the wet sock upon the radiator and sits on the bed while the sock sizzles and spits as it slowly dries out, at the same time staring through the window to a view of a brick wall.

Dennis Hopper has called Lynch 'the first American surrealist director', and this tableau has the intrigue of a Magritte painting with the despondency of Francis Bacon. Henry Spencer's first trial is the place he lives. David Lynch once described *Eraserhead* as his revenge on Philadelphia, 'the sickest city in America',[7] which was the inspiration behind the settings of Henry Spencer's world, even though the film was shot around Los Angeles.

Lynch's cinematographer, Frederick Elmes, who has also collaborated on subsequent Lynch productions, claims that *Eraserhead* was inspired by Lynch's experiences in Philadelphia. 'He draws on all those years of being an art student living in the factory part of town.'[8] Says Lynch: 'I love going into another world, and film provides that opportunity. *Eraserhead* way more than any other film, because I really did live in that world.'[9]

Henry opens the drawer, gets out two torn halves of a photograph and puts them together. It's the forlorn face of a girl, Mary X, staring through a window. Later, Henry approaches her house, sidling down an old disused railway line in the hours of darkness. Dogs bark, steam bellows through a ventilator shaft, and Mary's forlorn face stares down from the window once more. Henry looks up to Mary in the window. 'You never come around any more,' he says. 'Dinner's almost ready,' says Mary. 'Come on in.' He passes her in the doorway but there is no physical contact between them. In the living room Mary's mother sits on the corner of a sofa. On the floor, young pups whine frantically, feeding off a large motionless bitch. Henry seats himself cautiously, as does Mary – they are all at respectable distances from each other.

MOTHER: What do you do?
HENRY: I'm on vacation.
MOTHER: What did you do?
HENRY: I'm a printer. I work at Lapell's factory.

Mary has a kind of fit, clucking her tongue and rolling her eyes. Her mother pays no attention, and Mary's father, Bill, introduces himself.

BILL: We've got chicken tonight. Strangest damn things. They're man-made. Smaller than my fist. And they're new. Hello. I'm Bill.
HENRY: Hello. I'm Henry.

In the kitchen mother prepares dinner as grandmother sits passively on a chair. Mother places the salad bowl on grandmother's lap and they go through the motions of tossing the salad. Then mother lights a cigarette and places it in grandmother's mouth. Grandmother does not respond. A cuckoo clock strikes the hour. In the dining room, at the dinner table, Bill tells a strange story about his arm and asks that Henry carve the chickens. They're about as big as a fist.

HENRY: And you just cut them up like regular chickens?
BILL: Sure. Just cut them up like regular chickens.

Henry inserts the knife and a strange brown putrescent liquid bubbles over the plate as the legs swing up and down. Now it is Mary's mother who has a fit and she runs screaming from the room. Mary follows. Henry and Bill sit alone in silence at the table.

BILL: Well, Henry, what do you know?
HENRY: Oh, I don't know much of anything.

And so proceeds Henry's other trial. The atmosphere is as thick as the gravy oozing from the insides of the man-made chickens. Henry is the nonplussed innocent trapped in a microcosm of family dementia.

Mother returns and demands to speak to Henry, in private. Mary stands in the doorway and weeps. A floor lamp flickers precariously, and explodes. From this point until the next exploding light bulb which culminates with the infant's attack on Henry, any vestige of rationality dissipates. Together with Henry the viewer descends into a maelstrom of nightmarish improbability.

> MOTHER: Did you and Mary have sexual intercourse?
> (A bewildered Henry tries to extricate himself).
> MOTHER: You're in very bad trouble if you don't cooperate.

She forces Henry up against the wall and bites into his neck. Henry tries to force her off, then Mary appears in the doorway. This is a favoured Lynch sordid scenario, which he re-enacts in *Wild at Heart*, when Lula's mother, Marietta, attempts to seduce Sailor in a dance-hall toilet cubicle.

> MOTHER: There's a baby. At the hospital. And you're the father.
> MARY: Mom. They're still not sure if it is a baby!
> (Henry's nose begins to bleed. Mary's mother fetches some ice.)
> MARY: You don't mind, do you, Henry, about getting married?

Henry's mind races through the living room, past the dog and the floral curtains, and straight through the venetian blinds.

Henry's trial is over. He is found guilty. Next comes the sentence.

In his book *Kafka's Other Trial*, Elias Canetti describes how Franz Kafka's celebrated novel was influenced by his personal ordeal, his own 'trial' by the Bauer family as he courted Felice Bauer. Two months after Franz Kafka was officially engaged to Felice at the Bauer family home, in August 1914, he began work on *The Trial*, and according to Canetti, 'the engagement becomes the arrest in the first chapter; the 'tribunal' (when the engagement was called off) appears as the execution in the last.'[10]

In his diary, Kafka describes his engagement to Felice Bauer under the strict supervision of her parents; he 'was tied hand and foot like a criminal. Had they sat me down in a corner bound in real chains, placed policemen in front of me and let me look on simply like that, it could not have been worse. And that was my engagement.'[11]

Just as Kafka assimilates his anxieties into *The Trial*, Lynch empties himself into *Eraserhead* with a vehemence unparalleled in his other films. It was written and made when Lynch's girlfriend became pregnant and Lynch himself (a struggling art student), like Henry, became, first, the reticent husband, and then the reluctant father. Lynch describes *Eraserhead* as 'an abstract film... not just about one thing'.

Twenty years after the production was set in motion, Lynch's daughter, Jennifer, maintains that her birth inspired the film, that 'David, in no uncertain terms, did not want a family.' David Lynch acknowledges the events as 'a subconscious influence' but with characteristic diffidence suggests that the film 'be left alone to float in that pleasant abstraction.'[12]

Jennifer was born with club feet, and Lynch began filming *Eraserhead*, financed by a modest AFI grant, supplemented by delivering the *Wall Street Journal*. She appears in *Eraserhead*, filmed during its later stages, under the credit of 'little girl'. Jennifer was born two years before 'Laura Palmer', and encouraged by 'Dad' to write the fictitious diary of the model daughter, who, beneath the subterfuge, is promiscuous, a drug addict and murdered before she reaches eighteen. The story is expounded in *Twin Peaks: Fire Walk With Me*.

Elias Canetti says of Franz Kafka: 'He did not have for his private and interior processes that disregard which distinguishes insignificant writers from writers of imagination. A person who thinks he is empowered to separate his inner world from the outer one has no inner world from which something might be separable.'[13]

Joseph K. was taken out and shot for a crime he did not commit, for a crime that is never named. Henry is imprisoned in a dark cell with a mutant infant monster and a 'wife' who recoils at his touch. Mary's mother's question, as to whether Henry and Mary had sexual intercourse, remains unanswered.

Happy families and broken dreams

The paradox that runs through Lynch's body of work consists of the family idyll on the one side: wholesome, content and self-contained; and the 'diseases' which that idyll conceals, on the other. The paradox finds expression in Lynch's contrast of the 'closed' body – neat, formally dressed, 'whole', and the 'open' body – broken fissures revealing otherwise concealed matter: an unborn foetus, vital organs, diseases. If you break the skin which covers the 'perfect' body, all kinds of 'imperfections' are revealed; if you look behind the surface of the family idyll, you find many more imperfections.

Henry Spencer's family is as 'imperfect' as one is likely to encounter, yet Henry (like Lynch) attempts to conceal the broken skin, and create the idyll of television advertising and popular culture. Mary stands at the table of Henry's single-room apartment, dressed in a floral dress and, with bottle in hand, feeds the baby, swaying to the wurlitzer music of Henry's 78 rpm gramophone. The tableau is a pastiche of a 1950s magazine advertisement.

The baby is shown in close-up; a grotesque, deformed head is attached to a limbless trunk incarcerated in bandages. It is scarcely human, yet mimics the human infant as it sucks greedily on the milk bottle in Mary's hand.

Henry returns home and regards the domestic scene before him; mother feeding 'baby'. He smiles. The family idyll. He lies on the bed, still dressed in his suit and tie, and stares at the radiator. Slime gathers on the floor beneath it. Inside the radiator is a stage. The stage is empty. A single spotlight illuminates the scene.

In bed at night Henry reaches out and touches Mary's shoulder. The 'baby' is crying. She shudders and recoils in disgust. The baby still cries. Outside it rains and the wind howls. 'Shut up,' she shouts at the baby. She gets up, and screams: 'I can't stand it. I'm going home.' She drags the suitcase from under the bed and leaves.

Henry is now alone, and the 'baby' gets sick. He takes its temperature. It has a fever and boils appear over its face. The next morning, Henry, dressed in suit and tie, nurses the infant, but each time he tries to leave the apartment, the baby's frantic wailing drags him back. He is a prisoner in a domestic hell, a scenario born of Lynch's 'bond between the external hell of the world and his inner hell'.[14]

The burden of reality and the flight of fantasy

Up to this point, *Eraserhead*, for all its quirks and surreal absurdity, has proceeded along the lines of a conventional narrative. Burdened with a leaden reality, Henry's imagination seeks new avenues of diversion. As he stares at the stage behind the radiator, a deformed woman dances to Henry's wurlitzer music. She looks at the camera, smiles gleefully through her deformed and distorted cheeks, and clasps her hands before her over her frock. Serpent-like forms (umbilical cord/ spermatozoon) fall to the stage. She crushes them gleefully with her foot, and they spurt white liquid. Smiling, she disappears into the darkness behind the velvet curtain.

Henry observes a monstrous plant by his bed (echoes of *The Grandmother*), and suddenly finds that Mary is back in the bed. She is sleeping, grinding her teeth, slurping, twitching, groping at her eyes – brazenly executing the sounds and acts of conjugal irritation. Henry gropes under the sheets and discovers, to his horror, an umbilical cord/spermatozoon 'serpent' in the bed and casts it aside. Then another, then another – the bed is filled with these monstrosities. He throws them against the wall and they burst and spurt milky grey putrescence.

The doors of a cabinet open and Henry regards the animated antics of a maggot-like 'seed'. We return to the texture and furrows of another 'planet' from the opening sequence, once again emerging from a gaping hole. Henry stares at the growing planet. He pulls threads from his worn-out dressing gown. Everything is falling apart.

There's a knock at the door, and the seductive woman from across the hall enters. Her eyes and lips are painted and she smiles a wanton smile. 'I locked myself out of my apartment,' she says. 'Where's your wife?' 'She must have gone back to her parents again,' says Henry. 'I'm not sure.' She lures Henry to bed and they embrace, half-prone in the middle of the uncovered mattress. She is distracted by the infant's sounds of crying and cackling as they kiss, and Henry tries to divert her with enforced passion. The bed becomes a quagmire and they begin to sink. They sink into murky grey liquid, until they are submerged completely. Her hair floats on top.

In Fellini's film *City of Women* (1979), Marcello Mastroianni ascends the skies in a hot-air balloon formed in the shape of a large-breasted woman with a smiling face. A masked terrorist machine guns the balloon and Mastroianni plunges to the ground. The terrorist removes the mask and reveals the smiling face of a beautiful young woman. Mastroianni wakes abruptly, and looks into the same smiling face seated opposite him – he had fallen asleep on a train journey.

The dream finds a natural expression in the cinema; the dream sequences of both Fellini and Lynch evolve of anxiety, and are rooted in the tangible. 'There is nothing more honest than a dream,' says Fellini. 'And because it's honest it resists obvious interpretation.'[15]

The far side of madness

The deformed 'lady in the radiator' emerges from the dark. She stands centre-stage and sings: 'In Heaven everything is fine/You've got your good things and I've got mine.' Henry climbs on to the stage and the woman extends her hands. Henry seats himself in a theatre box and watches the stage where the deformed plant from his apartment now appears. He grinds his hands frantically when suddenly his head flies from his shoulders and bounces on the stage. A bizarre growth appears where his head used to be, and the plant begins to seep liquid. The growth replacing Henry's head becomes the 'baby's' head. The baby takes over Henry's identity – he is no longer himself, but a monster consumed by the monstrous infant.

Henry's detached head disappears into the pool of liquid seeping from the plant, then falls down the side of a building and crashes to the ground. An old tramp on a bench looks at the shattered head. A boy comes running along, picks it up and runs off with it.

The boy takes it to a workshop where it's examined by the assistant and the manager. They take it into the back room and drill it open. The 'substance' inside is extracted by a pencil-making machine and used as rubber tips on the end of pencils. Henry becomes 'eraserhead'.

The machine operator makes a test run, and scribbles on a notepad, then rubs out the scrawlings with the 'eraser' – the substance inside Henry's head. 'It's OK,' he says to the manager, and the manager counts out some notes from a wad of money and gives them to the boy. The machine operator brushes aside the bits of used 'rubber', which fly through the air, and shine like illuminated cosmic dust.

Henry has lost his identity, he no longer exists. An alien monster has consumed him utterly. Henry's nightmare is as terrifying as Ripley (Sigourney Weaver) confronting her own projection of parenthood horror in *Aliens* (1986). Like Henry, Ripley stares at the Alien monster before her, and reflects on her own loss of identity. With a little girl safely in her arms, Ripley faces her personal nightmare of motherhood – she sees the formidable Alien mother, imprisoned by her egg-laying appendage, surrounded by the offspring she's creating. For Ripley, the dark side of motherhood entails the sacrifice of her own ego for the single purpose of procreation. For Henry, the dark side of fatherhood similarly implies loss of ego – his identity is consumed by his progeny.

Apparently awakened from his dream, Henry lies on his bed, then is dressed and standing in his room. Steam billows outside his window; he looks outside – two figures wrestle in the dark. Footsteps echo in the corridor. Henry knocks on the door of number twenty-one, the woman across the hall, but there is no answer. He returns to his room.

The deformed infant cackles maliciously, Henry lies down and the wurlitzer music plays in the background. He gets up again and opens his door. The woman across the hall is outside her room, together with an ugly little man. They grope at each other vehemently. The woman looks at Henry and sees the head of the baby connected to his body. Even his identity to the outside world has been consumed by this monster. Because of the infant Henry has forsaken all – he is imprisoned in his room and once beyond the threshold of his own apartment he becomes merely an extension of the mutant infant he fathers.

Henry closes the door, turns off the light and looks through the keyhole, and slumps to the floor despondently. He takes out some scissors and cuts open the baby's bandages. Inside is an array of vital organs – there is neither skin nor bones. The baby whimpers desperately. Henry stabs at the organs with the scissors, the baby gasps and wheezes, spurts blood from its mouth, and its cut-open trunk oozes a thick porridge-like substance. The light flickers and electricity sparks.

The baby's neck elongates till it too seems like a spermatozoon. Henry watches in horror – giant baby heads leer at him from all directions. The flickering light explodes, connecting us to the moment at Mary's household when Henry was told he would have to marry.

The 'planet' which Henry observed before his 'seduction', shatters – a hole appears in its side and Henry stands surrounded by flying cosmic dust – the rubber granules of pencil erasers.

Inside the shattered planet, the man wrestles with the brake levers. The process which he began by releasing the levers in the first place, must now be halted. The brake levers scream and shudder, sparks fly in all directions, and his face becomes deformed and mutilated.

Henry has traversed his psychosis, for on the other side of madness lies redemption. He has regained his identity. Against a blinding white light the deformed lady appears and embraces Henry. Henry closes his eyes and drifts away.

An alchemical transformation

The alchemical term *nigredo,* blackness, in a psychological context refers to the darkness of despair, the leaden blackness of the human spirit. Alchemists aimed to transform the leaden blackness into gold – Jung translated this into the psychological process of transforming depression (blackness) into creativity (gold). Henry Spencer's ordeal is also the ordeal of David Lynch 'giving birth' to his own creativity by delving into the blackness of his own psychosis.

Nigredo signifies decay, suffering and death. 'It casts a blackness of despair which is not so much "of the ego" as "witnessed by the ego" and into which the ego is compulsively drawn and transformed,'[16] writes Jungian analyst, Robert Grinell, in *Alchemy in a Modern Woman.*

To understand a psychosis we must understand the primordial imagery; Lynch's ultimate nightmare – the brain (and the brain as a source of identifying the 'self' recurs throughout Lynch's films) is put into a pencil-making machine and made into erasers! Such an absurd image and yet such a logical one. The pencil is the essential prerequisite in conveying the creative impulse. A pencil writes, draws, doodles, sketches – it is the most basic extension of the creative 'self' to the outside world. As a symbol for the loss of ego Lynch chooses the eraser – the ultimate negation of the creativity proffered by the pencil. The pencil-machine operator who writes on a piece of paper and rubs the writing out with an eraser fabricated from the substance of Henry's brain, is committing the final travesty. Henry's brain no longer thinks, nor creates – it erases.

Eraserhead is an anxiety dream of a young man cast unwillingly into the role of father. It is also a portrayal of the creative process – of transforming the *nigredo* of despair and melancholy into the substance of 'art'. The opening sequence suggests the sowing of a seed and the painful process culminating in 'birth' – an eruption through the void, as the 'self' frees itself from the darkness and emerges into light.

In his notebook describing the genesis of *Persona* (1966 – also written during a period of personal crisis), Ingmar Bergman writes: 'I imagine a bleached white strip of film. It runs through the projector and gradually words can be made out on the soundtrack... Gradually just the word which I imagine. Then a face appears almost indiscernible within all the white...'[17]

In *Persona* the face is that of Alma Vogler, whose descent into *nigredo* has left her silent. In *Eraserhead* the face is that of Henry Spencer. *Persona* begins with a montage of images which refer specifically to the 'birth' of a film (a projector, film frames, upside-down animated sequences, sexual imagery); *Eraserhead*'s opening sequence suggests a descent into the dark recesses of the human spirit – of taking up the black matter of *nigredo*, and using it as the fuel to artistic creativity. Ultimately, Henry embraces the woman who teases him. Everything is fine in Heaven, but Henry has distinctly earthly issues to contend with.

The Elephant Man (1980)

*Was I so tall, could reach the pole,
Or grasp the ocean with a span;
I would be measured by the soul,
The mind's the standard of the man.'*

from Isaac Watts, *False Greatness*, quoted by
Joseph Merrick.

Synopsis: *London 1884. Surgeon Frederick Treves,
visiting a carnival sideshow, sees an exhibit entitled the
'Elephant Man', a grotesquely deformed figure of a
man. He persuades the exhibit's 'owner' to allow him to
take the man to the London Hospital for examination.
Like everyone else, Treves assumes the man is mentally
as well as physically retarded, but after some weeks
discovers that 'John Merrick' is articulate, well-read and
compassionate. Treves is unable to cure Merrick's
accelerating deformity, but provides him with a
sanctuary from the brutality beyond the hospital walls
and from those who wish to exploit him for profit.*

    *Treves meets with opposition from inside and outside
the hospital – Merrick is kidnapped by his former owner
and exhibited abroad. But he returns to Treves, becomes
the toast of London society, and following the fulfilment
of his greatest wish – a visit to the theatre – dies by
suffocation in attempting to sleep like a normal human
being.*

Shortly after John Merrick is befriended by Mrs Kendal,
a celebrated West-End actress, she pays him a visit and
presents him with a gift, a copy of Shakespeare's
Romeo and Juliet. He opens the book and begins
reading. They are Romeo's lines to Juliet. Mrs Kendal
Anne recites Juliet's lines and John Merrick continues to read
Bancroft, from the text, struggling to express the words with as
John Hurt much conviction as his deformed mouth allows.

MERRICK: If I profane with my unworthiest hand
This holy shrine, the gentle fine is this,
My lips, two blushing pilgrims, ready stand
To smooth that rough touch with a tender kiss
MRS KENDAL: Good pilgrim, you do wrong your hand
too much,
Which mannerly devotion shows in this;
For saints have hands that pilgrim's hands do touch,
And palm to palm is holy palmers' kiss.
MERRICK: Have not saints lips, and holy palmers too?
MRS KENDAL: Ay, pilgrim, lips that they must use in
prayer.
MERRICK: O, then, dear saint, let lips do what hands
do;
They pray, grant thou, lest faith turn to despair.
MRS KENDAL: Saints do not move, though grant for
prayer's sake.
MERRICK: Then move not while my prayer's effect I
take.
Thus from my lips, by thine, my sin is purg'd.

He reads out a scene instruction in subdued voice and
turns away awkwardly. 'Then it says, they kiss,' he says.
Mrs Kendal approaches Merrick and plants her lips
upon his deformed cheek.

MRS KENDAL: Then have my lips the sin that they have
took.
MERRICK: Sin from my lips? O trespass sweetly urg'd!
Give me my sin again.'

'Oh, Mr Merrick', says Mrs Kendal. 'You're not an
elephant man at all.'
'No?' says Merrick.
'No', she says. 'You are Romeo.'

It is a scene that externalises the inner turmoil of
Merrick's unexpressed fervour – a dramatic device
enabling this unlikely couple to articulate their feelings
through the lyricism of the bard. For Merrick the scene
expresses the desires concealed beneath his deformity,
emphasising the hopelessness of his condition. The story
of Merrick is of a man, whom nature has thwarted at
birth, struggling for love.
When Treves exhibits Merrick before the Society of
Anatomists (Merrick's silhouette is outlined through a
sheet draped before his body), still believing him to be
an imbecile, he notes to his colleagues 'that the genitals
are normal.' When Treves and Carr Gomm examine him

Treves concludes, 'An imbecile from birth.' 'Yes,' says Carr Gomm. 'A complete idiot. I pray to God he's an idiot.' The grim subtext to these lines is that were not Merrick so hideous to look upon, he would be capable of a normal sex life. As he is apparently 'an imbecile from birth' his appearance makes no difference.

In Treves' account, published in 1923, entitled 'The Elephant Man', upon which the screenplay is partially based, he wrote: 'I supposed that Merrick was imbecile and had been imbecile from birth... That he could appreciate his position was unthinkable. Here was a man in the heyday of youth who was so vilely deformed that everyone he met confronted him with a look of horror and disgust.'[2]

Better to be an imbecile, reasoned Treves, and be thus less conscious of fate's appalling blow, than to be aware of the hideousness of his appearance and the inhumanity of those around him. Better an imbecile than to feel the normal human desires for love and companionship and never assuage them.

Later Treves writes: 'It was not until I came to know that Merrick was highly intelligent, that he possessed an acute sensibility and – worse than all – a romantic imagination that I realised the overwhelming tragedy of his life.'[3]

Treves' observation – 'worse than all – a romantic imagination' is the inspiration to Lynch's film which elevates the narrative from the macabre to the sublime. It is the story of 'Beast' and 'Beauty', the inverse of Jean Cocteau's *La Belle et la Bete* (1946).

BEAST: My heart is good but I am a monster.

BEAUTY: There are many men more monstrous, but it doesn't show.

They are lines as appropriate to Merrick and Mrs Kendal as to Beauty and the Beast. Whereas *La Belle et la Bete* concerns the sexual awakening of a young girl – Belle integrating her projected animus, Merrick's story is of a man attempting to integrate the archetypal feminine.

Treves wrote: 'To secure Merrick's recovery and to bring him, as it were, to life once more, it was necessary that he should make the acquaintance of men and women who would treat him as a normal and intelligent young man and not as a monster of deformity. Women I felt to be more important than men in bringing about his transformation. Women were the more frightened of him, the more disgusted at his appearance and the more apt to give way to irrepressible expressions of aversion when they came into his presence. Moreover, Merrick had an admiration of women of such a kind that it attained almost to adoration. This was not the outcome of his personal experience. They were not real women but the products of his imagination. Among them was the beautiful mother surrounded, at a respectful distance, by heroines from the many romances he had read.'[4]

Many men more monstrous

The film begins with the image of the smiling and compassionate face of a young woman – the photographic portrait of Merrick's mother. The images which follow, the birth scene, parading elephants, swirling clouds and machine steam, are accompanied by the sounds of the rhythmic pounding of industry, steam-driven machines and the wailing of elephants which tone into her own screams, and the screams of a newborn infant. It is an opening charged with the intensity of *Eraserhead*'s more metaphoric birth, as a human soul departs the void. It marks the beginning of the film's cyclic passage moving towards the final images of the spirit leaving the body and returning to the void from whence it came.

The wails of despair and pain of birth dissolve into the screams of fairground amusement and people milling about carnival sideshows. The screams express both the isolation of pain and the collective shrieks of idle mirth.

A well-dressed gent, the surgeon Frederick Treves (Anthony Hopkins), surveys the carnival exhibits. He walks through a labyrinth of various exhibits, arriving finally at a dark cul-de-sac where police are involved in an altercation with a sideshow proprietor. They are closing down an exhibit. The freak on display is so grotesque it is causing offence and distress to onlookers.

At the surgery of the London Hospital, Treves is operating on a man's face mutilated by an industrial accident. 'Abominable things these machines,' he says, an ironic aside in light of the abominations to be perpetrated by Merrick's fellow human beings later in the film.

Treves walks through the squalor of London's East End to meet Bytes, the sideshow exhibit proprietor. 'This creature's mother was struck down by a wild elephant in the fourth month of pregnancy,' Bytes declares. It is a statement belonging more to the crowd-drawing patter of the showman (both in fiction and reality) with little basis on fact. Lynch's 'parade of elephants' is more of a visual and aural metaphor than an image giving credence to the sideshow explanation of Merrick's condition. (In 1930 Dr Parkes Weber diagnosed Merrick's condition as an extreme case of neurofibromatosis, an incurable disorder which in Merrick's case was most likely caused by a chance genetic mutation.)[5]

The character Bytes (Freddie Jones), and later the hospital porter (Michael Elphick) are apparently fictitious elements, melodramatic caricatures to provide dramatic contrast. (Tom Norman, one of Merrick's actual showmen, claimed the freaks with whom he had dealings were 'with very few exceptions, as happy as the days are long, and were very contented with their lot in life.')[6] Though Merrick no doubt suffered during his years as 'an exhibit', both Bytes and the hospital porter function more as token representatives of a 'nether world', in contrast to the wholesome and correct society inhabited by Dr Treves and his colleagues.

David Lean's Charles Dickens' adaptations, *Great Expectations* (1946) and *Oliver Twist* (1948) were, possibly, Lynch's inspiration for Bytes and the hospital porter. To the ear, the names Bytes and Sykes are not so far removed, nor is the former's character dissimilar to David Lean's manipulative and tormenting Fagin, or the convict Magwitch. In addition, the contrasting innocence and naivety of both Oliver and Pip are endearing qualities which John Merrick shares, and even the look and style of *The Elephant Man* resembles Lean's recreation of Victorian London in both films, including Lynch's choice to shoot the film in black and white.

When Treves beholds the creature – a shadowy figure in the corner of a darkened cell – for the first time, he weeps a single tear. He persuades Bytes to bring the 'exhibit' to his surgery at the London Hospital for examination. 'Life is full of surprises,' he says.

Later Treves discusses the case with his superior, Carr Gomm (John Gielgud). They are satisfied that the man is 'an imbecile from birth', and return him to the showman, Bytes. In a drunken rage Bytes beats Merrick viciously. Word gets back to Treves, and Merrick is returned to the doctor's care. The doctor is warned for contravening hospital regulations. Merrick must be taken elsewhere. A nurse takes a bowl of porridge into Merrick's room and screams in horror. Merrick screams back. The scene is vividly portrayed in Treves' memoirs. Lynch uses the incident as a dramatic climax – for the first time Merrick is revealed in the full light of day.

Treves briefly relinquishes his role as observer and becomes 'involved'. He attempts to communicate with Merrick. 'Nod your head if you can understand,' says Treves. Merrick nods. Treves teaches him to repeat a sentence. 'Hello. My name is John Merrick.' As Merrick's first utterance it is a line charged with savage irony: his real name was Joseph Merrick.

Merrick's birth certificate, which Treves saw following Merrick's death, reads: Joseph Carey Merrick b. Leicester 5.8.1862.[7] In his hand-written account, Treves wrote that according to the showman 'his name was John Merrick' and this was the name he used in his notes. Later, he did begin to use the name 'Joseph', but then crossed out these references, replacing them with the name 'John', presumably to keep his accounts in order, and prevent unnecessary confusion. The result was just the opposite.

Bytes comes back and demands the return of his source of income, his 'treasure'. Treves refuses to give Merrick up. 'All you do is profit from another man's misery,' he tells him, and Bytes leaves. Treves is still uncertain as to what level of 'humanness' is concealed by Merrick's disfigured form, but has established a bond with his new-found 'patient'. Treves teaches Merrick the 23rd psalm, beginning 'The lord is my shepherd...' Carr Gomm insists that Merrick be transferred to another hospital as the man is incurable and only capable of learning passages taught to him. He is incapable of thinking for himself. Carr Gomm leaves and outside the door Treves listens in astonishment. He calls Carr Gomm back. Merrick is reciting 'And yea though I walk in the shadow of the valley of death...' 'I never taught him that part...' says Treves.

Treves discovers that Merrick can read and write and learnt many biblical passages as a young boy. He is appalled to discover that Merrick has gone through life in this wretched state quite aware of his condition. Merrick is allowed to stay. No mirrors are allowed in his room.

News of Merrick travels quickly. From fashionable newspapers to pub gossip, interest in the 'Elephant Man' ranges from concern to idle prurience. The hospital porter assures Merrick of his 'interest', foretelling a grim unfolding of events, which dissolves into a montage of factories, steam and the sounds of industry. Merrick is as much a victim of his time as his deformity.

Treves invites Merrick home for afternoon tea and to meet his wife Anne. She smiles and shakes his hand. Later Merrick weeps. 'I'm not so used to being treated so well by a beautiful woman,' he tells her. Then he asks: 'Would you like to see my mother?' He shows her the photograph. 'Why, she's beautiful', says Anne Treves. 'I must have been a great disappointment to her,' says Merrick. 'My mother was so very beautiful.' His words accompany the image of 'mother's' photograph – a young and beautiful woman with a faraway gaze, more in keeping with the idealism of a pre-Raphaelite portrait than the impoverished woman from a Leicester working-class family who bore Joseph Merrick into the world. A musical coda, reminiscent of a music-box tune, intensifies the nostalgia and the delicacy of the image – in his mind Merrick opens up a figurative music box taking out the one precious memory of his past, admiring it, treasuring it. Anne Treves turns away discreetly and weeps in silence.

Treves' memoirs record the following: 'It was a favourite belief of his (Merrick) that his mother was beautiful. The fiction was, I am aware, one of his own making, but it was a great joy to him. His mother, lovely as she may have been, basely deserted him when he was very small, so small that his earliest clear memories were of the workhouse to which he had been taken. Worthless and inhuman as this mother was, he spoke of her with pride and even with reverence. Once, when referring to his own appearance, he said: "It is very strange, for, you see, mother was so beautiful."'[8]

Treves' account, written thirty-five years after Merrick's death, is, on occasion, guilty of melodramatic excess. Joseph's mother, for example, died when he was 10 years old. Nonetheless, the line is central to Lynch's concept of Merrick's story – a disfigured creature who carries with him an image of the idealised feminine – the 'Beast' and 'Beauty'. In *Dune*, Lynch portrays a similarly ambiguous mother-son relationship – following the death of his father, Paul's relationship with his mother (his father's mistress) is imbued with sexual tension, just as Merrick's evocation of the 'feminine' suggests desire rather than memories of maternal nurturing.

Back in his quarters, Merrick sketches a cathedral spire visible from his window. He begins constructing a model and Treves encourages him. 'I wish I could sleep like normal people,' says Merrick. 'Can you cure me?' he asks. 'No,' says Treves. 'We can care for you, but we can't cure you.' Part of Treves' 'caring' is arranging for the celebrated West-End actress, Mrs Kendal, to visit. As a result, Merrick finds himself a centre of attention under less exacting circumstances than his carnival sideshow days, as prominent citizens follow Mrs Kendal's example.

Merrick's fragmented dream images contrast the past – the workhouse and parading elephants – and the vaporous uncertainties of the present and future – the sky, clouds, steam...

Treves battles with his conscience. 'I've made Mr Merrick a curiosity all over again... why did I do it? Am I a good man or a bad man?' he asks himself. But Treves soon finds a more pressing conflict to resolve. The committee of the London Hospital wants Merrick evicted: 'He attracts unfavourable publicity – he does not belong here,' protests a committee spokesman.

Treves records; 'There were two anxieties which were prominent in his (Merrick's) mind... he often asked me timidly to what place he would be next moved... another trouble was his dread of his fellow-men, his fear of people's eyes, the dread of always being stared at, the lash of the cruel mutterings of the crowd.'[9]

The hospital committee scene is principally a dramatic contrivance – following the objections of committee members, and the threat to Merrick's precarious security, Princess Alexandra enters the chamber with the gusto of a theatrical denouement. She, Queen Victoria and the royal family are most interested in the Merrick case, she informs the committee. They trust the hospital will continue its support. Merrick is granted permanent residence.

Treves informs Merrick who is overcome with joy. The 'vanity set' Treves gives him as a present relates to an incident recorded by Treves as follows; 'I asked Merrick what he would like me to purchase as a Christmas present. He rather startled me by saying shyly that he would like a dressing bag with silver fittings...

'So the bag was obtained and Merrick the Elephant Man became, in the seclusion of his chamber, the Piccadilly exquisite, the young spark, the gallant... I realised that as he could never travel he could hardly want a dressing bag. He could not use the silver-backed brushes and the comb because he had no hair to brush. The ivory-handled razors were useless because he could not shave. The deformity of his mouth rendered an ordinary toothbrush of no avail, and as his monstrous lips could not hold a cigarette the cigarette-case was a mockery...still the bag was an emblem of the real swell and of the knockabout Don Juan of whom he had read.'[10]

Treves refers to the 'one shadow in Merrick's life', which is significant in light of one of the film's most poignant scenes in which the hospital porter organises a 'private show' amongst the clientele of the local public house. He makes good his earlier promise to Merrick in maintaining his 'interest'.

Treves writes: '(Merrick) had a lively imagination; he was a romantic; he cherished an emotional regard for women and his favourite pursuit was the reading of love stories. He fell in love – in a humble and devotional way – with, I think, every attractive lady he saw... He was amorous. He would like to have been a lover...when he talked of life among the blind there was a half-formed idea in his mind that he might be able to win the affection of a woman if only she were without eyes to see.'[11]

The paying customers the hospital porter lures to the basement quarters of the 'Elephant Man' consist of couples, well-dressed 'gentlemen' seeking to entertain their 'gentlewomen' escorts. A solitary elderly man joins the glad and intoxicated throng – Bytes.

The entourage of genteel spectators breaks into Merrick's room. He is passive and distressed. The men force their women to look, while they caress and slaver over them with sexual excitement. It is a scene of grotesque sexual perversity where the seemingly normal and well-dressed gentle folk display themselves as monstrous and 'deformed' while Merrick struggles to retain his composure and his dignity. Orchestrated music swells. One man forces his lady 'escort' to kiss Merrick upon his deformed lips. The hospital porter aided by the other men pins Merrick against the wall.

It is an obscene contrast with the tenderness and romance of the love scene played between Merrick and Mrs Kendal. If The Elephant Man is a horror film[12] here is one scene which is 'horrific' in the word's intended meaning. The kiss, from an expression of esteem and exaltation becomes degrading, subjugating – an act of humiliation and the defeat of John Merrick. It precedes similar scenes in Lynch's later films; tenderness becomes prurience, the pure, impure – closeness becomes estrangement, a bonding becomes isolation, the sublime turns obscene. Merrick, briefly liberated into hitherto unknown realms of romance and tenderness, is compelled once more to withdraw into the lonely enclaves of the monstrous.

His room is destroyed. The porter takes out a mirror

and encourages everyone to watch – he forces the mirror before Merrick's face to gloat over his reaction. Carousel music becomes more frantic. Bytes appears. 'My treasure,' he says.

The following morning Treves enters the room – it is in disarray and Merrick is gone. He encounters the porter in the cellar and attacks him in a rage. No one knows where Merrick is. The porter is dismissed.

The restrained and conventional mode of the film avoids sensationalism, is at times understated, at times contriving narrative devices and climaxes to comply with the traditional three-act drama of the commercial cinema. It's probably the most conventional screenplay with which Lynch has been involved – the chronology of Merrick's life has been re-arranged for the sake of the story.

In the terminology of the Hollywood screenplay, Merrick's disappearance constitutes the second-act climax – 'what will become of Merrick now?' The conflict between Merrick (protagonist) and the fictitious Bytes (antagonist), with Treves in the role of catalyst, together with the film's dramatic structure, are contrivances that obscure more suggestive themes.

Merrick's continental tour is factual – his abduction fiction; his arrival and collapse at Victoria station factual; his dramatic escape aided by fellow freaks, fiction.

The film proceeds with Merrick's return to the freak show; to avoid local prosecution Bytes undertakes a tour to Belgium. Merrick collapses. He is locked in a cage and monkeys attack from the other side of the bars. In scenes reminiscent of the camaraderie in Tod Browning's film, *Freaks* (1932), Merrick is released by other members of sideshow exhibits. A procession of freaks proceeds through the forest at night. They smuggle Merrick on board a boat from Calais to Dover. He returns to England. A steam boat. A steam train. The vapours and sounds of industry provide an ambience, a protective blanket – substance and noise as impermanent as life itself.

At Victoria station Merrick, dressed in cape and hood, is harassed by juveniles, and unmasked. He runs ungainly through the station pursued by a hostile crowd, and finally is cornered like a frightened animal. 'I am not an elephant,' he cries. 'I am not an animal. I am a human being.' He collapses. The police come to disperse the unruly crowd. In the pocket of the unconscious Merrick is a visiting card bearing the name Frederick Treves, London Hospital.

In the sanctity of his hospital quarters, Merrick's rehabilitation is swift, but the disease causing his deformities is accelerating rapidly. Merrick is now twenty-seven and dying. 'I am happy every hour of the day,' he tells Treves. 'I have gained my Self.'

But his final triumph is a visit to the Drury Lane Theatre, arranged by Mrs Kendal. It is a pantomime of *Puss in Boots* (this is no fiction – it was indeed *Puss in Boots* which Joseph Merrick saw at the Drury Lane Theatre in 1887).[13] Merrick becomes an observer of a spectacle rather than a spectacle himself, and he is enthralled. The fragments of the pantomime – the cat, the journey along a magic road, a little girl, a monster who turns into a lion, the carousel – could easily be interpreted as fragments from *The Wizard of Oz*, which features later in both *Blue Velvet* and *Wild at Heart*. Indeed the final scene we observe with Merrick, of the Princess Sweetheart descending to the stage, magic wand in hand, and concluding the performance with 'happily ever after' bears more than a slight resemblance to the final scene of *Wild at Heart*, when the Good Witch Glinda descends to transform a morally defeated Sailor Ripley. Princess Sweetheart's effect on Merrick is much the same. He is transformed, enchanted, uplifted.

At the end of the performance, as the players take their curtain calls, Mrs Kendal addresses the public and dedicates the evening's presentation to 'a very special guest', John Merrick. Merrick stands and the public applauds. A spotlight casts its light upon his deformed but well-dressed figure, and he bows.

It is an ambiguous moment – though for all of Treves' misgivings there is no suggestion, neither in the film nor in the records of Merrick's life, that he spurned the public gaze – on the contrary, he volunteered himself for exhibition in carnivals, and now, before the gaze of the theatre public, basks in the limelight as they applaud his presence. It is a moment of triumph, yet distinctly uncomfortable – Lynch makes us accomplices, lauding and validating the voyeur within us. Merrick is a spectacle once more – recalling Treves' earlier pangs of conscience; 'I've made Mr Merrick a curiosity all over again... why did I do it?'

After the evening, in Merrick's quarters, Merrick is overwhelmed with joy. He completes the last touches to his model of the cathedral. 'It's finished,' he says. He gazes at the picture on the wall of a sleeping child and re-arranges his pillows. Ordinarily, due to his deformed shape, he must lie half upright during the hours of sleep, in order to be able to breathe. Tonight he will sleep like a normal person.

Treves writes: 'He often said to me that he wished he could lie down to sleep "like other people". I think on this last night he must, with some determination, have made the experiment. The pillow was soft, and the head, when placed on it, must have fallen backwards and caused a dislocation of the neck. Thus it came about that his death was due to the desire that had dominated his life – the pathetic but hopeless desire to be "like other people."'[14]

In the swirling stars outside his window, his mother's young face appears, diffused with clouds and vapour, and she smiles and says: 'Never, no, never, nothing dies. The stream flows, the wind blows, cloud fleets, the heart beats. Nothing will die.'

From the void and returned to the void – where we come from and where we go; as in Lynch's earlier films, *The Grandmother* and *Eraserhead*, Lynch traces the cycle from birth to death and the unanswerable mysteries of before and after.

An elemental being

The Elephant Man is a self-consciously, old-fashioned styled narrative, enhanced by Freddie Francis's black and white cinematography (himself a director of low-budget Hammer horror films in the 1960s), told simply and directly with a minimum of cinematic effects. The opening, closing and central 'dream' montage sequences contribute to the illusion of form coming from the ether and returning to it. It emphasises a predominant existential theme in Lynch's films – the frailty of human existence – the transient brevity of human life made all the more poignant by the exemplary fate of the 'inhumanly' born Joseph Merrick.

'I found that I had to give my soul to the part,' commented John Hurt, who was nominated for the Best Actor Academy Award. 'It is so far beyond any ordinary human experience.'[15]

Paradoxically, by evaluating a life such as Merrick's, the 'rational being', whether doctor, scientist or magician is himself energised; the 'primitive' unleashes a creative drive, providing new-found purpose. 'Am I a good man or a bad man?' asks Treves of himself. Or as Sandy assesses Jeffrey in *Blue Velvet*; 'I'm not sure if you're a detective or a pervert.' Treves' interest in Merrick is an investigation on behalf of medical science, but are his motives as humanitarian as he maintains?

Lynch portrays the scientist as 'magician' and his relationship to his patient. On one level this is the relationship between a voyeur and the object of his gaze (a theme in which Lynch, like many film directors, finds a source of inspiration), or on another level, the roles of 'scientist' and 'object of study'. There exists a parallel with the relationship between the film director/ artist and the viewer, and also the archetypal relationship between the rational mind and the primitive life-force.

Merrick embodies the life-force; he is the misshapen monster that replenishes Treves with his unrelenting yearning. 'Savage, deformed slave' is the description attributed to Caliban in the *Dramatis Personae* of Shakespeare's *The Tempest*. Caliban is subservient to Prospero in the same way Merrick is dependent upon Treves. But just as Prospero's stature grows fuelling Caliban's strength, so does Treves' stature develop with Merrick's progress. The two are dependent upon each other.[16]

Treves, as presented by Lynch, is a Victorian romantic, seeing in Merrick 'the Noble Savage', a 'primitive creature.'[17] (Henry David Thoreau's *Walden*, published in 1854, which popularised the 'noble savage' concept, became a source of inspiration for the Romantic movement in the late 19th century.) For Lynch the tale of *The Elephant Man* is a social parable describing the affinity between the Enlightened and the Noble Savage. Merrick's creativity and desires feed Treves' reasoning mind – Treves 'lives' through Merrick's delight in the theatre, in romance, the acquisition of a dressing set, building a model cathedral, learning to articulate speech.

It is the relationship of Prospero and Caliban, and it is necessary to compare recent films treating this theme by so-called 'thinking' directors with *The Elephant Man* in order to understand why Lynch's film is thematically similar yet essentially different. Francois Truffaut's *The Wild Child (L'enfant sauvage*, 1969) documents, in the same objective straightforward way, the case of Cargol, a young boy found in the woods in central France in 1798. He was sent to the Institute for the Deaf and Dumb in Paris. Dr Jean Itard, played by Truffaut himself, teaches Cargol, who had been raised by wolves, to walk upright, wear clothes and speak. Like *The Elephant Man*, Truffaut's film was based on an actual account; Cargol was dubbed the wild boy of Aveyron, and the case received similar attention and notoriety as the case of Joseph Merrick.

Truffaut, like Anthony Hopkins, plays the doctor without sentiment – a man of science unravelling a mystery; ultimately the mystery of what makes us human – yet prodded by a conscience as to whether his subject is as much an object of the voyeuristic gaze in his jurisdiction, as elsewhere.

It is a dilemma encapsulated in the original title of Werner Herzog's film – *Jeder für Sich und Gott Gegen Alle* – Every Man for Himself and God Against All (*The Enigma of Kasper Hauser*, 1974). Also based on an actual case, it is the story of a young man who appears in the Nuremburg town square in the early 19th century. Kaspar Hauser's 'condition' also drives him to the carnival sideshows. Finally he is taken under the kindly wing of Herr Daumer – and Kaspar's education begins. It traces the relationship between the mentor and protégé – making human the 'freak'. Herr Daumer teaches Kaspar speech and logic, delighting in the progress he makes with his unlikely pupil. Like Merrick, Kaspar came under public scrutiny, 'a fascinating case' of his day. He was killed by an unknown assailant when in his late 20s.

'He was an elemental being, so primitive that he might have spent the twenty-three years of his life immured in a cave.'[18] The words are an accurate description of Kaspar Hauser's life, yet they are written by Frederick Treves describing his impressions of Joseph Merrick. They echo Lynch's view of himself – that 'there was nothing much going on upstairs until the age of 19.'[19]

Truffaut dedicated *The Wild Child* to Jean-Pierre Leaud, the young actor who featured in Truffaut's debut film, *The Four-Hundred Blows* (*Les Quatre Cents Coups*, 1959). *The Enigma of Kaspar Hauser* is Werner Herzog's tribute to the remarkable personality of Bruno S., who plays the title role. He spent twenty-two years in prisons and institutions, before being discovered by Herzog, playing an accordion in a Berlin square.

These films concern the film director's preoccupation with the outsider, the social misfit, and the developing relationship between mentor and protégé. They are dramatisations entrenched in the tradition of social realism.

Padre Padrone (Paolo and Vittorio Taviani, 1977) is also a true-life account based on the life of Gavino Ledda, who is forced into the isolated life of a goatherd by a domineering father. He is deprived of language and companionship until his late teens. Ledda himself introduces the film – in his 20s he taught himself to read and write and, fascinated with language, continued his studies, finally becoming a teacher of linguistics.

Arthur Penn's 1962 film, *The Miracle Worker*, tells the true-life story about blind, deaf and mute Helen Keller and how she is taught speech and literacy by her teacher, Anne Sullivan. (Anne Sullivan is played by Anne Bancroft, who plays the role of Mrs Kendal.) *Awakenings* (Penny Marshall, 1990), also based on actual events, traces the career of a research doctor (Robin Williams) who works in a chronic care ward. A comatose patient (Robert De Niro) responds to his treatment and awakens from a 30-year coma, now compelled, under the good doctor's guidance, to contend with life as an adult. The story is based on the book and experiences of Dr Oliver Sacks in the late 1960s.

Awakenings and *The Miracle Worker*, and the many similar well-intentioned films of the commercial cinema, are straightforward Hollywood bio-pics, complying rigidly with the conventions demanded by the genre – sentimental and sufficiently socially conscious to attract appreciative comment at Academy Award functions. The films of Taviani, Truffaut and Herzog relate to actual people, but also to actual relationships between the director and the subject – Leaud is Truffaut's 'wild child', Bruno S. is Herzog's Kaspar Hauser, and Gavino Ledda himself is the driving force that inspired the Taviani brothers to make *Padre Padrone*. In each case the protagonist is driven by a spiritual hunger – striving to realise 'logos' – the word.

The Elephant Man, like these other stories, based on an actual case, nonetheless remains Lynch's 'fiction'. Behind the mask of the Elephant Man is a gifted performer – John Hurt – and behind him is the Gothic vision of David Lynch.[20]

For Herzog, Truffaut, Arthur Penn, Penny Marshall and the Taviani brothers, the story's emphasis is on social adjustment – social outcasts struggling against deprivation, in order to attain knowledge. They are narratives that bear the implications of social critique – castigating the inadequacy of social systems incapable of accepting the 'Kaspar Hausers' of the world – who are redeemed only by the efforts of another social outcast – the devoted 'teacher'.

The narrative ingredients are the same but *The Elephant Man* is a different kind of story. David Lynch is the romantic seeking the sublime in the imperfect – realising the grandeur and nobility of the human spirit concealed in the superficial distortion of corrupted flesh. For beneath the surface of Lynch's hitherto most conventional film narrative lies a netherworld of decay and decomposition, of inhumanity and brutality. Merrick, estranged in the exclusively male domains of carnival entrepreneurs and medical science, is seeking something else other than knowledge.

John Merrick is also driven by a spiritual hunger. Literacy, however, he has.[21] His literacy remains hidden beneath his deformity. Merrick is driven, not by logos – the word; but by eros – the touch, representing physical love.

His longing is embodied by the portrait of his mother – the idealised image of the feminine. The ideal is finally realised in the appearance of Mrs Kendal, who unlocks his own feminine side with the romance of drama, a few words of love and a kiss upon the cheek.

Dune (1984)

"I was happy. It was so awful."
Alejandro Jodorowski.

Synopsis: *'A beginning is a very delicate time. Know then that it is the year 10,191. The known universe is ruled by the Padishar Emperor Shaddam IV – my father. In this time the most precious substance in the universe is the spice, melange. The spice extends life, the spice expands consciousness, the spice is vital to space travel...'*

Princess Irulan begins narrating the story of the conflict between the Emperor, in league with House Harkonnen, and House Atreides. Young Paul Atreides is to be killed, and House Atreides defeated. That they are to take over the production of the spice on Planet Arrakis – Dune – is a ploy of the Emperor's, designed to bring about their demise.

On Dune the deformed and malevolent Baron Harkonnen leads the assault on House Atreides – Paul's father, the Duke, is killed, but Paul and his mother, Lady Jessica, escape into uncharted desert. Here the giant sandworms devour all living things. But Paul and his mother come under the protection of desert dwellers, the Fremen, and Paul's arrival fulfils an ancient prophecy.

Both Paul and Jessica possess occult powers and teach the Fremen warriors the means by which to defeat the Harkonnen.

In the final battle, Baron Harkonnen is destroyed and the Emperor defeated. Paul has become all-powerful, and true to his promise to change the face of Arrakis, summons the rain, which begins to fall on the planet's surface where no drop of rain has ever fallen before.

Kyle MacLachlan, Francesca Annis

John Merrick, the Elephant Man, yearns for respite from the masculine world of carnival entrepreneurs and medical scientists in an alternative feminine world, imbued with compassion and feeling, which is denied him. Paul Atreides, the young hero of *Dune*, is also the solitary and socially estranged hero – with a destiny as the only male to be granted entry into an otherwise exclusively feminine realm. In Lynch's next film, *Blue Velvet*, Jeffrey is the male intruder stealing his way into the forbidden domain of 'Aphrodite's' boudoir.

Dune is concerned with male politics, male militarism and male power plays. Beneath the surface of these male orchestrated inter-galactic conflicts is a 'feminine' network, called the Bene Gesserit, orchestrating political manoeuvres of their own, with subterfuge and cunning, plotting to produce a female messianic leader. However, it is Paul who, through an accident of birth, is destined to be the Kwisatz Haderach – a male child combining psychological attributes of masculine and feminine.

At the beginning of the story, Paul undergoes a two-fold initiation; trial by combat to satisfy his male peers, and trial by psychic suggestion to satisfy the Reverend Mother Gaius Helen Mohiam, Proctor Superior of the Bene Gesserit. The Duke, and the patriarchal system he represents, must ascertain the credibility of the youth as a political and military leader. The Reverend Mother must determine whether or not Paul is to become the Kwisatz Haderach. At the end of the story he once more undergoes two 'trials' – one masculine, one feminine; proving his military strength to the Emperor, and demonstrating the powers which prove that he *is* the Kwisatz Haderach.

On one level the conflict in *Dune* is between good and evil; House of Atreides and House of Harkonnen; on another level it concerns the psychological conflict between masculine and feminine. David Lynch's interpretation of one of the most successful science-fiction novels of all time is at once faithful to the novel, and incorporates themes of his earlier films. Ultimately the compromises necessary to combine Lynch's vision and Frank Herbert's narrative with the demands of the movie business proved unrealisable. What remains is a quasi-David Lynch film within a $45 million de Laurentiis production – some outstanding sequences within a disjointed whole.

'I sold out from the start,' says David Lynch six years later, 'by not having final cut, and by attempting to provide the producers with what they wanted more than what I wanted.'[1]

Parts of Frank Herbert's novel appeared in science-fiction magazines during the 1960s, and it was published in its entirety in 1965. Ten years later, the same year the novel was voted 'the greatest science-fiction novel published,' the Latin American film director, Alejandro Jodorowsky (*El Topo* – 1971, *Santa Sangre* – 1989, etc) began the preparatory work to make 'the greatest film ever made in the history of Hollywood.'[2] He assembled the talents of the Belgian illustrator, Morbius (Jean Giraud), the special effects expert, Dan O'Bannon, and H. R. Giger (best known for the *Alien* monster design), and they began a three-year collaboration on the project. Morbius sketched a storyboard containing three thousand drawings: 'he was the cameraman and I was the director,' says Jodorowski. Escalating costs proved too much even for the Hollywood financers and the project was abandoned in 1978.

The rights having expired, Dino de Laurentiis bought the property and in 1979 assigned Ridley Scott as director, who in turn assigned Rudolph Wurlitzer to write the screenplay adaptation. He opted for a personal interpretation – Alia was the result of an incestuous relationship between Paul and Jessica. Once again, an escalating budget led to Scott's departure from the project, and in 1981 de Laurentiis, following the success of *The Elephant Man*, assigned David Lynch, 'the one man who could maybe make the movie better than me', according to Alejandro Jodorowski.

When Lynch was engaged, the $45m budget was one of the cinema's largest ever. For Lynch it involved three-and-a-half years' work – 18 months on the script, first in collaboration with his co-scriptwriters from *The Elephant Man*, Christopher de Vore and Eric Bergren, though the final screen credit is Lynch alone; then a full year's shooting, and twelve months' post-production work. In 1983 filming began in Mexico – six months' principal shooting, studio and location, then six months' special photography and miniatures.[3]

Lynch claimed later that his main problem was too much material to edit into a two-hour film; 'I would like to make it more like a long poem. Just let it be abstract in some places, with no dialogue, and let it be more of a mood.'[4] Some years later a special 190-minute version of the film was edited for US television, despite protests from Lynch, containing new narration and previously unused footage. Lynch disavowed the project and direction is attributed to pseudonym Allen Smithee.

The film that was finally released in 1984 was a failure of magnificent proportions, castigated by critics, audiences and even Lynch himself, who 'died a thousand deaths'.[5]

Yet what remains is David Lynch's pictures to Frank Herbert's words; the story's themes are as central to the novel as they are to the film, and Lynch's interpretation, for all its shortcomings, embellishes, on occasion transcends, the source material. *Dune* is the story of 'George and the Dragon'.

Irulan

Dune begins where *The Elephant Man* ended. A young woman's kind and compassionate face is superimposed over the swirling stars of the cosmos. The final words of *The Elephant Man*, 'nothing ever dies' spoken by Merrick's mother, become 'a beginning is a very delicate time'. Princess Irulan, the daughter of the emperor, is ushered away at the arrival of the Third Stage Guild Navigator, then does not return to the narrative until the very end. Her presence pervades the film throughout in the nebulous manner of the idealised image of Merrick's mother in *The Elephant Man*.

Princess Irulan's voice-over provides the viewer with some necessary, though complicated exposition, ('You know you're in trouble when the film's opening narration setting up the story is completely incomprehensible,' wrote critic Leonard Maltin)[6] in which, amongst other things, the importance of the spice 'melange' is emphasised. It is only found on the desert planet, Arrakis, known as Dune, and 'he who rules the spice rules the universe.'

It is an opening which suggests a 'literary' style to the narrative – Lynch sets out to recreate the chronicle feel of Frank Herbert's epic novel. Lynch uses the voice-over device throughout the film, adhering to Herbert's 'externalising' process. The voice-over is often criticised as an intrusive non-cinematic device – Deckard's voice-over in *Blade Runner* (1982) was a post-production afterthought, considered necessary to clarify complications within the plot. In the case of *Blade Runner*, the effect, even if by default, is to emphasise the *film noir* style of the story – the solitary protagonist wrestling with his own despair and isolation, telling his tale with dispassionate gloom to an anonymous 'listener' (Deckard in Philip K. Dick's novel was a married man pursuing the luxury of a non-mechanical sheep – Deckard in the film was divorced, an emotionally 'cold fish', about to be ensnared by a humanoid *femme fatale*).

In *Dune*, the voice-over is not from the perspective of a single person – it may be the story of Paul Atreides, but just as Herbert reveals the inner thoughts of many characters, Lynch uses this essentially literary device for the same reason, to externalise the inner thoughts of principal 'dramatis personae' – sometimes several within the same scene. Even the Baron Harkonnen reveals his bloody intent with the aid of inner monologues in David Lynch's *Dune*.

The image of Princess Irulan, like that of John Merrick's mother, returns our gaze, but her initial frozen stillness is a deception – she is not a photographic portrait but a personality, the story-teller. She is the woman Paul Atreides will later marry – not for the sake of love, but for the sake of restoring and maintaining political balance and bringing an end to intergalactic conflict. Irulan is the quintessential projection of the feminine; passive, beautified and challenging the masculine gaze with her look to the camera. As the head-on gaze of John Merrick's mother pervades *The Elephant Man*, so the image of Irulan is a constant element in contrast to the turmoil of the characters and situations pitted against each other on Dune.

Frank Herbert describes her as, 'a tall blonde woman, green-eyed, a face of patrician beauty, classic in its hauteur, untouched by tears, completely undefeated. Without being told it, Paul knew her – Princess Royal, Bene Gesserit – trained, a face that time vision had shown him in many aspects: Irulan.'[7]

The Third Stage Guild Navigator

In Frank Herbert's novel, the conflicts between the Emperor, House Atreides and House Harkonnen are subtly manipulated by an unseen 'Guild'. David Lynch makes characters of the Guildsmen, calling them 'navigators', portrayed in various stages of mutation. Following Irulan's prologue, the complexities of *Dune*'s plot are outlined in a Guild report.

Lynch's use of computers to clarify complicated exposition is a further diversion from Frank Herbert's concept. 'A Secret Report Within the Guild', and a computer screen, are accompanied by a computer voice. The computer describes the four worlds which make up the story: Arrakis (Dune) – the desert planet on which the spice, melange, is mined. It is a world inhabited by the desert people, the Fremen, and administered by the Atreides's sworn enemy, House Harkonnen.

Kaitain is the home planet of the Emperor, Shaddam IV, Irulan's father; Caladan – home of House Atreides; and Giedi Prime – home of the sinister House Harkonnen, under the rule of the tyrant Baron Vladimir Harkonnen.

The sequence describes the complex political situation at the outset of the story. However, in doing so, Lynch abandons the novel's concept of worlds without machines. So-called 'thinking machines', principally computers, had been abolished as a result of the 'Butlerian Jihad', also known as the Great Revolt, many centuries before. This led to the establishment of the Bene Gesserit – a training school for female students to develop psychic powers, and the Mentat – humans trained as 'human computers'.

Similarly, the weirding modules are a fabrication of the film – the 'weirding way' described by Frank Herbert consists of the power of the voice, an occult force mastered and taught by the (feminine) Bene Gesserit. In the film, when Paul leads the Fremen, he constructs modules – machines – from plans salvaged after the Harkonnen's attack on Dune.

Whereas Frank Herbert is deliberately vague about the appearance of Guildsmen – 'No-one sees a Guildsman," the Duke tells Paul. "Do you think they hide because they've mutated and don't look... human any more?" "Who knows?" The Duke shrugged. "It's a mystery we're not likely to solve." '[8] – David Lynch, with Carlos Rambaldi's design, portrays the Third Stage Guild Navigator as the definitive form of asexuality.

Black-dressed First Stage Guild Navigators direct a massive black steel vessel to the court of the Emperor. The First Stage mutants already show distinct signs of the Lynchian 'open body', with broken skin, intruding tubes, protruding mechanical devices and hairless skulls. The removal of the black plates reveal a roving eye imbedded in an aquatic slug far removed from Rambaldi's E.T. creation.

This slug is one more Lynch misshapen biological throwback, like Henry's genderless mutant infant in *Eraserhead*, like the umbilical cord forms that plague Henry's dreams. Whereas gender is clearly defined on Kaitain by dress and adornments, the Navigator is repulsively naked, floating around a glass tank like an internal organ in an alcohol-filled specimen jar. It is sexless, like Henry Spencer's 'monsters', and like the

Arrakis sandworm on Dune. And just as Henry's genderless monstrosity determined his fate, so does the 'genderless monstrosity', in the form of the Navigator, determine the fate of Paul, the protagonist of *Dune*.

Through the voice of a First Stage interpreter, the Navigator, from his glass-paned water tank, tells the Emperor that, 'the spice must flow.' The Emperor relates his plot to incite conflict between House Atreides and House Harkonnen. He will allow Atreides to assume power over Arrakis, so they then may be destroyed by Harkonnen. The Guild Navigator sees a flaw – the untimely birth of a male to a sister of the Bene Gesserit. And his father is the Duke Atreides. The boy may be the foretold messiah, the Kwisatz Haderach. For the Space Guild, Paul might unbalance the established order of things based on the ongoing conflict between patriarchy and matriarchy. 'Paul Atreides must be killed,' says the Navigator.

The Reverend Mother

The initial conflict – that Harkonnen should defeat Atreides – is contrived by the Emperor in league with the Space Guild. The Guild wants Paul killed because, as Fremen leader, he could threaten spice production. The intrigue initiated by the emperor is the attempt of a patriarchal order to eliminate a matriarchal power which threatens it. Although the Bene Gesserit plot demanded a noble-born woman they can still use Paul because of his Bene Gesserit (feminine) powers.

The matriarchal order is unconcerned with political boundaries, or race, or House. Bene Gesserit Reverend Mothers are amongst the Fremen, House Atreides, and Planet Kaitain, home of the Emperor.

The initiation sequences that begin the story test the two sides of Paul's character. He proves control over his body (a battle with his instructor, Gurney, who fights to the maximum; and with a machine, as a test of reflexes). Then he must prove control over mind, and withstand the test of the Bene Gesserit Reverend Mother. He passes this test too. Paul is in control of both mind and body – he is the Lynchian 'perfect body' protagonist *par excellence*; whole as opposed to broken, 'closed' as opposed to 'open'. He is the antithesis of Lynch's version of Baron Harkonnen, who has no control of his body, is ravaged by disease, is frequently unclothed, and 'open' in that his skin is ruptured, revealing matter and blood beneath the fissures. An anti-gravity machine is necessary to transport the Baron as he is too overweight to transport himself; his desires control his mind, hence the ravishing and cannibalising of young boys, and the hysterical madness which accompanies his deeds.

Paul may be in control of body and mind, his thoughts and deeds, but he has no control over his fate – the Reverend Mother has decided his destiny; she is his 'Moira'. Paul is the means to an end; the matriarchal conquest over patriarchal dominance.

The 'psychomachia', the struggle between souls, is not the conflict of opposites, but the conflict of polarities. The polarity of male and female defines them both, as does that of patriarch and matriarch. The Emperor's conflict with the Bene Gesserit Reverend Mother represents a struggle for supremacy between two sides – their 'opposite' is all-powerful, yet genderless.

Caladan

A towering dark castle on a cliffside above a raging sea and silhouetted against a stormy night sky introduces the home planet of Paul Atreides, his father, the Duke Leto, and his mother, Jessica. Jessica, in a hooded black cape, walks briskly across a windswept cobble-stoned courtyard to the giant wooden portals. The Duke sits at the mahogany desk of his book-lined study, rain beating against the lead-rimmed glass panes, and a well-groomed bull terrier waiting at his boots. 'I'll miss the sea,' says Paul's father, when they finally leave for Arrakis.

The images combine the visual splendour of *The French Lieutenant's Woman* (Reisz, 1981) and the ambience of a turn-of-the-century European royal family. Lynch's choice of a Victorian scenography and production design is more than mere kitsch delight in monstrous metallic machines of the past, brass knobbed devices, contraptions lifted from the illustrations of Jules Verne stories, stylish military clothing, long dresses and plunging necklines. The costumes and production design of the film's early sequences (on the planet Kaitain, home of the Emperor, and the planet Caladan, home of House Atreides) emphasise sexual contrasts and gender-defined social status. Men dress militarily, women dress domestically, and with sexual allure. Men are the social instruments of power and violence, women are the bearers of sexuality. There are clear and rigid lines of demarkation between the biological roles of male and female; between the social roles of men and women.[9] Less apparent are the psychological attributes of masculine and feminine – Paul Atreides is a symbiosis of the two opposites; his 'wholeness' is the means by which harmony can be restored.

In analysing the novel, Derek Longhurst maintains that: 'Herbert's narrative can be read as an exploration of the ways in which masculine identity often conceals conflict, uncertainty and ambivalence. On the one hand, the pull of aggression, competitiveness and desire for dominance and on the other the need and desire for tenderness, intimacy and sharing. This uneasy dichotomy of public identity and private self is registered in Herbert's fiction together with an examination of the relationship between militarism and masculinity.'[10]

Lynch accentuates the story's 'uneasy dichotomy' by emphasising Paul's 'masculine/feminine' duality. As the Duke's son he undergoes a male (physical) combat test with his trainer, Gurney. Dagger to dagger, each penetrating the other's shield, it is a display of masculine bravado, preparing Paul for his manly role in forthcoming trials of strength. As the offspring of a 'Bene Gesserit' he undergoes a female (mental) test, adminstered by the Reverend Mother. Under the threat of death he places his hand in a box and must withstand the pain of flames burning his hand to cinders. This psychic technique illustrates the telepathic powers of the Bene Gesserit, and a sequence verifies young Paul's resolve – he doesn't move his hand.

Military power and politics in *Dune* are exclusively male patriarchal issues between the Emperor, the Duke and the Baron. There are no empresses, duchesses or baronesses in *Dune*. The archetypal feminine is represented by the Reverend Mother (Magna Mater – The Great Mother) who directs Paul's initiation. She is a forbidding high priestess with a resolve bordering on the sadistic. Jessica is the Duke's concubine; Chani is to become Paul's concubine. In David Lynch's *Dune*, Alia, Paul's young sister, is as merciless as she is powerful – it is she who defeats Harkonnen, sending him reeling into the gaping orifice of an open-mouthed sandworm.

Giedi Prime

In contrast to the Gothic lyricism of Caladan, the Baron's home planet is a world of steel girders, mammoth structures and imposing edifices. All surfaces are manufactured and, unlike Caladan, here exists no evidence of 'nature'. Sea, sky and earth are obliterated by towering man-made forms, which are overwhelming and as unsightly as the most vast of industrial complexes. It is the landscape of *Eraserhead* gone mad with power.

David Lynch's interpretation of the Baron Vladimir Harkonnen continues his explorative characterisations of the perverse and psychopathic. Bytes, John Merrick's persecutor, is a parodic representation of the grotesque; the Baron's psychopathy borders on the absurd – an obese figure covered in boils and abscesses, who plots to destroy Atreides, rule Arrakis, the galaxy, the universe. 'He who controls the spice controls the universe,' he exclaims to his nephew protégé, Feyd. A servant brings him a young boy, who glares at him open-eyed in terror and repulsion – the Baron rips open the boy's chest and drinks his blood. 'This is what I'll do to the Duke and his family,' he says, for not only his violence will eliminate the Atreides, but the Baron's flagrant homosexuality will ensure the end of a progenitive line of rule.

There is no ambiguity in the portrayal of Harkonnen and Atreides. The Baron is evil, sadistic, gluttonous, avaricious – he is without redeeming features. Most significantly, the disorder he represents is bereft of a social structure, specifically, the family. Frank Herbert goes to some lengths to explain the interwoven family relationships between the Emperor, Harkonnen and Atreides; Jessica is Baron Harkonnen's daughter, Alia – who kills him – is his granddaughter; Leto Atreides is related to the Emperor; '... we are Harkonnens,' declares Paul after the Baron defeats the Duke.[11] In the film, Harkonnen and Atreides are two opposing sides – good against evil, order against chaos.

The Baron's gluttony extends to his sexuality, which in the film is exclusively homosexual and sadistic. When Jessica is bound, trussed and gagged before him the Baron dribbles spit onto her cheek, articulating jovially, that this he must do. It is a Lynchian excess as repellent as the Baron's festering boils. There are no women or children in the traditional family structure within the Baron's entourage.

The Duke, by contrast, is the traditional family patriarch – ruling his domain and his domicile with benevolence, yet naive about the political subterfuge which threatens his position. The Duke resembles Tsar Nicholas II, and the Caladan decor bears more than a passing resemblance to the court of Imperial Russia.

The departure of the Duke and his family as they

leave Caladan for Arrakis in a space convoy, removes us abruptly from the political chicanery of a quasi turn-of-the century Europe, and back into space opera.

The contrast between Atreides and Harkonnen is one of polarities, not opposites; for Atreides the family unit represents a 'wholesome' social order, for Harkonnen its perversion belies madness. The 'psychomachia' pits the benevolent dictator against the mad tyrant. Their opposite is the tribal structure of the Fremen; in which there is no 'lineage' or family exclusivity – the community at large is an all-embracing family.

The Fremen

Lynch has largely disregarded the political and ecological aspects of the novel, for which it won so much acclaim in the late 1960s (it was published in 1965). Herbert portrayed the Fremen as 'fremd/fremmende' – foreign, as foreign as the Bedouins are to Europeans. Herbert researched desert cultures in detail to create an authentic and alien sub-culture; the language, customs, rituals, history, and, above all, the appearance of Frank Herbert's Fremen are estranged from other galactic inhabitants.

For Lynch the Fremen are 'free-men'; displaced Californians in both appearance and language. Lynch himself plays the part of a Fremen machine operator to emphasise they are a race like you and me, only displaced and altered by their having to adapt to the planet's harsh and waterless environment.

David Lynch's *Dune* is less concerned with Paul's initiation into the ways of an alien culture, and more concerned with the masculine/feminine dichotomy.

Paul's experiences on Dune rekindle past memories and dreams – the geography, the people, and events which befall him, are familiar – he is like a sleepwalker going towards a predetermined destiny. As Paul and Jessica flee from the sandworm amongst the rocks, even the sudden appearance of blackgarbed and staring blue-eyed distinctly hostile Fremen poses no threat to Paul. Ordained for the task he assumes the role of leader. He takes the name 'Muad'Dib', after the second moon that orbits Arrakis.

Meanwhile, a new trial awaits Paul. He must drink the 'water of life' in a Bene Gesserit initiation in the desert. The 'water', deadly to mere mortals, will provide the chosen one with a rush of insight. For Paul it is that 'the worm and the spice are one.' Paul has integrated both masculine and feminine within himself.

The Dragon

Male and female define one another. They represent gender, the opposite is androgyny, in which the polarised genders are assimilated. In *Eraserhead* Lynch devised a singular metaphor, combining the spermatazoon with the umbilical cord. With the literary source of Frank Herbert's Shai-hulud, the Arrakis sandworm, David Lynch has devised a similarly disconcerting metaphor of androgyny.

On his first flight into the desert, Paul sees a sandworm, 150 metres long, rise from the sands and devour an entire mining plant. Later, after the Harkonnen overthrow of House Atreides, Paul and Jessica, trussed and bound, are taken out into the middle of the desert to be consumed by sandworms. By using the telepathic commands of the 'voice', and Jessica's sexual allure, they overcome their captors, crash land the vessel, and flee across the uncharted desert seeking refuge in the rocks. They are alone in a vast wasteland. Paul is enthralled by the sight; 'Never one drop of rain on Arrakis,' he says. 'The sleeper must awaken.'

A sandworm attacks, and Paul faces the gaping-toothed orifice of the monster that rises up from below the planet's surface. The Dune sandworm is a giant serpent which opens up into an engulfing cavity, devouring everything. It is a paradoxical combination of the phallic, with what mythologist Joseph Campbell refers to as 'the toothed vagina – a recurring motif in primitive mythologies; the vagina that castrates'.[12]

In *Return of the Jedi* (Marquand, 1983), Hans Solo and Luke Skywalker also face the 'toothed vagina', the ultimate threat, or what Freud refers to as '*horror feminae.*' Solo and Luke are 'taken to the Dune Sea' to be 'cast into the Pit of Carkoon, the nesting place of the all-powerful Sarlacc...' – a tooth-rimmed palpitating orifice in the middle of the desert. In saving themselves they re-establish their male bond.

Paul, who has been attempting to establish a connection between the sandworms and the spice, experiences a revelation: 'The spice and the worms are one,' he tells himself, the significance of which is not made apparent until later – when 'the sleeper does awake.'

The image of the sandworm is ambiguous –
integrating both masculine and feminine; just as Paul is
'ambiguous' – born to assimilate the psychological
functions of both masculine and feminine. Later Paul
must 'conquer' the sandworm in order to prove himself
a 'Fremen' leader. It is a portrayal of an age-old tale of
the hero defeating the dragon – which in many versions,
St George included, is the hero's quest to rescue the
maiden. Psychologically it can be interpreted as the
hero releasing the feminine.[13]

Paul must fulfil the prophecy in order to prove his
leadership by 'riding the sandworm'. It is an initiation of
manhood, primarily to affirm his masculinity before the
Fremen men.

The story begins with 'initiations' – trials by which
Paul must prove his worth – and ends in trials by which
he must demonstrate his worth. In his trial in the desert
Paul weeps blood. The women who witness the trial
bleed from the nose and mouth. The sandworms are
summoned, but don't attack. The destructive side of
male energy has been harnessed, and 'the sleeper has
awakened.' The union of masculine and feminine
energies unleashes a power to subdue and control the
monsters beneath the planet's surface (unconscious),
and integrate this powerful and lethal energy into a vital
'conscious' force.

Unfortunately, by this stage, the film's preoccupation
with its symbols and images has left the story stranded
somewhere in the Arrakis desert. For the dozing cinema
goer, Paul's cry of 'the sleeper has awakened', is a cue
to wake up and view the pyrotechnics of the culminating
battle scene.

Restoring the family

Dune, full of promise and potential, now proceeds
along a narrative course as limp and flaccid as a dead
sandworm. Irulan's voice-over, rather than emulating a
literary device, is a means to hasten along an
unnecessarily protracted plot: two years later, the spice
production is halted, Alia further develops her powers
and the Fremen launch attacks upon the Baron's
stronghold.

Disorder prevails. The Third Stage Guild Navigator
tells the Emperor to remedy the situation and restore
spice production. The Emperor decides to destroy all life
on Arrakis.

Paul summons a meeting of the Fremen and they

prepare for battle with the forces of the Emperor. The Emperor comes to Arrakis and Paul summons the sandworms. The Emperor chastises the Baron for his ineptitude and inability to quell the Fremen uprising. The Emperor takes control.

The final part of *Dune* is the pyrotechnic excess demanded of the genre – battles, explosions and long-suffering extras flung into the mouths of waiting sandworms, and stuntmen cavorting through shattering windows.

Paul leads the Fremen attack. With the aid of the sandworms, the Harkonnen forces are swiftly defeated. The Baron is destroyed by Alia who demobilises him with a lethal Bene Gesserit needle, the Gom Jabbar, and ushers him through the broken Arrakeen walls and into the tooth-lined orifice of a sandworm.

Paul takes over and Emperor Shaddam allows Feyd (played by Sting) to do battle with Paul. This seemingly meaningless encounter provides Sting with an opportunity to embarrass himself further with a fixed pixie-like grin and a woodland prance choreography. The forces of 'good' have already won and the fight merely reaffirms Paul's heroic status. Paul kills Feyd and the Emperor concedes defeat.

'Muad'Dib has become the hand of God.' Paul summons the rain and it rains. Arrakis is transformed. Alia exclaims: 'And how can this be? For he is the Kwisatz Haderach!' This last line is symptomatic of one of the film's unresolved obstacles. Frank Herbert provides a 20-page glossary for readers of the novel – a luxury not available to first-time viewers of the film.

Dune ends with the restoration of family order, unbalanced though that family may be. With the Emperor rendered politically impotent, Paul is the solitary male among a court of potent women; his concubine, the Fremen warrior, Chani; his wife, the Bene Gesserit Emperor's daughter, Irulan; his mother, now a Reverend Mother 'high priestess'; a surrogate grandmother; Reverend Mother Gaius Helen Mohiam; and most potent of all, Alia, his tiny younger sister.

Words to pictures: Herbert's novel, Lynch's film

In condensing a five-hundred-page novel to a two-hour screenplay there are omissions and compromises which complicate an already complex plot. Whereas the novel is hailed as 'one of the monuments of modern science fiction', with a worldwide sale of more than ten million copies, the film has received its fair share of disparaging criticism.

'Huge, hollow, imaginative and cold,' according to *Variety*. 'This movie is a real mess,' wrote critic Roger Ebert, 'an incomprehensible, ugly, unstructured, pointless excursion into the murkier realms of one of the most confusing screenplays of all time.'[14]

Although Lynch has infused the literary universe of Frank Herbert with the idiosyncracies of his own universe, the fact that he so faithfully retained Herbert's plot structure reveals the director's low priority for narrative. Lynch's skill as scenographer (the overall production design for *Dune* was closely supervised by Lynch) is as apparent in *Dune* as in *Eraserhead* and *The Elephant Man*. Unlike the worlds of these films, *Dune* proved to be a world Lynch could not make his own.

In spite of *Dune*'s spectacular failure, Dino de Laurentiis had sufficient faith in David Lynch to provide a $7 million budget for Lynch's next project – and this time Lynch would have 'final cut'. It is a film which begins with the happy family of middle-American suburbia and charters the wayward son's swift descent into chaos and darkness.

Blue Velvet (1986)

'Give me Love and Desire,' she said, 'the powers by which you yourself subdue mankind and gods alike.'

Aphrodite in Homer's *Iliad*

Synopsis: *Jeffrey Beaumont's father collapses while watering the garden outside his suburban Lumberton home. Returning home from visiting him in hospital, Jeffrey finds a human ear in a field. He takes it to Detective Williams at the police station and, with encouragement from Williams' daughter Sandy, investigates the intrigue. It transpires that the human ear may belong to the missing husband of nightclub singer, Dorothy Vallens.*

Jeffrey seeks evidence in Dorothy's apartment while she is away. She returns home unexpectedly, however, and finds Jeffrey hiding in the closet. At knife-point she forces him to participate in sado-masochistic sex games, then forces him back into the closet when the psychopathic Frank Booth pays a visit. Jeffrey witnesses Frank brutally assault Dorothy.

Jeffrey investigates the intrigue further, uncovering Frank Booth's criminal drug dealings. Once again visiting Dorothy, he is discovered by Frank and taken for a 'joyride' to a bleak industrial area of town, where Dorothy's son is being held captive. Jeffrey is severely beaten and left bruised and bleeding in a timberyard.

Prompted by Sandy he reports his findings to her father, hoping to extricate himself from the murky affair with which he has become involved. At night, however, Dorothy appears naked in the street, outside Sandy's house, proclaiming that Jeffrey 'has put his disease in me'.

Kyle MacLachlan, Isabella Rossellini *Jeffrey takes Dorothy to the police and returns to her apartment to discover the bodies of Dorothy's husband and a police investigator. Frank is on his way to the apartment to kill Jeffrey, and once more Jeffrey hides in* *the closet. As Frank attacks, Jeffrey shoots him.*

The next day Jeffrey awakens in the sanctity of his suburban home – Sandy makes him lunch and an artificial robin sings in a tree. Dorothy sits in a sunlit park embracing her young son.

Aphrodite is the irresistible blue-eyed seductress of Greek mythology, a temptress who could arouse desire in any man she chose. She is associated with the colour turquoise-blue. She married a smith named Hephaestus, and, according to the myth, embarked upon a romantic liaison with the warrior god, Ares.

Ares is the brutal, insensitive and belligerent god of war. He is accompanied by his three cohorts; Deimos, Phobos and Eris (Fear, Fright and Strife), and his unpredictable bouts of violent temper strike the fear of the gods into mere mortals. Ares makes a point of being seen, whereas Hades, who shares Ares' predeliction for power and sex, rules the underworld, hidden well away from prying eyes.

In *Blue Velvet*, Jeffrey ventures into a dark and secret world, an inquisitive mortal in forbidden territory, the hidden realm of the 'gods'. For his curiosity he must reap the consequences: with experience – pain, with knowledge – the loss of innocence.

The 'Aphrodite' who introduces him to the pantheon of the gods is the nightclub singer, Dorothy Vallens (Isabella Rossellini). Between the jalousie slats of the wardrobe door, Jeffrey (Kyle MacLachlan), furtively watches her 'adulterous' relationship with the psychopathic Frank Booth (Dennis Hopper). Frank in turn introduces Jeffrey to his three cohorts; Raymond, Paul and Hunter, (Brad Dourif, Jack Nance and Michael J. Hunter), and takes him on a 'joyride' to the underworld, where Ben (Dean Stockwell) rules with benign malice.

David Lynch describes *Blue Velvet* as 'a film that deals with things that are hidden within a small town called Lumberton and things that are hidden within people.'[1]

From the rolling folds of the blue velvet curtain – a textured layer of wilful subterfuge – drapes hiding secrets – over which the opening credits appear, the film ritualises Lynch's predominant theme, 'that everything has a surface which hides much more underneath.'[2] 'Symphony No. 15 in A Major', Dmitri Shostakovich's final symphony, was to have accompanied the opening and recur at various points in the narrative. *Blue Velvet*, however, marks the beginning of Lynch's fruitful collaboration with Angelo Badalamenti, whose haunting soundtrack accompanies the title credits, then weaves through the narrative, accentuating the *noir* mood of the film. The story begins in the bright light of suburban day and descends swiftly into netherworlds of crime, disease and Jeffrey's 'dark side'.

Exterminating bugs

Bobby Vinton's song 'Blue Velvet' plays over the opening sequence, as the blue velvet curtain dissolves into blue sky. Against the sky we have a white picket fence, red roses and yellow tulips. A fire engine passes slowly by. A fireman smiles and waves. At us. Kids cross at a school crossing. Mr Beaumont waters the garden and Mrs Beaumont watches television, drinking coffee. The television shows a close-up of a hand-held gun. In the garden, Mr Beaumont has an attack. He sinks to the ground, water spraying from the hose. A dog laps greedily at the water, and a toddler watches enthralled. Mr Beaumont is writhing on the green and newly trimmed suburban grass in the throes of a coronary thrombosis. Bobby Vinton's song fades swiftly into the background, and the grinding torturous sounds of subterranean conflict accompany the camera's excursion beneath the blades of grass. Something is stirring down there, something black and grotesque.

Bugs! Black beetles plough through the grass with their serrated pincers and waving antennae. A pair of them are locked in mortal combat, tearing each other apart. Later Jeffrey will dress up as a bug exterminator to gain access to Dorothy Vallens' apartment. Bugs form the hidden virus of restlessness and disease that plagues the tranquillity of suburbia. 'It's only a bug man,' says Dorothy to the man in the yellow jacket as Jeffrey goes through the motions of spraying her kitchen. A pest in human form, that gets under all the surfaces and makes a nuisance of himself. Bugs remain a menace until the end of the film when the robin sits in the tree with a bug in its beak. 'Ugh!' says Jeffrey's Aunt Barbara, 'I could never eat one of those.'

'The sound of the falling tree' announces the local radio over a 'Welcome to Lumberton' poster, as Jeffrey strolls across a field on the way to the hospital. His father is in traction; arrested by an array of metal arms with tubes piercing his flesh and his mouth forced open by medical apparatus. Jeffrey holds his hand, stays a while and says goodbye.

Returning through the same field, looking for stones in the grass to throw at a tin drum, Jeffrey finds an ear. A human ear, half rotten around the edges where it has been severed from someone's head with strands of black hair, wrested from the temples, still attached. Jeffrey brushes off the insects and places the ear in a brown paper bag. More bugs.

Jeffrey presents the ear to Detective Williams, a friend of his father's, at the local police station. 'Yes,' says Williams. 'That's an ear all right.' Jeffrey accompanies Detective Williams to the coroner's office, where the coroner assures Jeffrey that the ear has been cut off with a pair of scissors, and that 'after tests we can identify the person.'

'It had to be an ear,' says Lynch, 'because it's an opening. An ear is wide and you go down into it. It goes somewhere vast.'[3] For Lynch the ear is an aperture for getting inside the head. For Jeffrey listening is as integral to his investigating as watching. He listens to Dorothy sing, he listens to her cries behind a closed door at Ben's place, and his overhearing Frank abuse Dorothy is as informative as his watching. Throughout the film Jeffrey's curiosity is appeased by both his eyes and ears.

Later that evening, assuring his aunt he won't go near 'Lincoln' (the sinister side of town), yet burning with curiosity, Jeffrey leaves the house to visit the Williams who live nearby. The Williams' home is introduced by a large gold-framed photographic portrait of their daughter, Sandy, placed before red velvet drapes. Detective Williams warns Jeffrey of the dangers of being too curious, in a memorable exchange of 'discourse of obviousness', the kind of Lynchian dialogue that pervades the *Blue Velvet* screenplay:

> WILLIAMS: Curiosity. That's what got me into this business.
> JEFFREY: It must be great.
> WILLIAMS: It's horrible too.

Outside the house, Sandy, a blonde blue-eyed innocent of seventeen, emerges from the darkness of a suburban night, like Mary X in the black-framed window staring down at Henry Spencer in *Eraserhead*, John Merrick's mother from the dark memory of the past in *The Elephant Man*, and Irulan from the depths of space in *Dune*. As Irulan is the chosen wife of Paul Atreides, so will Sandy become bonded to Jeffrey. For most of the story however, Jeffrey's interest in Sandy is as the bearer of secret knowledge. She takes Jeffrey to see the apartment block of a woman believed to be implicated in the 'missing ear' case. It's on Lincoln.

Jeffrey and Sandy agree that 'it's a strange world', and Jeffrey tells a story about a kid he knew who had 'the biggest tongue in the neighbourhood'. The next day, at his father's hardware store, he jokes with two of his father's employees, both negroes, one of whom is blind, yet can still count the number of fingers Jeffrey holds up.

Sandy has a boyfriend (Mike), but she meets Jeffrey anyway, who convinces her that his plans provide 'opportunities for learning knowledge'. He is going to get inside Dorothy's apartment dressed as a bug exterminator, leave a window open, and sneak in again at night. Sandy resists but Jeffrey persuades her by condemning the suburban disease of ordinariness which tarnishes them both.

> JEFFREY: No one will suspect us. Because no one would think two people like us would be crazy enough to do something like this.
> SANDY: You have a point there.

The tranquil idyll of suburbia creates restlessness – kids cruise the streets in old cars at night, Mrs Beaumont watches murder mysteries on TV, Jeffrey's idea of a large afternoon is throwing stones at tin drums, and parents warn of the dangers of being too curious, and getting too close to the seedy side of town. Lumberton might just be Santa Rosa (*Invasion of the Body Snatchers*, 1956) after the body snatchers have taken over, only no one's noticed.

In the guise of a bug exterminator Jeffrey climbs the stairs to the seventh floor of the Deep River apartment block. Briefly we are back in the world of *Eraserhead* – a neon light falters, the lift is out of order, the stairs and corridors are dark and menacing. He knocks on the door of 710 and Dorothy answers – a frightened painted face behind a chained door.

Jeffrey sprays the kitchen, and while Dorothy answers a knock at the door to a man in a yellow coat, Jeffrey, 'the bug man', steals a spare key and leaves.

In the realm of the senses

Jeffrey and Sandy sit at a table of The Slow Club and

discuss brands of beer, just as Sailor and Lula in *Wild at Heart* discuss brands of cigarettes. Sandy's father drinks Budweiser, Lula's father smoked Camels. Sailor prefers Marlboro and Jeffrey favours Heineken. 'Here's to an interesting experience,' says Jeffrey, and the Master of Ceremonies introduces 'The Blue Lady'. She sings 'Blue Velvet' in front of a blue star, bathed in blue light, in front of a red velvet curtain. Jeffrey watches enthralled, Sandy is restless.

Outside the apartment block Sandy attempts to dissuade Jeffrey from going in, without success, then promises to sound the car horn as soon as Dorothy arrives. 'I don't know if you're a detective or a pervert,' says Sandy as Jeffrey sets off.

'I'd always had a desire to sneak into a girl's apartment and watch her through the night...' says Lynch,[4] and has accordingly structured *Blue Velvet* around this central sequence of Jeffrey inside Dorothy's apartment. The sequence lasts twenty minutes, and four different scenarios, each about five minutes long, are played out. Jeffrey watches Dorothy, Dorothy watches Jeffrey, Jeffrey watches Dorothy and Frank, and finally, Jeffrey and Dorothy are united through Frank's brutality.

Until Jeffrey's entry into Dorothy's flat he relates to the senses in a purely abstract manner – a story to Sandy about the kid with the biggest tongue; joking with the blind man who works at his father's hardware store, a severed ear in a field, drinking beer, but only interested in which brand it is; these are representations of the senses either redundant or deformed (eyes that can't see, an ear that can't hear, a tongue that's too big, etc). Lynch presents each of the five senses misused, corrupted or perverted in some way.

For Jeffrey, Dorothy's boudoir is the realm of the senses – it is the scene of Jeffrey's initiation of the post-adolescent accepting the adult body. From the outset, once inside the apartment, Jeffrey's senses take over, from the sensual relief of urinating, ('Uh! That Heineken!'), which makes him miss Sandy's warning, to answering Dorothy's pleas to strike her. He is subject to a broad range of sensation experiences, far removed from the realm of abstracts, which, up to this point, has been his refuge.

Jeffrey watches Dorothy

'That's the fantastic thing about the cinema,' says Lynch. 'Everyone can be a voyeur.'[5] Jeffrey plays voyeur from behind the jalousie of the wardrobe door. He watches

Dorothy undress down to her underwear, then as she answers the telephone.

> DOROTHY: Frank, Frank let me speak to him... Don? Don. Is little Donny all right... You mean Madeleine? Mummy loves you...

Dorothy walks around the floor, like a cat on all fours. She removes her wig, goes to the bathroom, and returns naked but for a towel. She opens the wardrobe door and Jeffrey hides himself amongst the clothes as she removes a robe of blue velvet, closes the door, and puts it on. He remains undetected. He watches and listens.

Blue Velvet, distinct from other examples of voyeuristic cinema, does not focus on watching alone. For L. B. Jeffries in *Rear Window* (1954), his fiancée, Lisa Fremont, only becomes arousing when he watches her on the other side of the courtyard through the telephoto lens of his camera. For Michael Powell's *Peeping Tom* (1960), arousal lies in filming his female victim's fear before killing her with a blade concealed in the camera's tripod. Tomek (about the same age as Jeffrey) in Kieslowski's *A Short Film About Loving* (1989) watches a woman in the window opposite through a telescope, stolen expressly for the purpose. But when they meet, and he succumbs to her sexual manipulations, he is so defeated by the experience that he attempts suicide.

Sound is as arousing for Jeffrey as sight. We watch as he associates deeds to off-screen sounds; Dorothy's telephone conversation, her visit to the bathroom, her unseen wanderings around the apartment. Jeffrey's voyeurism is imbued with tension – he may be discovered at any moment. An early version of Lynch's film script established Jeffrey as a voyeur at the beginning of the story, when he is in the school furnace room 'fascinated by a sight, beyond in the darkness',[6] of a girl student fighting off the sexual advances of a male student. Although this sequence was subsequently dropped, there is no mistaking Jeffrey's pleasure hidden inside Dorothy's wardrobe; this is his sought-after 'opportunity for learning knowledge'.

Jeffrey is not curious about Sandy – she is 'the girl next door', without secrets, devoid of mystery. Dorothy is the love-goddess, Aphrodite, arcane and beyond the reach of mortals. She sings on stage, bathed in blue light, where anyone can watch her, but no one can touch her. Now her 'performance' is solely for Jeffrey's eyes, and already he has uncovered secrets, not only concerning her situation (missing husband, missing son), but her nature. She prowls like a cat because she is a cat-woman, predatory and unpredictable. That her hair is not her own is just one more secret Jeffrey has all to himself. Not for long, however. He bumps some coat hangers, and gives himself away.

Dorothy watches Jeffrey

Armed with the flashing blade of an oversized kitchen knife, Dorothy opens the door, and demands that Jeffrey get out, get down on his knees, and place his arms above his head. Watching and listening, which began as abstract voyeuristic pleasures, now exact their price.

'What have you heard? What have you seen?' demands Dorothy. She nicks Jeffrrey's cheek with the knife and draws blood. 'Get undressed!' she says, 'I want to see you.' Jeffrey undresses and when he stands she falls to her knees and removes his underwear. 'Don't look at me!' she commands.

The goddess Aphrodite is renowned for her skills in the arts of love, and she is considered irresistible to all men. Moreover, she is no passive lover, but assumes control over the man, ensuring gratification both for herself and her lover. According to the myth, Aphrodite has a darker side, an irrational vengefulness whereby she derives pleasure from provoking and tormenting mortals with vindictive intent. Should Aphrodite make love with a mortal man, he is at once stricken with old age.

There is little doubting Jeffrey's mortality – 'Don't look at me, or I'll kill you,' screams Dorothy, as she arouses him orally, then drags him to the couch, and, assuming the dominant position, with the knife over Jeffrey's throat, renders him passive.

One of the most striking images of Nagisa Oshima's film *In the Realm of the Senses (Ai no Corrida*, 1976), is of Eiko Matsuda, in red kimono, leaning over her lover and former employer, Tatsuya Fuji, with a knife held in her mouth hovering over his exposed throat. Her sexual domination leads to his death. In *Basic Instinct* (Verhoeven, 1992), Michael Douglas's character describes the experience of sex bound and tied to the bed, in the supine position, and with a knife at his throat, as the 'fuck of the century'. The distinction between the little death and the big death for one brief moment becomes inseparable.

Jeffrey doesn't find out. There's a knock at the door

and Dorothy forces Jeffrey back into the wardrobe.

Jeffrey watches Dorothy and Frank

Jeffrey peers through the jalousie once more, with, as
the word suggests, misgivings about the proceedings
acted out before him. Frank Booth enters and demands
his bourbon. He sits on a chair and tells Dorothy to
spread her legs. All Jeffrey can do is watch and listen.
Now it's Frank who demands of Dorothy, 'Don't look at
me,' and he erupts with a torrent of obscenities. (Dennis
Hopper later commented that for every 'fuck' in David
Lynch's screenplay, he'd add six more...) He inhales gas
which stimulates him further, intensifying his ritualised
abuse of Dorothy.

He clutches a blue velvet cord, a perverse mockery of
an umbilical cord (echoes of *Eraserhead*), as he sobs;
'Hello, baby. It's daddy,' then inhales once more,
whimpering, 'Mummy... mummy,' followed by further
obscenities. 'Don't look at me...' he shouts, from which
we realise the source of Dorothy's 'performance'.

'Baby wants blue velvet,' shouts Frank, striking
Dorothy and pulling her to the floor, taking out a pair of
scissors and snapping them wildly. The severed ear, the
piece of velvet from Dorothy's robe, the blue cord.
Frank cuts anything and everything, yet is unable to
sever himself from the primordial pre-cognitive state of
demanding everything and yielding nothing.

During a mad and frantic simulated sexual act he
shouts, 'Daddy's coming home,' strikes Dorothy once
more, and shouts; 'Don't you fucking look at me...'

Frank's use of obscenity is an expression more of
impotence than rage. His infantile manner in both word
and deed again echoes the spiteful vindictiveness of
Henry Spencer's child. Jeffrey's 'psychomachia' with
Frank Booth parallels Henry's confrontation with the
infant in several ways. They are both contests of the
infantile and irrational against 'reason'. Henry and
Jeffrey, both 'closed-body' Lynchian heroes, are
seemingly powerless against the malevolence of their
infantile adversaries; and finally both Henry and Jeffrey
destroy their respective miscreants through violence
exposing their internal organs. (The Lynch 'open-body'
antagonist.)

Frank's obscenities are exclusively sexual; his use of
language is a futile attempt to validate his sexuality. As
the plot develops his misogyny becomes more
pronounced, just as his 'male bonding' becomes more
pronounced. Frank Booth, along with Bytes and Baron

Harkonnen, joins Lynch's pantheon of homosexual antagonists.

'You stay alive, baby,' Frank tells Dorothy as he leaves. 'Do it for van Gogh.' These are further sinister references to her husband's severed ear.

Jeffrey and Dorothy united

Jeffrey leaves the wardrobe and helps Dorothy; Dorothy, shaken, bruised and traumatised, collapses into Jeffrey's arms, 'Don. Hold me. Hold me. I'm scared.' Throughout the scene she refers to him by her husband's name, they embrace each other on the sofa, and Dorothy's embraces become more fervent. She demands that Jeffrey feel her breasts, and Lynch employs his favoured close-up of the red-painted half-parted and sexually enticing lips as she whispers, 'Hit me.'

Jeffrey declines, gets up, and while Dorothy goes to the bathroom he notices the missing patch of material from the bottom of her blue velvet robe. He finds a photograph of husband Don and their son, together with a marriage certificate. Jeffrey leaves as Dorothy stares into the bathroom mirror and whispers, 'Help me,' with a vacant stare. She is a woman seeking an identity.

We never find out who Dorothy is; we only know her through her performances – either on the stage of the nightclub, or on various other 'stages' to specifically male audiences, all of which she provides with a different scenario. The victim to Frank, the dominatrix to Jeffrey, and later, the self-ingratiating lover. To her son she performs 'mother', but even that performance is as much for the benefit of Frank, Ben and the curious assembly at Ben's place. The nearest Dorothy comes to a natural representation of herself is in the final sequence – the slow-motion image when she embraces her little boy. In this sequence the camera is performing on her behalf.

Meanwhile, her performance with Frank has shaken Jeffrey, who, once outside, sees himself as a savage beast in the guise of Frank.

Trouble till the robins come

Sandy and Jeffrey meet. She too has a performance for Jeffrey. But, unlike Dorothy, she believes it herself. Outside a church, at night, they meet in the car and Jeffrey tells his story. Once more they agree 'it's a strange world,' and Sandy reveals the dream she had the night she met Jeffrey. 'There is trouble till the robins come,' she tells him. 'The robins will bring love into the world...' As they drive away, the church remains in the background and the soundtrack of church organ music wells up to a mocking crescendo.

For once, Sandy is centre-stage, when she acts rather than reacts, is expressive, rather than passive. Yet her eloquence is embarrassing, comic in its naivety. Jeffrey is neither convinced by, nor dismissive of, the suggestion that the psychopaths will perish in one fell swoop, and the suburban American dream will be restored, once 'the robins come'. Shortly afterwards, not surprisingly, he visits Dorothy.

'I looked for you in that closet last night,' she says, and leads him to the bedroom. Dorothy likes to be watched (like Lisa Fremont in *Rear Window*, like the woman across Tomek's window) – Dorothy wants to perform.

At The Slow Club Jeffrey drinks 'Blue Velvet' cocktails and watches Dorothy perform for her male audience. Jeffrey's pleasure is short-lived, however, as at another table Frank listens to Dorothy singing, clutching the piece of her blue velvet robe, sobbing into it, and manipulating it in surrogate masturbation.

'Why are there people in the world like Frank?' asks a troubled Jeffrey, prior to Sandy's consoling vision of 'everything all right when the robins come back'. He seems less concerned with why Frank should be tormenting just Dorothy. Lynch's assembly of psychopaths are motivated by greed – Bytes wants his 'treasure', Merrick; Baron Harkonnen wants Dune and the spice; Bobby Peru wants his 'silver dollar'. What drives Frank, it seems, is the desire for pleasure – he is the 'sensualist' in contrast to Jeffrey's asceticism, but his sensuality is uncontrolled. He takes what he wants, whether it is drugs or a desirable woman.

As the plot unfolds, it transpires that Frank and Dorothy's husband, Don, have had drug dealings together. Frank, driven by his desire for Dorothy, holds Don and their young son prisoner in order to blackmail Dorothy for sexual pleasure. The severed ear is both a token of Frank's seriousness of intent and a perverse interpretation of van Gogh's 'sacrifice' in the name of unrequited love.

Now Jeffrey, as he watches Dorothy, and watches Frank watching Dorothy, is troubled by the thought that the desire he feels for the woman performing before him is not so far removed from Frank's desire. 'You're like me,' says Frank later to Jeffrey, as Jeffrey becomes more attuned to his physical senses, both the pleasure they provide, and the pain.

Similarly, Jeffrey's desire for Dorothy, who is dark-haired, voluptuous ('overweight' remarked some critics in regard to Isabella Rossellini's naked scenes), contrasts with the lean and ascetic form of Sandy.

Jeffrey plays detective, watching Frank's movements and taking photographs. The next day at Arlene's Diner, he summarises Frank's complicated dealings with the 'man in the yellow jacket', among others. 'A drug dealer shot to death and a woman had both her legs broken.' Jeffrey is breathless: 'I'm seeing something. I'm in a mystery and it's all secret.' He kisses Sandy passionately, then goes to Dorothy's to make love with her. A whole new world has opened up for Jeffrey.

In Dorothy's flat red velvet curtains billow, and thunder rumbles ominously outside. 'Blue Velvet', sung by Bobby Vinton, fades out swiftly at the same point it faded out in the opening sequence, as the song's delicate chords dissolve into a subterranean rumbling as Jeffrey's father collapses.

'I want your disease in me,' Dorothy says, and later, 'Are you a bad boy? You want to do anything? Anything?' With Dorothy's coaxing Jeffrey strikes her, over and over. He is engulfed with the image of burning flame and for a few short seconds Jeffrey becomes the monster he saw in Frank. 'I have your disease in me now,' says Dorothy, and as they part company outside her apartment, she smiles wistfully. 'I still have you inside me,' she says.

A joyride to Meadow Lane

Frank Booth and his cohorts appear outside the apartment as Jeffrey is about to leave – Ares, accompanied by Fear, Fright and Strife. 'Who is this fuck?' demands Frank and, with Dorothy in tow, decides they must see Ben. 'We're going on a joyride,' says Frank.

Ben is the suave, well-dressed and effeminate ruler of a netherworld of drug and prostitution, the benevolent dictator in the manner of Hades and his rule over the underworld.

Ben is a more sinister representation of the forces of chaos than Frank – Frank is a brutal thug, who raises a toast ('Let's drink to fucking. Here's to fuck. Here's to Ben'), and smacks Jeffrey across the face, enraged that Jeffrey should be watching him. (Jeffrey's problem from the outset has been that he can't *not* watch.) Ben, on the other hand, refined, well-groomed and courteous, approaches Jeffrey with a sympathetic smile before punching him in the stomach and asking politely, 'Did that hurt?'

Dorothy goes into another room and Jeffrey listens to the cries from behind the other side of the door: 'Donny. Mamma loves you.' Just one more of Dorothy's performances.

Jeffrey's 'joyride' is his journey into an unknown realm where he is vulnerable and mortal, at the mercy of the gods' mean-spirited games. Dorothy gives him pleasure, Frank – pain. Ben leaves him winded and bewildered. The 'surrealism' with which Lynch portrays the familiar territory of the middle-class suburban community, dissolves into the 'anti-realism' of Ben's underworld. Jeffrey is disorientated – nothing seems real, not the place, not Ben, not Frank and his three thugs, not even Dorothy. There's nothing to suggest that there really is a little boy behind that closed door.

To emphasise the 'unreality', Ben picks up a wire-encased light globe, and in a parody of Dorothy's night-club performance, mimes to Roy Orbison singing 'In Dreams'. Frank listens in a kind of ecstasy, and the characters gather around Jeffrey like archetypal projections forcing themselves into his conscious state. The detached peculiarity of the scene evokes an otherworldness, a sense that Jeffrey finds himself divorced from reality.

Although it is Ben, then Frank, miming the lyrics of the Roy Orbison song, the line: 'I close my eyes then drift away into the dark night...' equally serve as Jeffrey's inner voice.

Frank insists on continuing Jeffrey's joyride 'into the dark night': 'Let's hit the fucking road,' he says, and they depart, Jeffrey in the back with Fear, Strife and Fright; Dorothy in the front with Frank. 'You're like me,' says Frank to Jeffrey, while molesting Dorothy, abusing their shared icon of desire. Jeffrey, outraged at Frank's treatment of Dorothy, *does* become like Frank – he lashes out with his fist and strikes him in the face.

Lynch's most explicit 'psychomachia' is the conflict between Jeffrey and Frank. Jeffrey has flashes seeing himself in the roaring bestial guise of Frank, as he hits Dorothy. Frank creeps through the fissures of Jeffrey's normality, and becomes his dark self.

The car stops and Jeffrey is dragged out – Frank paints himself with red lipstick (later to become Marietta's signature of dementia in *Wild at Heart*), then kisses him. 'You receive a love letter from me,' says Frank, 'and you're fucked forever.' As a girl dances on the bonnet of the car to the tune of Roy Orbison's 'In

Dreams', Frank recites the text, wipes Jeffrey's face with the torn piece of blue velvet, and instructs his thugs to hold Jeffrey down while he beats him savagely.

In the light of morning Jeffrey comes to, and finds himself in a timberyard off 'Meadow Lane'. Originally, Lynch had written the scene showing Jeffrey with his trousers around his ankles and 'fuck you' written on his legs with lipstick. Although this scene was filmed and later deleted,[7] there is much to suggest that Jeffrey was nonetheless raped. Frank's continuous references to Jeffrey's 'joyride'; his thugs referring to Jeffrey as 'a pussy Frank, our pussy'; Frank's insistence that 'when you get a love letter from me, you're fucked forever'; and in Frank Booth's final sequence as 'the well-dressed man', he enters the apartment looking for Jeffrey, saying: 'I know where your cute little butt is hiding.'

Jeffrey's rape, the final degradation, marks his entry into the netherworld realm of the senses – if Dorothy gave pleasure (they have made love once), then Frank's 'joyride', as Frank promises, is the love letter that has 'fucked him forever'.

Suburban American dream

Blue Velvet, released in the latter half of 1986, was one of a number of films delving beneath the surface of the American suburbs, uncovering displeasing elements, psychopaths, brutality, sickness – the elements that had been successfully hidden away for more than a generation with wholesome television situation comedy, melodramas, the Mickey Mouse club and Elvis Presley movies.

River's Edge (Tim Hunter – see *Twin Peaks*), photographed by Lynch's photographer, Frederick Elmes, and featuring Lynch's psychopath, Dennis Hopper, begins with a teenage high-school student sitting on a river bank smoking a cigarette beside the naked corpse of a girl. The story develops into a conflict of loyalties, where the friends of the boy who murdered 'for kicks' decide to protect him from incrimination. The film was based on an actual incident, claim the credits. The Dennis Hopper psychopath contains his acts of bestial violence to a rubber doll.

Predatory women with hidden soft sides feature in *Black Widow* (Bob Rafaelson, 1986) and *Crimes of Passion* (Ken Russell, 1984). In *Something Wild* (Jonathan Demme) the male hero is attracted to the wild dark-haired Lulu – she also assumes the dominant position when making love to him in a motel room – only to find that in her suburban enclave she is blonde, obedient and wears floral dresses. In the city she is the predator, back home in the suburbs she is the prey, hunted by a psychopathic ex-boyfriend who intends to kill her new-found city lover, but dies himself in an empty suburban house, watching himself expire in a bathroom mirror, a romanticised coda enforcing the illusion of the suburban dream.

In David Cronenberg's *The Fly*, Jeff Goldblum embarks on a casual love affair, impressing his lover with his scientific prowess. His sexual relationship coincides with the beginning of his transmutation into a fly – as if the two scenarios are related. Cronenberg's script is the antithesis of the 1958 original, where Henri's scientific prowess results in the breakdown of the established family unit. Just as *Blue Velvet* contains 1950s ideals, perverted by a mid 1980s cynicism, the two versions of *The Fly*, separated by twenty-eight years, illustrate a transition of social anxieties, from what threatens 'the family', to what threatens 'me'.

It is this anxiety, 'an anxiety of the ego', that underlies *Blue Velvet*'s 'wholesome' cousin, Francis Ford Coppola's *Peggy Sue Got Married*, another entry into the 1986 list of 1950s 'time trips'. In this film the time trip is quite literal; Kathleen Turner attends a 1986 high school reunion, collapses under the pressure of, amongst other things, a divorce, and wakes up in 1958. We find ourselves in a sub-Lynchian world of 'happy family' suburban kitsch in which Turner salvages her failed marriage, and wakes up back in 1986 to a 1950s-style 'happy family'. The 1986 Hollywood movie perspective oscillates between cynicism and sentiment; *Blue Velvet* encapsulates both, yet parodies both. (The dementedly brutal 'Jeffrey watches Frank and Dorothy' sequence, Lynch claims, had him rolling on the floor with laughter.)

Blue Velvet's 'good twin' (*see Introduction*), Frank Capra's *It's a Wonderful Life*, celebrated its fiftieth anniversary when *Blue Velvet* was released. George Bailey's (James Stewart) burning curiosity about the world beyond Bedford Falls is constantly thwarted by Henry Potter, a wheelchair-bound 'psychopathic' town mogul. Like Jeffrey, George ends up with 'the girl next door' by default, and perpetuates the sanctity of small-town life by integrating himself into it. George puts a stop to Potter by enlisting the support of the community and shaming him out of existence; Jeffrey stops Frank Booth with a bullet between the eyes.

This mid-1980s cinema, vilifying the myths of suburbia and the small-town idyll (*River's Edge, Something Wild, True Stories*, etc), succeeds the *noir* revivalism of the early 1980s: *Blood Simple* (Joel and Ethan Cohen, 1984); *Body Heat* (Lawrence Kasdan, 1981); and the gritty remake of *The Postman Always Rings Twice* (Bob Rafaelson, 1981), three films influenced by the Cain school of sexual subterfuge, betrayal and treachery between lovers.

The themes and elements of *Blue Velvet* have precursors in the small-town *noir* films of the 1950s (*see Introduction*) but the world of *Blue Velvet* draws equally from American television. Situation comedies like *The Adventures of Ozzie and Harriet* (1953), *Life with Father* (1953), *Father Knows Best* (1954), *The Eve Arden Show* (1957), *Bachelor Father* (1957), *Leave it to Beaver* (1957) – Hugh Beaumont plays Beaver's dad, *The Donna Reed Show* (1958), *The Ann Sothern Show* (1958) – this is the world of white picket fences, 'Arlene's Diner', teenage parties and characters named 'Aunt Barbara'. These are the half-hour servings which Lynch draws from, parodies, idealises; the values of an American 1950s childhood – the myth of the family unit played out with every new US television network sitcom. *Blue Velvet*'s opening sequence, Lynch claims, is inspired by an American school book, *Good Times on Our Street*. 'It's about happiness, about everyday surroundings, good neighbours. For an American kid who comes from a well-to-do home, heaven must look like the street where he lives...'[8]

Jeffrey's return to the Beaumont residence is a return to the Cleavers, the Nelsons, or any one of seventy-two middle-class households in the 'traditional family' sitcoms produced between 1948 and 1955, or one of more than a hundred different middle-class family households in the 'nuclear family' sitcoms produced between 1955 and 1965.[9] Jeffreys's return is a return to normality as prescribed by American television fiction. Jeffrey joins his mother and Aunt Barbara for breakfast and idle conversation. Yet whatever innocence Jeffrey had is lost forever. The normality he once took for granted is torn asunder with fissures of corruption. When Jeffrey goes to the police station to tell all to Detective Williams, he sees the man in the yellow coat, and discovers that he's a policeman – Detective T. R. Gordon, Williams' colleague.

He visits Williams at his home instead, who responds by becoming abusive. Jeffrey has had enough. He abandons the world of intrigues and returns to the pleasures suburban life can offer – watering the garden, visiting father in hospital, and going to a Friday night teenage party with Sandy.

Sandy's party is the contrast to Ben's, sufficiently wholesome to prompt an exchange of dialogue between Jeffrey and Sandy as they dance to a tune called 'Mysteries of Love' (lyrics by David Lynch, sung by Julee Cruise). Sandy and Jeffrey exchange the most favoured suburban cliché of all:

> SANDY: I love you, Jeffrey
> JEFFREY: I love you too.

But Jeffrey's return to ordinariness is not an easy one. When Jeffrey and Sandy drive home, Sandy's former boyfriend, Mike, and his buddies, give chase through the suburban streets – Jeffrey is convinced Frank is on his tail – and outside the Williams' residence Mike and his buddies rough him up. They take off when Dorothy appears, emerging from the darkness as Sandy had, only Dorothy is naked and confused. She is the love-goddess, descended from celestial heights to stir up trouble in a Lumberton household.

Inside the house, unashamedly naked before Sandy, and Sandy's mother, Dorothy points to Jeffrey and claims: 'My secret lover. He put his disease inside me.' Sandy is upset. When an ambulance comes to take Dorothy away, Sandy strikes Jeffrey.

Jeffrey returns to Dorothy's apartment; the door is open and a record player plays 'Love Letters', sung by Kitty Lester. Gordon, 'the yellow man', is shot, apparently dead, yet still standing, blood dripping from his arm, and brain matter seeping through a head wound. A dead man, minus an ear, is seated in an armchair with a piece of blue velvet stuffed into his mouth – Dorothy's husband, Don.

While the police, led by Detective Williams, raid Frank Booth's place, Jeffrey is about to leave Dorothy's when he sees a man with a moustache ascend the stairs – Frank in disguise. Jeffrey returns to Dorothy's flat, and to the wardrobe from where he first watched Dorothy undress. Now he watches Frank as he shouts and rants. Frank opens the wardrobe door and Jeffrey shoots Frank through the head.

We return to the blue skies, green lawns and white picket fence – Jeffrey bathes in sunlight and looks at a bird in a tree. Jeffrey's father and Sandy's father chat in the lounge room. Jeffrey embraces Sandy, and from the kitchen, together with Jeffrey's mother and Aunt

Barbara, they watch the bird which holds a large black beetle in its mouth. 'Maybe the robins are here,' says Jeffrey, but somehow 'the blinding light of love' Sandy had described earlier has made the picket fence a little too white, the lawn too green and the sky too blue. The bird is a mechanical device, although according to Lynch 'it's not an artificial bird; it's a real bird. That's just the way it turned out.'[10] The scene is as pretty as it is artificial, as artificial as the charade of security and normality which the suburbs proclaim.

Dorothy and her little boy, also illuminated by sunlight, embrace; the blue sky becomes blue velvet, Bobby Vinton sings the 1950s song, and harmony returns to the once troubled community of Lumberton.

According to the Aphrodite myth, Ares' adulterous liaison with Aphrodite resulted in a daughter, named Harmonia. The lesson in the Aphrodite story is that brute force can be subdued by love and can bring 'harmony' to the world. In *Blue Velvet*, chaos and disorder prevail until Dorothy and her child are united. Brute force is defeated, harmony reigns.

In a scene which Lynch later deleted from the film, Dorothy and Jeffrey make love while 'a very sad forlorn version of "Over the rainbow" creeps through the wind'.[11] Another Dorothy, who has secured her place in American popular 'mythology', travels down 'a yellow brick road', is pitted against wicked witches, and finally realises that no other place can compare to her home in Kansas.

In the final cut, *The Wizard Of Oz* had no place in *Blue Velvet*, but this most American of tales found its niche in Lynch's next project, based on a sprightly little novel of contemporary America. Barry Gifford's book was barely off the printing presses before Lynch had written his screen adaptation.

Wild at Heart (1990)

> *A film that doesn't have a happy ending is misunderstanding the basis of all cinema.*

William Boyd, *Brazzaville Beach*

Synopsis: *Sailor Ripley is released from prison after a two-year sentence for the manslaughter of Bob Ray Lemon. He is reunited with Lula and the couple leave North Carolina and head south for New Orleans in a red convertible. Lula's mother, Marietta, is determined to split the couple up and enlists the aid of boyfriend Johnnie Farragut, then a hired killer, Marcello Santos.*

During their road journey Lula and Sailor recall fragments of the past – the death of Lula's father (who supposedly burnt himself to death), Marietta's attempted seduction of Sailor. From New Orleans they drive to Big Tuna, a small and sleazy community, where Sailor meets a former underworld contact, Perdita.

To get money Sailor is persuaded by the psychopathic Bobby Peru to join him in a bank robbery. Unknown to Sailor the robbery is a set-up orchestrated by Santos to have Sailor killed. The robbery becomes a bloodbath and the unexpected intervention of the police results in the death of Bobby Peru and the arrest of Sailor. He's sent to prison and, as at the beginning of the film, Lula meets him when he is released. However, six years have passed, Sailor has a young son he's not met before, and walks away feeling that a reunion would be impossible. At this point the Good Witch from The Wizard of Oz descends from the heavens and inspires him to return to Lula.

They are reunited. He sings 'Love Me Tender'.

Laura Dern, Willem Dafoe

It's midday in Big Tuna and Lula (Laura Dern) lies alone on the bed in provocative black lingerie. Sailor (Nicolas Cage) is out fixing the car. The psychotic Bobby Peru (Willem Dafoe) enters her motel room, in order to use the bathroom. He makes suggestive remarks while he urinates and, instead of leaving, approaches Lula, and forces himself upon her.

'Y'know,' he says, 'I sure do like a woman with nice tits like yours who talks tough and looks like she can fuck like a bunny. Can you fuck like that?'

Lula, indignant, tells him to leave, but he heaps upon her one obscene proposition after the other, grabs her by the waist and pushes his face into hers: 'Say "fuck me", then I'll leave.' She turns away repelled by his disfigured jagged teeth imbedded in his bloated gums – a pencil-line moustache across his protruding upper lip. 'I'm not leaving till you say "Fuck me",' he says, mauling at her breasts and groping between her legs. 'Say "fuck me",' he repeats, his mouth almost touching hers: Lula's red-lipped and enticing, his protruding and repellent.

Her eyes closed, her body trembling, she finally whispers the words. He pushes her away, shouting, 'Someday, honey, I will, but I got to get going.' He leaves, laughing to himself – Lula holds herself and cries out for Sailor.

The episode is grotesque, unsettling and perverse – and it's all David Lynch. In Barry Gifford's novel Bobby Peru makes no advance on Lula. Lynch wants Lula to betray Sailor, and to be betrayed by her own sensuality, just as Sailor, in colluding with Bobby Peru, betrays Lula.

At night, when the couple share the same bed, they are unable to share these, their darkest and, as it transpires, their final moments together, before Sailor sets off to participate in the robbery the next morning.

Sailor is released from prison six years later and Lula is there with their young son, Pace, to meet him. But Sailor soon feels ill at ease, and decides to make his own solitary way.

'"You been doin' fine without me, peanut. There ain't no need to make life tougher'n it has to be." He picked up his suitcase, kissed Lula lightly on the lips and walked away. She let him go.'[1]

Barry Gifford ends the story there, but, says Lynch: 'I didn't buy the ending of the book. In the first script I wrote, the ending was true to the book. [Sailor and Lula part company] [which was] a real defeat... I almost wanted a miserable ending just to show that I wasn't trying to be commercial. And that's wrong... it's got to feel honest...'[2]

In Lynch's final sequence, Glinda, the Good Witch from *The Wizard of Oz*, appears *deus ex machina* to Sailor and says, 'Don't turn away from love.' (Lynch insists it is not him talking, but the Good Witch.) Sailor returns to Lula and sings 'Love Me Tender', a token act of commitment for which he was 'not ready' at the beginning of the story.

Apart from being a 'happy ending', Glinda's appearance (with the face of Sheryl Lee – *Twin Peaks'* Laura Palmer) confirms Sailor Ripley's acceptance of Lula's world. *The Wizard of Oz* is, Lula tells Sailor, her favourite film. She gives him fantasies and dreams, Sailor has both feet on the ground. His anecdotes describe past acts of violence, conflicts and traumas. Just as Mrs Kendal, in *The Elephant Man*, opens up the 'fantasy' world of pantomime, theatre and drama as an alternative to the dreadful reality of John Merrick's earlier life, Lula provides an alternative reality for Sailor. That this is a 'feminine' role was the basis of *The Kiss of the Spider Woman* (Hector Babenco, 1985), another MGM production which reverses the sepia and colour schema of *The Wizard of Oz*, in which the effeminate homosexual 'sexual' prisoner (played by William Hurt) re-enacts Hollywood melodramas for Raul Julia, who plays the brutalised 'masculine' political prisoner. In the same way that Julia is fascinated and frustrated by William Hurt, Sailor is tantalised by Lula's flights of fantasy: 'You never fail to fascinate me, peanut,' but suitably cynical within the masculine mould to which he adheres, refusing to share or incapable of sharing her 'feminine' fantasy world until the end of the picture. Lula's Good Witch, Glinda, descends from the heavens, inspiring him with moral fortitude, but also finally making him accept Lula's alternative reality, affirming his love for her.

Lynch has transformed the Hollywood 'happy ending' cliché into pastiche, yes; and in doing so emphasises the narrative form of the cinema – 'The essence of all art is positive. So in the one great popular art form, *the* art form, this motive has to be even more powerful.'[3]

'Fire walk with me'

The film begins with the sound and image of a striking match, followed by an engulfing fire. Through the wall of flame the film title explodes across the screen. This image recurs at key points in the narrative, ostensibly to describe the death of Lula's father, but also as an image to describe the relationship between Sailor and Lula; a single match, a single cigarette – Sailor's individuality; one match, two cigarettes – unity; sharing the same cigarette – intimacy.

Fire, indeed, does walk with both Sailor and Lula through the story – Lula watched her father burn, and Sailor watched the fire, not aware of exactly what it was he was watching. 'Maybe you got too close to a fire – maybe you're gonna burn,' says Lula's mother to Sailor. Both of them had unwittingly witnessed the murder of Lula's father, engineered by her mother and carried out by an underworld psychotic, Marcello Santos.

The story opens at a place that has already made its way into film mythology, Cape Fear, somewhere near the border of North Carolina, where Sailor meets Lula at a swanky dance hall. Glenn Miller's 'In The Mood' is playing and Lula's mother, Marietta (Diane Ladd; Laura Dern's real-life mother) watches from behind a pillar as Bob Ray Lemon pulls a knife on Sailor, accusing him of 'trying to fuck your girl's mamma in the toilets!' At the end of the fight Bob Ray's brains seep over the marble floor. Sailor points an accusing finger at Marietta, who leers as she hides herself in the shadows, and Lula collapses in tears. Sailor is sent to the Pee Dee Correctional Institution.

'22 months 18 days later' reads the text, and Sailor telephones Lula. Marietta answers and warns: 'If you try to see her you're dead,' then tells Lula not to see him, pressing her red lips to a dry martini.

Lula, in a tight red dress, meets Sailor outside the prison and presents him with his snakeskin jacket, which Sailor declares, and not for the first time, 'represents my individuality and my belief in personal freedom.' They get in Lula's convertible and drive away.

The fire that 'walks' with Sailor and Lula is in both the past and the present: each time they make love their passion dissolves into a blazing image, either from a cigarette lighter, a match or the memory that ties them both. After their first round of lovemaking in a hotel room, the frame dissolves to red which in turn dissolves to the flame from a cigarette lighter. They share each other – they share a single cigarette. Lula's fiery memories transport her to her sexual debut with a wicked uncle, the wicked uncle's demise in a burning car as it crashes down a hill, and to the burning house in which her father perished.

As Marietta enlists the aid of her boyfriend, Johnnie Farragut (Harry Dean Stanton), to be rid of Sailor Ripley, Sailor nurtures fiery flashbacks of his own. Marietta confronts Sailor in a cubicle of the men's toilets and tells him, 'I'd sure like to fuck.' Sailor declines and Marietta threatens him with, '... maybe you're gonna burn.'

Sailor Ripley, Elvis Presley and Marlon Brando

On the dance floor a young rival makes a pass at Lula, and Sailor intercedes. Sailor beats up the interloper, apologises for embarrassing him in front of the crowd and once more declares the significance of his snake-skin jacket. (An unscripted prop supplied by Nicolas Cage.) He picks up the microphone and with the accompaniment of the stage band sings to Lula an Elvis Presley song, 'Love Me'.

They make love in their hotel room and Lula asks Sailor why he didn't sing 'Love Me Tender'. He'd always promised that one day he'd sing 'Love Me Tender'. 'Not ready yet, babe,' says Sailor, and two separate matches light two separate cigarettes.

'Love Me' is a raunchy Presley number full of meaningless lyric and sexual undertone; 'Treat me like a fool/treat me mean and cruel/but love me...' Sailor Ripley, like his American mythological mentor, begins as the wild untamed rebel and is forced to become the compassionate sentimentalist. Sailor's story parallels Elvis's development from *Jailhouse Rock* (Richard Thorpe, 1957), where Elvis learns to play guitar in prison, and once outside begins a career as an ill-tempered, surly rockstar with all the nostril-flaring insolence of his Sun Records career, to *Girl Happy* (Boris Sagal, 1965), a formula Elvis musical set in Fort Lauderdale, Texas, where a subdued Elvis undertakes the task of chaperoning the beautiful young, but spoiled daughter (Shelley Fabares) of a notorious Chicago mobster. In compliance to the formula, romance ensues, the girl is tamed and family unity restored. Sailor begins as the nostril-flaring, untamed jailbird (with rockstar aspirations), and ends up as the guy who ran off with the mobster's daughter. Like Elvis, Sailor's story begins with 'Mystery Train' and ends up as 'Teddy Bear'.

'What really grabbed me,' says Lynch, 'was the characters of Sailor and Lula. Sailor could be wild and like a rebel and be masculine, and Lula could be wild and like a rebel and feminine. They treated each other with respect, they were in love, they were equals in the relationship... a modern romance.'[4]

Sailor's masculine role models, Presley and Brando, are wild and rebellious in 1950s Hollywood movies – a decade later they were tame icons, sanitised for general consumption. Brando's last 'rebel role', after his 1950 debut in *The Men* (Fred Zinneman), *A Streetcar Named Desire* (Elia Kazan, 1951), *The Wild One* (Laslo

Benedek, 1954) and *On The Waterfront* (Elia Kazan, 1954), was Sidney Lumet's *The Fugitive Kind* (1959) in which he wears a snakeskin jacket 'representing his individuality and freedom'. The film, based on Tennessee Williams' play *Orpheus Descending*, has Brando, a wayward drifter, persuading Joanne Woodward to cruise the highways of America's southern states in an open-top car. Lula and Sailor's journey through Texas in Lula's convertible leads to the same kind of small-town hell-on-earth that Brando drifts into.

Marietta engages Santos to rid her of Sailor, and in doing so unintentionally sanctions Johnnie Farragut's death at the same time. While she paints her entire face with red lipstick, Johnnie, in New Orleans on the trail of Sailor and Lula, watches television in his hotel room: screeching hyenas tear apart and devour a gazelle. Marietta telephones him. 'I've done something real bad,' she says, her hands and face bright red. She tells Johnnie she's coming to New Orleans, hangs up, then vomits into the toilet bowl.

Lula Pace Fortune, Momma Marietta and the Wicked Witch

After Sailor tells Lula he's not ready to sing 'Love Me Tender', Lula tells Sailor the story of the Wicked Witch from *The Wizard of Oz*.

Throughout her adventures, Dorothy Gale, the heroine of *The Wizard of Oz*, remains a good-hearted, conventional, home-loving Kansas girl. The virtuous resonance of Frank L. Baum's books, and later, the MGM musical with Judy Garland, is due to Dorothy – she is forthright, wholesome, even sententious, but that Good will invariably triumph over Evil can be attributed to Dorothy's moral fibre. She reacts to bewildering characters and events with interest rather than fear, and she admonishes those who do not meet with her expectations of down to earth moral resolve.

Like Sailor's, Lula's archetypes are firmly planted in the mid-fifties, when *The Wizard of Oz* was first screened on American television, finally gaining the accolades it was denied on its release in 1939. In 1939 the film was not only poorly received, its box office barely covered production costs. When the film was screened on television in 1956 (the year Elvis first appeared on television) the film gained a status by which other musicals are measured, and a permanent place in American popular culture.[5]

An International Wizard of Oz Club was formed in 1957, and the film has since had an airing on American television almost every Thanksgiving. The story is known universally as *The Wizard of Oz*, yet of the fourteen 'Oz' books, seven written by the creator, Frank L. Baum, none of them bear this title; the film fable has a place in popular culture the story books could never attain. And it is the influence of the film acknowledged by contemporaries (and Lula), which has found its way into Anglo-Saxon culture. British author Salman Rushdie claims this was the film that inspired him to be a novelist – he perceives the Wicked Witch of the East as a possible benevolent dictator, and the Wicked Witch of the West as a positive woman role figure, compared to the frail and delicate Glinda: 'frilly pink versus slimline black. No contest.' The 'no place like home' motif, says Rushdie, conceals the film's subtext – escaping from the inadequacies of adults to find one's own maturity.[6] John Boorman's oddity, *Zardoz*, made in 1974 and set in the year 2293 portrays a primitive, Sean Connery, who unmasks the god he worships to reveal an insignificant technocrat who has taken his name from the disparate syllables of *The Wizard of Oz*.

Baum himself filmed the first version of *The Wizard of Oz*, in 1925, produced by Chadwick Pictures, with Oliver Hardy in the role of the Tin Man. It is a thoroughly American fable; a quest story which leads to a journey down a gold-lined road in search of a Wizard who turns out to be a charlatan. A parable of blind faith, innocence and the American dream.[7]

'It aspires to being a modernised fairy tale, in which the wonderment and joy are retained and the heartaches and nightmares are left out,' wrote Baum of his first 'Oz' book, *The Wonderful Wizard of Oz*, published in 1900. In fact, the 'nightmares' are part and parcel of the stories, and even the MGM film culminates with the grisly death of the wicked witch as she dissolves into liquid putrescence. The nightmare visions of the Wicked Witch terrorise Lula, but only the Good Witch shows herself to Sailor.

But there is more than the Wicked Witch of the West to terrify Lula, who sees omens of ill-fortune strewn along the yellow brick road.

First, the radio plays an old 1940s melody, 'Smoke Rings', while Lula and Sailor fill up Lula's car at a petrol station straight out of an advertisement for jeans: a nail varnish ruby red automobile is set against blue sky and green trees. Sailor naps in the back of the car as Lula drives, cruising down the yellow brick road, on the way to Emerald City.

Now the car radio issues forth its own version of the American dream – like Baum's fable, with the heartaches and nightmares, only little else besides: news items about a mother who killed her three children: a local judge who praises the defendant John Roy but 'was dismayed to learn that Roy had had sex with the corpse...'; crocodiles released into the Ganges to devour floating corpses... Lula goes crazy, stops the car, wakes Sailor and demands that he find music on the radio. He tunes in to a heavy rock station and they dance wildly in the desert against the red dusk sun.

Driving by night to the tune of Chris Isaaks' song 'Wicked Games', Sailor tells Lula that he knew her daddy, Clyde; that he did some driving for Santos, and that he saw Lula's house go up in flames. Lula sees the same image, only 'daddy Clyde' is inside all those flames. Why didn't Sailor tell Lula before? 'We all got a secret side, baby,' says Sailor, one of the few dialogue lines that Lynch added to those taken from Barry Gifford's novel.

Lula sees the Wicked Witch of the East cackling on a broomstick flying beside the car. In *The Wizard of Oz*, the Good Witch Glinda (Billie Burke) tells Dorothy, 'Close your eyes and tap your heels together three times. And think to yourself, there's no place like home.' Only for Lula, Marietta rules the roost, and her life pales before the ultimate Hollywood product – a film which boasted many writers (Herman Mankiewicz was one of the uncredited writers), many directors (mainly Victor Fleming, but also King Vidor, George Cukor and Richard Thorpe), and many compromises; Judy Garland was a substitute for Shirley Temple, and in the first cut the song 'Over the Rainbow' was deleted because it slowed the story down.

Lula's Hollywood-fabricated dream insists home is best; 'If ever I go looking for my heart's desire again,' says Dorothy (Judy Garland), 'I won't look any further than my own backyard, because if it isn't there, I never really lost it to begin with.' Only Lula's 'home' is burnt down, 'daddy Clyde' included, by a psychotic mother, so that all that's left is Emerald City, whatever horror that may be, whatever villain runs the place.

Emerald City

Santos has arranged for Sailor's demise at the small Texas town, Big Tuna. Mr Reindeer (W. Morgan Sheppard) is a David Lynch character, a sinister Oz

Wizard eccentric who sits on the toilet talking on the telephone, watching naked girls dance in his bathroom. He is a contract killer who lives in a brothel, with three fellow assassins, and who exhibits the gratuitous perversity of a mind gone rampant in an Emerald City of his own. Reindeer gives Santos one of two silver dollars for the assassination of Sailor, while a black woman in a blue-sequinned dress stands before a blue velvet curtains and sings 'Up in Flames' (lyrics by David Lynch).

The other silver dollar is for Johnnie Farragut, who is thumped on the head at his New Orleans hotel, taken out into a desolate patch of Louisiana night, tied to a post and shot between the eyes.

Meanwhile, for Lula and Sailor, the yellow brick road is strewn with clothing and dead bodies, not gold. 'One bad car accident,' says Sailor as he looks at the two crashed cars off the roadside. Two dead bodies lie beside each other, then another. A girl wanders dazed clutching her bleeding head. 'Robert,' she screams (as though all acts of violence, in a Lynch film, must be perpetrated by a character with that name), and as Sailor tries to calm her down she complains about 'sticky stuff in my head...' and inserts a finger into her head wound. She collapses by a tree, bleeds from the mouth, then dies. Sailor and Lula watch helplessly, then drive off down the road, red lights on black.

In Barry Gifford's novel, just before Sailor and Lula arrive in Big Tuna, Lula tells Sailor that she doesn't appreciate being called 'peanut' so much. It puts her, she says, 'so far down the food chain'. Lynch's road accident sequence, which occurs halfway through the film, gives a darker tone to the rest of the story, in the same way that Lula's objection to being called 'peanut' marks the beginning of a disintegration of her relationship with Sailor, in the novel.

'Big Tuna, Texas. Pop 603 Elev 3700' reads the road sign in the middle of a Texas wilderness, and the reverse side of the tin plate 'Big Tuna' sign is emblazoned with the legend 'fuck you' in red spray paint. 'I know it's not exactly Emerald City,' says Sailor.

He knocks on the door of a white-bleached cabin and skeletal trees blow in the wind. A bleached blonde with dark eyes and a smug smile answers. Her name is Perdita (Isabella Rossellini), an 'old flame' of Sailor's who assures him, falsely, that no one has a contract out on him. Perdita provides her own flashback of the burning house.

SAILOR: I didn't see nothing.
PERDITA: Don't you know that Santos burnt your little girl's daddy?

Marietta returns to Sailor's flashback, just to remind him, 'so maybe one night you got too close to a fire and maybe you got burned.'

Flies take off from a pool of vomit as Sailor opens the door to the motel room where Lula lies prostrate on the bed. 'My favourite shot in the film,' relates Lynch, who, during the course of the plot, has both mother and daughter throw up.[8]

The Big Tuna sequence is a study in Lynchian 'abjection' – the place itself is abject from the social mainstream, 'cast up' from social normality. It is the antithesis of Lynch's suburban white picket fences, new cut lawns and yellow tulips. There are no families in Big Tuna – only social outcasts and misfits.

Lula vomits because she is pregnant and in the isolation of the motel room the 'abject' scenes of her past are cast up like the contents of her stomach; the rape by her 'Uncle Pooch' and the subsequent abortion in which the red embryo is cast into a stainless-steel repository. Later Lula writes out a note to Sailor telling him she's pregnant. Sailor responds by lighting two cigarettes with one match. He gives one to Lula (solidarity), and says:

SAILOR: It's OK by me, peanut.
LULA: I'm not so sure it's OK by me.

Sailor and Lula have been copulating wildly across the southern states of America but their sex life comes to a brisk halt in Big Tuna, where sex is as 'abject' and repulsive as everything else. Apart from Bobby Peru's mock seduction of Lula, which is linked to his urinating, and his play on the use of the word 'head' ('I'm not gonna piss on your *head*, I'm gonna piss in the toilet'), sex in Big Tuna is a dirty business.

At night Sailor and Lula drink beer with the locals, an underworld ensemble straight from the residence of Ben in *Blue Velvet*. 'People over there making a pornographic movie,' one of them says, and the film team walks by beneath a string of coloured lights, thin men in suits and wide-brimmed hats, accompanied by Felliniesque oversized women who parade their nakedness lewdly before the nocturnal gathering. Jack Nance (who played Frank Booth's cohort, Paul, in *Blue Velvet*) tells an absurd story about his dog. What kind of dog do you imagine, he asks; 'perhaps you might even picture Toto', Dorothy's dog from *The Wizard of Oz*.

A man introduced as Bobby Peru ('like the country') joins the company, and as he recollects his participation in a Vietnam massacre it becomes clear he is unhinged – a deformed Lynch psychopath with his protruding lip and a pencil-line moustache over jagged teeth embedded in a mass of pink gum. (In 1992 Lynch published a book of photographs just of teeth and gums.) Bobby Peru's use of obscenity is more colourful than Frank Booth's, and his utterances are accompanied by a permanent snide grin. Bobby Peru shows no anger – just the deranged giggle of pleasure in the style of the Richard Widmark psychopath in *Kiss of Death* (Hathaway, 1947).

'I hope seeing that girl didn't jinx us,' says Lula when they arrive in Big Tuna, recollecting the car accident as an ominous sign. Sailor sits beside her and this time he sees the Wicked Witch. He gives Lula a candy necklace, 'four different colours – one for each reason I love you.'

Later, when they both have their secrets to conceal (Lula's near seduction, Sailor's planned hold-up) Sailor tells Lula; 'I promise I ain't gonna let things get no worse. Not in a million years.' The Wicked Witch laughs in the distance; Big Tuna, as Sailor observed on their arrival, is 'not exactly Emerald City'.

Over the rainbow

Sailor goes out to fix the car and Bobby Peru forces himself upon Lula. Then he joins Sailor and invites him for a beer. At the bar a man in the background is singing to a guitar and Bobby Peru proposes a robbery at the Lobo foodstore. Sailor says no.

Outside Bobby shows Sailor the armoury in his car trunk. 'How much you got?' he asks. 'Forty dollars,' says Sailor. Through the opaque glass of a crystal ball Sailor says OK; 'The money will get us a long way down the yellow brick road.' A woman's hand drapes across the crystal ball – the hand of Marietta, 'Moira', manipulating Sailor's fate from disaster to catastrophe. Sailor returns to the motel room where Lula sits in bed and smokes. Sailor lights up his own cigarette – each has betrayed the other – they are alone.

> LULA: That Bobby Peru is a black angel – don't get mixed up with him.
> SAILOR: I love you but I gotta get some sleep now.

LULA: This whole world is wild at heart and weird on top. [Crying] I wish you'd sing 'Love Me Tender.' I wish I was somewhere over that rainbow.

The following morning Sailor has his regrets, but it's too late for him to extricate himself from the hold-up. Perdita, Sailor's perdition, drives the car.

Inside the grain store Bobby Peru and Sailor hold up the two shopkeepers, while outside a policeman stops to chat with Perdita. Bobby takes the loot, shoots the two men behind the counter, points his double-barrelled shotgun at Sailor and smiles, 'You're next.' Sailor dives through the door to the waiting sheriff, Bobby runs out, gets shot once and blows his own head off with the shotgun. The contents of his skull are spilled over the desert ground, as Bob Ray Lemon's head was split open at the beginning of the picture. Sailor's mouth is in the dust. 'Lula, I really let you down,' he says.

Inside the grain store the two men from behind the counter, blood streaming from their wounds, search for the shot-off hand of one of them. 'Don't worry,' says his colleague. 'They can sew them back on again.' A dog runs out the door with the hand in his mouth, an image from Kurosawa's film, *Yojimbo*, and one which is imitated in Sergio Leone's *A Fistful of Dollars* (1964).

Once again Sailor is put behind bars, and Marietta and Santos come to take Lula home. 'Can you give your old friend Santos a hug?' says Santos and hugs her. Lula screams.

'Five years, 10 months, 21 days later' reads the text, superimposed over a gold-framed photograph of Lula in front of red velvet curtains. Lula, with their nearly six-year-old son, Pace, drives off in her open-top convertible to pick up Sailor after his release from prison. The journey is interrupted by a grisly car accident, where blood and internal organs colour the roadside and a delirious bleeding male victim attempts to converse with Lula. The accident may be a herald of ill-fortune, as Lula perceived the delirious girl accident victim, en route to Big Tuna nearly six years earlier, to be.

Sailor stands at the station with a stuffed lion in his hand, Lula and Pace join him, and for a brief moment there is a family in the couple's otherwise family-less lives. Marietta, at her place, in front of a picture of Lula and with a martini in her hand, screams 'No!' And sure enough, as they drive down the road, Sailor stops the car, tells Lula 'it don't feel right,' bids farewell to Pace, picks up his suitcase and walks away.

In the middle of an empty street Sailor is suddenly surrounded by nine punks. He takes out a Marlboro cigarette and lights up with studied deliberation. 'What do you faggots want?' he says, and gets soundly beaten. As he lies on the ground, Glinda the Good Witch descends in a luminous bubble and tells Sailor that Lula loves him. 'Don't turn away from love,' she says three times, in the same hypnotic tone with which Bobby Peru made sexual advances towards Lula.

Sailor gets up with a swollen nose, apologises to the punks for calling them homosexuals and sprints down the road, running over cars stuck in a traffic jam, finally planting himself on the bonnet of Lula's convertible. They embrace. 'I just met the Good Witch,' he tells Lula, then sings 'Love Me Tender'.

Do we 'buy' Lynch's ending? Or is it as 'gratuitous' as a number of disparate scenes that intersperse the plot? The *Sight and Sound* critic, Jonathan Rosenbaum, writes that 'Lynch is only interested in iconography, not characters at all,' and the happy ending 'seems sadly to demonstrate only the desperation of a surrealist vaudevillian stuck for a finish.'[9]

Lynch purports to embrace the convention of the form – a Hollywood movie must have a 'happy ending'; yet the parodic extravagance of the ending appears as an ironic commentary on the narrative's singular lack of resolution. Apart from Sailor singing 'Love Me Tender', and the demise of Bobby Peru, not a lot is resolved. Santos is alive and kicking, unpunished for the murder of Johnnie Farragut, Perdita is back in the purgatory of Big Tuna, and if Mr Reindeer was ever the Wizard of Oz, he remains 'undebunked'. Marietta's photograph may have disappeared in a puff of smoke, but Marietta herself is more unhinged than ever, and, presumably, more adamant than ever that Sailor and Lula don't remain together.

The loose threads of matters undisclosed lie at the heart of Gifford's novel; Sailor taking off alone is just one more loose thread. The very artifice of Lynch's ending may suggest the opposite of its intention. For Lula and Sailor, Emerald City is the prospect of playing 'happy families', a game in which, according to the David Lynch book of rules, everyone loses.

Lynch's ending to *Wild at Heart* is a playful departure from 'road movie' genre conventions. Traditionally, the couple on the run, whether from the law, or from the underworld, meet an ill-fated end. The protagonists of *You Only Live Once* (Fritz Lang, 1936), *They Live By Night* (Nicholas Ray, 1949), *Gun Crazy* (Joseph Lewis,

1949), *Breathless* (Jean-Luc Godard, 1959), *Bonnie and Clyde* (Arthur Penn, 1967) all die violent deaths. In Godard's *Pierrot le Fou* (1965), *Wild at Heart*'s twenty-five-year-old 'cousin', Ferdinand (Jean-Paul Belmondo) retrieves the bullet-strewn body of his girl, Marianne (Anna Karina), ties two rows of dynamite sticks around his head and lights the fuse.

These films depict 'the worker-hero rejected and penalised by society, the girl who identifies herself with his plight, their attempts to find happiness together frustrated by poverty and an inescapable past.'[10] The summary describes *Wild at Heart* as much as the many successors to *You Only Live Once*, which ends with Eddie (Henry Fonda) set up by the law to rejoin his wife, only to be gunned down by the police.

Lula and Sailor are spared, family intact, ready to partake of the mad consumerism they observed from the front seat of their open top convertible. Their driving days are over.

David Lynch describes Lula and Sailor as 'struggling in darkness and confusion like everybody else... The idea that there's some room for love in a really cool world is really interesting to me.'[11]

Awarded the Palme d'Or at Cannes 1990 for its cinematic virtuosity, *Wild at Heart* is a 'film film', says Lynch, with no other purpose than being just film.

The Wizard of Oz's dedication to all those who are 'young at heart', applies to David Lynch's *Wild at Heart* – to the contemporary 'young at heart' who absorb the fragmented narratives of rock videos and television advertising, uninterested in resolved intrigues and plot development. The loose ends can stay loose. Isn't that what 'love in a really cool world' is about?

Twin Peaks: Fire Walk With Me (1992)

> *She was a maiden of rarest beauty, and not more lovely than full of glee. And evil was the hour when she saw, and loved, and wedded the painter.*

Edgar Allan Poe, *The Oval Portrait*

Synopsis: *Special FBI Agents Chester Desmond and Sam Stanley are sent to Deer Meadows in Washington State to investigate the murder of a young woman named Teresa Banks. In the course of his enquiries, Desmond mysteriously disappears, and Special Agent Dale Cooper is sent to investigate. Cooper has a premonition of the next victim in what appears to be the work of a serial killer. A seventeen-year-old schoolgirl, foresees Cooper, sexually active and taking drugs – a description of half the schoolgirls in the United States, his colleague suggests.*

A year later, in the community of Twin Peaks, Laura Palmer is on her way to school, and sniffs cocaine before the day's lessons begin. She is the homecoming queen, much loved by all, but her innocent looks conceal a hedonistic lifestyle. She keeps a record of her sexual encounters with a character named 'Bob', who has been 'having her' since she was twelve. She is shocked to discover that 'Bob' is her father, Leland.

After two nights of sexual depravity and drug excesses (on the first of which her friend Donna attempts to follow in Laura's footsteps so she may lose her innocence), Laura is kidnapped by her father and beaten to death. He wraps her body in plastic and pushes it into the river.

Within a mysterious place in the forest, called 'the lodge', a place Laura has already visited in her dreams, she sits in an armchair with Agent Cooper by her side, and smiles and watches a white dressed angel ascend into the heavens.

Sheryl Lee

Few viewers of the film are unaware of Laura Palmer's fate, which has been the subject of thirty episodes of a television series, stretched over two seasons and broadcast in sixty countries. The series became a 'media event', the fate of Laura Palmer became material for newspapers, magazines, TV chat shows and radio programmes. The intrigue of the film lies not in 'what' happens to Laura Palmer, nor even 'when and where', nor 'how' or 'why' – these questions have already been answered. What remains is the way in which David Lynch shows these events – information becomes pictures; abstracts are made concrete.

Portraits of Laura

The focal point of the film and the television series is the 'image' of Laura Palmer – both figuratively and literally. Her photographic portrait is an icon of 'the feminine' which pervades Lynch's previous films; John Merrick's mother in *The Elephant Man*, Princess Irulan in *Dune*, Dorothy Vallens in *Blue Velvet*.

The portrait of Laura Palmer (Sheryl Lee) stands framed in the Twin Peaks High School glass cabinet along with school medallions and trophies. Laura is a prize. Bobby Briggs (Dana Ashbrook) trips into the corridor, gloats before Laura's picture, presses his lips to the glass and says, 'You're all mine, baby.' In the television series Laura's picture is an image of ambiguity that pervades not only the high school corridor, but the Palmer residence; the bedroom of her best friend, Donna; the home of the introspective Harold Smith; the outsider, James Hurley; and the desk of Twin Peaks' elder, Benjamin Horne. Laura belongs to everyone.

The smiling portrait of Laura is the image of youthful beauty and innocence – she is the pride of the Twin Peaks community, (the face of Glinda the Good Witch in *Wild at Heart*), an 'American sweetheart' straight out of a 1950s copy of *True Romance*. Laura and Laura's image, dissected extensively through thirty episodes of television melodrama, is the principal subject of *Twin Peaks: Fire Walk With Me* – her character oscillates violently from predatory vamp, to sorrow-strewn incest victim, to raging junkie, to wayward innocent.

Laura's problem, which soon becomes the film's problem, is that she has no identity, only an image. The creator of the image, David Lynch, claims he made the film 'because I love Twin Peaks. Twin Peaks is a land of mystery...'[1] He is a painter beset with his painting, and 'evil indeed is the hour' when 'the painting' weds the artist.

A portrait of Laura is also central to the *film noir Laura* (Otto Preminger, 1944), the story of a 'dead' woman and the effect her 'image' has on men. Her portrait dominates her apartment, as her image dominates the men who come into her life. The power of the image becomes most apparent when Laura is believed dead. 'The power to incite murder which is visually ascribed to Laura's magnificent portrait is revealed to be a product of the neuroses of the men around her, not of the power she wields.'[2] Film critic Janey Place is describing here the Preminger film, but the observation is as valid if applied to Laura Palmer, who functions as a catalyst to perverse forms of male desire. The name of the painter is Jacoby, which is also the name of Laura's analyst in *Twin Peaks*. According to the story's narrator, Waldo Lydecker, 'Jacoby was in love with her when he painted it, but he never captured her vibrancy, her warmth.' Similarly, it transpires, Jacoby the analyst's verbal portrayal of Laura Palmer fails to capture 'her vibrancy, her warmth'; like other residents of Twin Peaks, he knows Laura primarily through her image.

Bobby Briggs covets the 'school prize', and 'daddy', consumed by an 'evil spirit', harbours sexual desires which culminate in murder. The men in between include bar drifters and drug pushers (Jacques Renault, Leo Johnson), the customers of the whorehouse across the border, young innocents (James Hurley, Harold Smith) and the man 'who owns the town', Benjamin Horne.

The sanctity of the image is countered by the depravity of its subject, and its power contrasts with the weakness of the beholder. The sexual 'victims' of Laura Palmer all lack moral fortitude in the face of her appeal: they are men corrupted, either by power, drugs or sex. Only the 'law' is above reproach: Special Agent Dale Cooper foresees her plight and, through dreams, tries to warn her.

In Preminger's *Laura*[3], the image is glamorous and Laura herself a poor imitation. When Laura Hunt appears from the 'dead' to the detective investigating her 'murder', she stands before him a drab figure in a raincoat; wet, bedraggled and unpainted. Her portrait shows her made-up to an ideal of sexual allure, with naked shoulders, painted lips and a helpless 'come-hither' glance. The detective, Mark McPherson, has already fallen in love with Laura's image, and when she turns up alive, he must abandon the preconceptions suggested by the picture in order to be involved with the real Laura Hunt. Janey Place describes the portrait of Laura as an 'impotent powerless form, powerless to move or act,' a form in which 'the sexual woman is no threat to the *film noir* man.'[4]

In her photograph, displayed alongside the high school trophies, Laura Palmer is safe, passive, controlled, but in real life, she refuses to comply with the fantasies inspired by the image. She is the picture of innocence concealing guilt, an icon of purity who incites murder.

Lynch completes the 'enantiodromia' of Laura Palmer, the conversion from one extreme to the other, in two scenes: from her walk to school with best friend, Donna, to her retreat into a toilet cubicle before lessons where she hastily sniffs cocaine. This is hardly a revelation, however; Laura Palmer's cocaine habit was revealed by Cooper in the first episode of the television series. In fact, there is no information in *Twin Peaks: Fire Walk With Me* that hasn't been disclosed in the television series, and Lynch makes it clear from the start that the film and the TV melodrama are inextricably linked.

Exploding a television myth

The film begins with a haunting subdued melody, with the resonance of 'Smoke Rings' or the theme to *Chinatown*, playing against a pulsating blue-grey haze – a close-up of television static. The title credits appear against this nebulous background, white on grey, and as the 'Directed by David Lynch' credit appears, the camera pulls back to reveal a television set. No sooner has the text faded than an axe plunges through the screen and Leland Palmer's mad face appears.

A body wrapped in plastic floats down a river, the body not of Laura Palmer, but Teresa Banks; a river not in Twin Peaks, but in Deer Meadows.

The first words we hear, and the first face we see, belong to Lynch himself, in the role of FBI Regional Supervisor, Gordon Cole.

These three disparate shots are familiar territory – images plundered from the television screen, as indeed most of the film is. Leland Palmer has been identified as Laura's murderer, and the 'bearer' of Bob's evil spirit. Leland met his demise in Episode Nine of the second season, and his funeral was held in Episode Ten. The floating corpse we associate with Laura – the opening shots of the first episode when Pete Martell discovers the plastic enshrouded corpse on the river bank. We have also seen Laura's cousin Madeleine despatched in the same manner. David Lynch as Gordon Cole appeared intermittently; along with Cooper, Sheriff Truman and others, a further specimen of the inviolate upholder of the law. But in the role of a hard-of-hearing supervisor, Lynch plays the role of a boss who goes his own way regardless, a benign fellow deaf to the ideas and criticism of subordinates. A malfunctioning hearing aid becomes a convenient excuse not to have to listen to anyone. Leland Palmer's axe through the television promises that *Twin Peaks: Fire Walk With Me* will be a radical departure from the television medium, but it is a promise unfulfilled. The film ploughs through an already harvested crop, serving new versions of familiar material.

Cole's meeting with agents Chester Desmond (Chris Isaaks) and Sam Stanley (Kiefer Sutherland) on a Dakota airstrip provides us with some eccentric exposition – a woman in a red dress, contorting and grimacing irregularly, transpires to be a semiotic coding of plot detail which the two men decipher on their drive from Oregon to Washington State. Cooper's Tibetan detection method was a wittier and less gratuitous eccentricity, satirising television's means of contriving plot and character summaries in each episode to refresh the viewer's memory.

But the most blatant exploitation of the television series occurs twenty-five minutes into the story, when at the end of the Deer Meadows prelude, the familiar chords of the Angelo Badalamenti theme resonate over the Twin Peaks highway sign, the establishment coda for each one of thirty television episodes. From now on the viewer is in familiar territory – the characters, the locations, the situations are all readily identifiable.

Twin Peaks: Fire Walk With Me also sounds and looks more like TV than cinema. The film is David Lynch's first since *Eraserhead* not to be shot in wide-screen Panavision (2:35:1 ratio); the film's 1:85:1 ratio, photographed by Ron Garcia, the principal photographer of the television series, is pre-packaged for television transmission.

Also, this is the first feature film in which Lynch has not collaborated with sound designer Alan Splet. Sound design on the film is attributed to Lynch alone; in the words of William Blake, 'the sound is forc'd, the notes are few.' Following the moody and nostalgic chords of Badalamenti's opening theme, the soundtrack quickly descends into a cacophony of sudden shocks and blaring noise, lacking the subtlety and finesse of the earlier Alan Splet sound designs. Screeching tyres and blasting engines which accompany the one-armed man's pursuit of Leland in mid-town traffic only serve to highlight the banality of the images, and the dramatic weakness of the situation. To overcome the familiarity of 'Bob' to viewers of the television series, Lynch has apparently deemed it necessary to introduce thunderous roars to accompany his menacing appearance.

Demystifying the feminine

The story begins in Deer Meadows, North Dakota. Special Agent Chester Desmond investigates the murder of Teresa Banks. 'A drifter...' according to the local sheriff, 'no-one knew her.' Despite local hostility, Desmond, with the aid of Agent Stanley, conducts his own autopsy, in the provisional morgue, a wooden shed behind the sheriff's office.

Teresa Banks, 'Bob's' murder victim twelve months prior to the murder of Laura Palmer, is being cut open on a marble slab. Repeated blows to the head are given as the 'cause of death', and a ring is missing from a dirt-ingrained finger. Her painted mouth and eyes are open wide in the obscene pose of a rubber doll manufactured for male gratification. Her unruly mop of artificially-bleached blonde hair intensifies her synthetic appearance. Stanley removes one of her red varnished fingernails – the varnish scratched and faded – to recover an implanted letter, a 'T'. The body of Teresa Banks is a discarded sexual object, to be dissected by a coroner's scalpel as if by cutting her open men in suits and white coats could comprehend the nature of sexual desire.

The autopsy scene of Laura Palmer in the television series turns into a wild parody of *The Texas Chainsaw Massacre*, as FBI pathologist, Albert, resolutely wields his electrical saw above Laura's cranium. The protests of outraged Twin Peaks officials, Dr Hayward, Sheriff Truman and Deputy Brennan result in a near brawl over Laura's corpse, prevented only by the intervention of Agent Cooper.

Transgressing males in a Lynch film meet their demise through violence; their split-open skulls invariably spilling brain matter (Bob Ray Lemon and Bobby Peru in *Wild at Heart*; Frank Booth and Don 'the yellow man' in *Blue Velvet*, a Canadian drug courier in *Fire Walk With Me*). Transgressing women are beaten to death, then taken apart in autopsy. Lynch pries behind a smiling portrait to expose ugliness, strips away flesh to expose vital organs, removes the skull to examine brain matter. Yet his delving beneath surfaces in an unholy quest for knowledge, his attempts to divine the mystery of the feminine through dissection, yields only blood and organs. Similarly, Laura's promiscuity reveals that sexual experience does not necessarily equal knowledge: when she tells Harold Smith that 'Bob' has been 'having her since she was twelve', it implies his possession of her as much as his having sex with her.

Diner by night

Roadside diners feature consistently in Lynch's pictures; usually in the clear light of day; Arlene's Diner in Lumberton (*Blue Velvet*) where Jeffrey and Sandy first plan, then later analyse Jeffrey's intrusion into the apartment of Dorothy Vallens; Norma Jennings' Double R Diner in *Twin Peaks*, the 'heaven where cherry pies go to', and Bob's Diner in Los Angeles where David Lynch and his daughter, Jennifer, executed a daily two-thirty ritual of coffee and hamburgers for six years, from 1978 to 1984. Lynch claims his inspirations were jotted down on Bob's Diner paper serviettes; outlines of forthcoming film scenarios.[5]

That agents Desmond and Stanley visit Hap's Diner in the darkest hours of night is singularly appropriate in Deer Meadows, the dark sibling of Twin Peaks. A flickering blue neon light casts sinister shadows over all who leave and enter; Chester and Sam drink coffee. Behind the counter Irene describes the death of Teresa Banks as a 'freak accident'. An obese male customer with a pretty waif of a girl interjects constantly but has nothing to say. 'Three days before she died,' says Irene, 'her left arm went numb.' Three days before Cooper disappears into a patch of forest outside Twin Peaks, his arm turns numb and trembles, Pete Martell's arm trembles, Benjamin Horne's arm trembles and the third last episode of the television series ends with the extended left arm of 'Bob' dangling in the woodland night air, his body concealed within the so-called 'Black Lodge'.

The David Lynch diner is the setting for the mandatory rite of coffee drinking, a hallmark of the television series, in which the quality of coffee is a measure for the quality of life. In the Lynch world the worst that can happen to a cup of coffee is the presence of a fish in the percolator, as in the television series (I.1), so it's little surprise that coffee at the Fat Trout Caravan Park doesn't meet with FBI standards.

When Desmond and Stanley investigate the caravan of Teresa Banks, caretaker Carl Rodd (Harry Dean Stanton) prepares a pot of 'joe', which becomes both the subject of a prolonged conversation and a male initiation rite ('Strong enough?' 'Yuh!' 'Whoa!', etc). In between they scrutinise a polaroid snap of Teresa Banks, and confront the mute stares of an eccentric old lady, a sinister version of the Twin Peaks 'log lady'.

Their presence in Deer Meadows, from their arrival onwards, provokes local antagonism mediated through the coffee pot. 'Help yourself to the coffee,' says the deputy. 'I'm sure it's fresh... like two, three days old...' as the two agents are kept purposely waiting. When Desmond goes on the attack, by twisting the deputy's nose, he suggests, 'time to start with that fresh pot of coffee'. So sacrosanct indeed is coffee, that when the *Twin Peaks* series ends, the gold-framed portrait of Laura is replaced by a cup of solidified coffee (presented to Cooper inside the 'lodge') upon which the image of Laura is gradually superimposed.

The Feds

The Federal Bureau of Investigation is a division of the US Department of Justice and was created in 1908 to investigate violations of federal law. These include espionage, sabotage, bank robberies, fraud, kidnapping and, in special cases, such as serial killings, murder. Under the directorship of J. Edgar Hoover (1924–1972) the FBI came under increasing attack for political activities and interfering in the constitutional rights of US citizens.

David Lynch's portrayal of a Bureau of sympathetic well-dressed males, eccentric but goodhearted, can be attributed to a degree of poetic licence, but more to the underlying conservatism of the Lynch world. Men working within the law are 'white' and those outside the law are 'black'. The White Lodge is reserved for FBI agents, local lawmen and air-force majors. The Black Lodge is for psychopaths.

David Lynch's Philadelphia FBI consists of Regional Supervisor Gordon Cole (played by himself), an eccentric romantic who finally falls for Shelley, the waitress at Norma's Double Diner; the brilliant but belligerent pathologist, Albert Rosenfield, who, after a number of altercations with the slow-thinking Sheriff Truman, embraces and declares his love to the bewildered lawman; the sexually confused but capable transvestite, Denis(e); and Dale Cooper, mystic, dreamer, resolute, incorruptible.

The FBI is also a place of mysterious and inexplicable goings on: Cooper must confide in Gordon Cole; it's 10:10 am on 16 February, and Cooper is 'worried about today because of the dream I had.' A missing agent, Phillip Jeffries (David Bowie), appears, utters a few words in an appalling parody of a southern accent, and disappears, though his image, together with the image of Cooper, fastens itself to the electronic impulses of a video monitor. In the hazy timewarp between his coming and going, a brief insight into the red-velvet chamber, 'Bob' appears, the young Chalfont boy, and 'the man from another place', the dwarf, who says, 'we live inside a dream.'

Cooper, investigating Desmond's disappearance in Deer Meadows, finds the agent's car, upon which the words 'Let's rock' are daubed in red – words uttered by the dwarf to Cooper as he dreams the name of Laura Palmer's murderer in his room at the Great Northern Hotel, Twin Peaks, one year later. (I.3)

Red velvet

The familiar chords of Angelo Badalamenti's theme and the Twin Peaks road sign returns us instantly to television – Laura walks to school with her best friend Donna, says hello to a parade of familiar characters in the school corridor, and disappears into a toilet cubicle to sniff cocaine. The following few scenes quickly establish Laura's dual character; the traumatised incest victim and the vengeful predator unleashing her venom on unsuspecting male victims. But she is neither one character nor the other – she attempts to fulfil and subvert the ideal of her photographic image which is displayed so prominently publicly and domestically.

When she discovers that some pages are missing from her diary, she visits a young man, an introspective wayward soul called Harold Smith, whom she has befriended, and confides in him her fears. She breaks down and weeps as she shows him her diary from which the pages have been torn.

HAROLD: But who would do that?
LAURA: Bob!

HAROLD: But Bob's not real.

LAURA: He IS real. He's been having me since I was twelve.

Laura turns into a fierce, red-gummed, red-eyed vampire and hisses 'Fire walk with me,' then breaks down and weeps. Laura cannot be one character or the other – she is both victim and persecutor; Harold sympathises with her, yet fears her. Laura has no identity of her own; she is both traumatised and possessed by an 'evil spirit'. She asks Harold to hide her diary, and as she leaves, turns in the doorway, crying, 'I may never come back.' The shot dissolves to red velvet curtains as a premonition of Laura's destiny. Like a sleepwalker, Laura walks to her inevitable death. But first she must meet with those who dwell behind the red velvet curtains; the instruments of fate that usher her on her way.

Laura promises to help out on the Meals on Wheels round, and while she is doing so, an old lady and a young boy approach her. The old lady gives her a painting which shows a half-open door in a room decorated with floral wallpaper. 'This would look nice on your wall,' she tells Laura. Then the boy looks up and says: 'Someone is looking in your diary now.' Laura runs home and sees 'Bob' in her bedroom, tearing out pages of the diary.

The old lady and the boy are the Chalfonts, referred to by Carl as the people who left the Fat Trout Caravan Park immediately after the disappearance of Chester Desmond. They appear again in the television series (II.2), when Donna covers Laura's Meals on Wheels round trying to uncover details about the mystery surrounding her death. Now their name is Fremont, and the little boy performs magic tricks while the old lady tells Donna about Laura's secret diary hidden in the home of the introspective Harold Smith, next door. When Donna takes Cooper to meet them, they have disappeared, and no one has ever heard of such a couple. The little boy appears before Leland Palmer shortly before he murders Teresa Banks in Deer Meadows. He wears a white mask and hops up and down like a kangaroo. And they appear again to Laura, inside her dream, inside the painting the old lady gave to her.

Laura, having discovered 'Bob' is her father, visits Donna and weeps uncontrollably. At the dinner table that evening, Leland grabs Laura's hands: 'You haven't washed your hands – look, your hands are filthy –

there's dirt way under this fingernail,' he says, prying at the fingernail beneath which he will later insert a letter 'R', in the manner that the letter 'T' was inserted under the fingernail of Teresa Banks. Laura's mother, Sara, interjects, but Leland persists. He pulls the broken heart locket from Laura's neck: 'Did you get this from your lover?' he demands. Laura runs to her room weeping.

Subdued, Leland goes to Laura and consoles her: 'Laura, I love you – goodnight, princess,' he says, and leaves. Laura cries (her two modes of expression throughout the film consist of hysterical weeping and hysterical laughing) and looks at a painting on her bedroom wall. It shows a white-robed, blonde-haired angel feeding a group of children seated around a table. 'Is it true?' she asks, then places the painting she received from the old lady on the wall.

As Laura sleeps she is absorbed into the painting. She enters the room and meets the old lady and young boy once more, as they beckon her through other doors, and finally into the room lined with red velvet curtains and the presence of the dwarf, 'the man from another place'. Cooper sits beside the dwarf, and next to them is a table, on top of which lies a ring bearing a mysterious emblem. It's the same ring which Desmond picked up beneath the Chalfonts' caravan in Deer Meadows prior to his disappearance, and the same ring worn by one-armed Mike as he shouts at Leland Palmer, warning Laura: 'It's him. It's your father.' As Laura approaches Cooper says: 'Don't take the ring, Laura. Don't take the ring.'

Laura 'awakens'. She is in her bed, but next to her lies the body of a girl covered in blood. The violation of nocturnal sanctity is a recurring Lynch anxiety. In *Eraserhead*, Henry Spencer awakens to find the departed Mary next to him, executing an entire range of connubial irritations, and then discovering she is 'giving birth' to a bed full of severed umbilical cords. In a later scene, Henry embraces the girl from across the hall, and they are both submerged in the watery depths which suddenly open up in the middle of the bed.

Laura's bed companion introduces herself: 'My name is Annie,' she says. 'The good Dale is in the Lodge and he can't leave.' When Laura awakens, the ring she was warned not to touch is on her finger.

This enigmatic line, spoken by an even more enigmatic character, only makes sense in connection with the final episode of the television series. Dale Cooper has fallen in love with ex-convent girl, Annie – she is kidnapped by Cooper's adversary, Windom Earle, and taken to the 'Black Lodge'. Cooper enters the lodge and in return for Annie's life yields his soul to the evil spirit of 'Bob'. The Dale that has left the lodge is 'evil', and Annie's few brief words are a consolation to Twin Peaks viewers left with the final image of the 'pure' Dale Cooper transformed into the psychopathic 'Bob'.

The red-velvet chambers of the lodge make up the arena for the 'psychomachia' between Cooper and 'Bob', but also the consoling scenes between Cooper and Laura, and later Laura's vision of the ascending white angel. The old lady and the boy act as functionaries leading chosen souls into this otherworldly dimension – a place where dreams and reality collude. Guests of 'the man from another place' have included Leland Palmer, Windom Earle, Cooper, Major Briggs, Annie and Laura Palmer. In the unlikely event of Twin Peaks II, it's a safe bet that future guests will include the missing Chester Desmond, and the enigmatic Phillip Jeffries.

That it is a place where men go by choice, and women go to be murdered, suggests 'the place where women fear to go' in *Dune*, the place where Paul (later the face of Cooper), not only 'goes', but conquers, in order to become the 'supreme being of the universe'. The emergence of the character Annie refers to as the 'good Dale' may have similar implications.

However, for all Cooper's warnings, for all the warnings and omens that foretell the fate of Laura Palmer, there is no avoiding fate. When the 'lord of the underworld' summons, Laura responds.

Persephone's descent into Hades

Laura drinks a large whisky in front of her gold-framed photograph as homecoming queen, before heading off for The Gun Bar, unaware that her friend Donna has followed her. Outside the entrance, Margaret, the 'log lady', warns Laura that 'all goodness is in jeopardy.' Inside Julee Cruise is singing a wistful ballad, 'She would die for love' (lyrics by David Lynch). Laura sits at a table and weeps.

Donna watches from a distance as the barman, Jacques Renault, sends over two men to Laura's table. She is now composed and greets them with a smile and a challenge. 'So you want to fuck the homecoming queen,' she says, leaving little doubt as to how she finances her cocaine habit. Donna approaches and shows she is determined to join in Laura's 'games', and together they seduce the two men.

They move into an inferno-like discotheque, drink spiked beer, and dance provocatively. Laura discards her jacket on to the floor and dances bare-breasted – Donna, whose resolve fails her, picks up Laura's jacket and ties it around her waist. She is now imbued with the valour to have sex with her partner on top of a beer table. Laura sees her and, in a furious tantrum, has her thrown out. Laura cannot share the secrets of her nights, nor can she share her journey. She is the lone traveller into her own darkness.

The next day, as father and daughter drive into town, Mike, the one-armed man, a 'messenger from the underworld', warns Laura, pointing at Leland and saying: 'Miss, it's him; it's your father.' Mike wears the ring which Cooper told her not to pick up.

As Laura dissolves into hysterical shrieking, Leland recalls his encounters with Teresa Banks at the Deer Meadows motel room, ending with him beating her to death. The flashback is crosscut with Laura's screaming, as though she is witness to her father's memories and deeds.

Back at school Bobby promises Laura a fresh supply of cocaine – he has arranged a meeting with his supplier in the forest that night. The forest as a place of dark secrets is a recurring Lynch theme, and several sequences of the television series feature the suggestive play of torchlight over trees. Laura and Bobby giggle in a half-drunken stupor as Laura casts eerie shadows over the swaying branches, and she continues to giggle as the courier approaches with a bag of cocaine. He pulls a gun, but Bobby shoots first and kills him. Laura regards the brain matter oozing from the dead man's skull, and giggles all the more uncontrollably.

The next day James Hurley talks to Laura outside her house as Leland watches from the doorway. In her bedroom Laura sniffs cocaine, while her mother, Sara, envisions a white horse in the living room. (A casual reference to heroin or a Lynchian touch of the surreal? The image recurs several times throughout the series, and Sara's role as medium becomes clear when we share her visions of, among other things, Laura's missing necklace, and the face of 'Bob'.)

'Bob' crawls serpent-like through Laura's bedroom window, and as they copulate on her bed, she demands several times: 'Who are you?' When 'Bob's' face becomes the face of her father she screams loud and long. How do we account for her reaction when she has already seen that 'Bob' is her father? This can only be attributed to Laura's denial of reality. 'No, it can't be,' she kept telling herself as she watched her father leave the house, after having witnessed 'Bob' tear pages from the secret diary hidden in her room. They are both obviously one and the same person, yet Laura denies the truth, choosing to live in self-manifested illusion. 'Victims of incest... learn secrecy and subterfuge in order to conceal the extent of their pain even from themselves...' writes analyst, Claire Douglas. 'Victims of incest need help in calling things by their real names...'[6]

For all the film's shortcomings, the portrayal of an incestuous father/daughter relationship is a credible one – Laura creates a bestial face for her nocturnal intruder rather than associate it with the face of her father. She leads a duplicitous life of drugs and promiscuity; drugs to avoid facing reality, and a promiscuity borne of the 'separation' from her body.

Laura's perception of reality dissolves into vagaries – school is a haze of dutch angles (oblique camera angles used to suggest discord) and blurred images. The monster of her dreams has erupted forth into her waking life, to drag her down into the underworld. Just as Persephone, the maiden of spring in Greek mythology, eventually eats the fruit of the underworld, the pomegranate, Laura's 'addiction', is just one more means of surrendering her identity to the darkness. Persephone (her name means 'bringer of destruction') is the virtuous maiden, untouched by life, until Hades, the lord of the underworld, takes her down to his subterranean realm and rapes her.

The myth of Persephone's rape is also a key to understanding the nature of the 'beast' – for it is her image of unblemished innocence which arouses the savage desire of Hades. Persephone yields to her fate, but, according to the myth, the compassion of the gods allows her to spend two-thirds of her time in Olympus with the gods, while in the other third she must fulfil her obligations and remain in the underworld. In psychological terms above ground represents the 'conscious' and below ground the unconscious – the states of 'wakefulness' and 'sleep'. For Laura, her period of 'sleep' is the one-third of her life dominated by 'Bob'; but now he has come to claim her 'conscious' state as well.

Laura's last night

Laura sniffs coke, puts on her sexiest underwear and half-heartedly arranges to meet James Hurley outside the house. Before she leaves she looks at her bedroom picture of the angel feeding the children. The angel disappears before her eyes and she weeps bitterly. Leland watches from the window as Laura disappears on the back of James' motorcycle.

They stop on the roadway in the middle of the forest:

> JAMES: What's wrong with us. We have everything.
> LAURA: Everything but everything.
> JAMES: You always hurt the one you love.
> LAURA: Or the one you pity.

Laura vacillates from nasty to kind; they embrace and then she runs off into the forest, with James calling after her.

In the forest she meets Jacques, Leo Johnson and Ronette Pulaski. They go to Jacques' place, sniff cocaine and Laura strips off and dances in her underwear. To the accompaniment of overpowering euphonic discord, Jacques ties up Laura on the mattress, and in the process she gets bitten on her shoulder by a caged bird named Waldo. ('Waldo' is the name of Laura Hunt's would-be murderer in the film *Laura*, 1944). These details are all pieced together later by Agent Cooper. All the events portrayed in the sequence of Laura's last night have been scrupulously outlined by James Hurley, Agent Cooper and others, in the first episodes of the television series.

Leland watches the sordid proceedings through the cabin window and when Jacques walks outside the cabin to relieve himself, Leland slugs him over the head. When Leo comes out in a drug-induced stupor, and sees Jacques, unconscious and bleeding, he gets in the car and drives off. Leland takes Laura and Ronette. One-armed Mike gives chase.

Leland ties up both the girls inside a disused railway wagon, and before Laura's eyes he is transformed into Bob. Laura screams, but then sees her ascending angel. The murder becomes a sacrificial rite: the father must sacrifice the daughter to appease the gods of the underworld. 'Forgive me,' he says, as he clubs her to death. Leland throws Ronette's unconscious body out of the compartment, then disappears into the patch of forest known as the 'Black Lodge'.

Laura's body, shrouded in plastic, floats down the river, to be washed up on the shore and discovered the following day, as portrayed in Episode One of the television series. Laura herself is seated in an armchair in a chamber lined with red velvet curtains. 'Bob' is here, her father, Leland, one-armed Mike and 'the man from another place', the dwarf. Cooper stands beside her, his hand on her shoulder, as she gleefully observes the white angel from her bedroom picture, ascending into the sky.

The final image of Laura's smiling face in misty half-tones (a recurrance of some of the images of women that occur in his earlier films), shows that for all his efforts to demystify the feminine, David Lynch remains confounded and his women have survived endless dissections, prevailing as the unknowable 'other'.

The Beast devours Beauty

The sacrifice of Laura by her father is a reworking of the scenario of Beauty and the Beast, as seen in *La Belle et la Bete* (Jean Cocteau, 1946). In Cocteau's film, the father has plucked a rose from the garden of the beast, and for that he must forfeit his life, or sacrifice his daughter. For the sake of the father, Belle sacrifices herself; she presents herself to the beast at his enchanted castle.

Leland Palmer, at a point prior to the murder of Teresa Banks, has transgressed in the garden of the Beast, and is consumed by a spirit that embodies evil. He carries the Beast within himself, and Laura sacrifices herself to it, for the sake of her father.

In *La Belle et la Bete*, Beauty not only confronts the beast but tames him, and transforms him into the prince. It is the story of a young girl's initiation, symbolising her release from her father so that she can integrate her own erotic 'animal' nature. The Prince and Beauty are united and ascend into the heavens together. (The film was criticised for its explicit overstated and excessively sentimental 'happy ending',[7] but doubtless won over Lynch who describes Cocteau as 'the heavyweight of the surrealists'.)[8] In *Twin Peaks: Fire Walk With Me*, the equally explicit and overstated 'happy ending' has Laura's angel ascending alone, and Laura herself, a ghostly presence in a ghostly place, also alone. Seen figuratively, she has been unable to heal the traumatic wound – the separation from her erotic side caused by the incestuous relationship with her father. As long as he remains 'the beast', she is unable to integrate the 'animal' side of her nature, which prevents her from having a reciprocal relationship with a man.[9]

At the outset of *La Belle et la Bete* the beast is a heartless monster demanding the life of any that

142

trespass in his garden. But just as the story concerns Beauty's awakening to her femininity through accepting the beast within the masculine, it also concerns the beast's change through his love for Beauty.

The 'beast' of *Fire Walk With Me* is forever a beast – there is no possibility of redemption or transformation. 'Bob' is an all-consuming evil spirit – through Leland he has claimed Teresa Banks, and now the perfect maiden, the embodiment of Persephone, Laura. Later he will consume Laura's cousin Madeleine, Leland Palmer himself, and, finally, his 'pure' counterpart, Cooper.

Unfortunately the story fails to resolve the dramatic problem of a submissive protagonist and attempts to compensate through sequences of depravity and revulsion. (Teresa Banks' autopsy, Laura at The Gun Bar, Leland's roadside dementia, etc.) The passive 'goalless' character arouses not sympathy, not empathy, but indignation. Discussing the commercial failure of his film *Patty Hearst* (1988), writer/director Paul Schrader said that, 'the definitive problem... is that it deals with a passive protagonist. Movies are about people who do things. The number one fantasy of the cinema is that we can do something – we are relatively impotent in our own lives so we go to the movies to watch people who are in control of their lives. *Patty Hearst* violates the cardinal rule of the cinema.'[10]

When Laura watches her white-dressed angel ascend into the heavens, she is just one cardboard character gleefully observing another; a character without an identity, without a story.

'And evil was the hour...'

Why did David Lynch make this film? His photographer Ron Garcia, 'unsure of Lynch's true motive', claims that 'the people who are really following David Lynch's ongoing story of Twin Peaks are still out there...'

'The plot of the film dovetails perfectly into the pilot. David was adamant about the details of the script and how they merged with the series,' says Garcia.[11]

'I happened to be in love with the world of Twin Peaks and the characters that exist there,' said Lynch at the press reception following the premiere screening at the 1992 Cannes Film Festival. His diffidence could be attributed to the hostile reception when he entered the press room – people jeered and booed; but Lynch's 'love of the world of Twin Peaks' was reiterated some four times during the press conference, yet remains unconvincing. Is the final episode of the television series the work of a man who 'loves the world of Twin Peaks'?[12]

Equally suprising is David Lynch's accolades for Sheryl Lee, an actress ostensibly hired to play a corpse, whom he describes as 'an unbelievable actress – there are things she's done in this movie that are truly incredible.'[13] Alas, acting was not one of them. Bearing the full burden of the film's ponderous script proved an insurmountable task for Sheryl Lee's two modes of projection. 'From A to B', as Dorothy Parker once quipped.

To a critic who felt 'great discomfort at the end of the film because of what I see as a sort of puritanical, religious, right-wing attitude' Lynch replied that he doesn't 'like to give interpretations...'.

Interpretations, however, are not an issue. As the same critic concluded, 'I feel that we are not allowed to ask you these questions because we won't get answers.'[14]

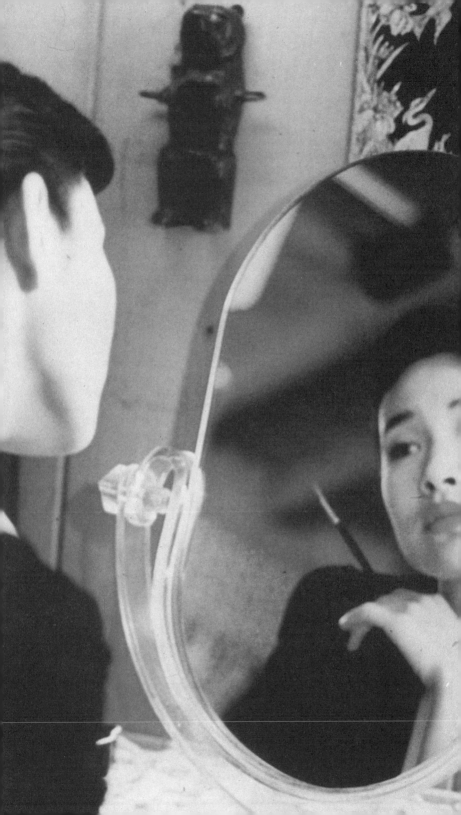

Twin Peaks (1989–1991)

> 'It is spring, moonless night in the small town, starless and bible-black.'

Dylan Thomas, *Under Milk Wood*

Synopsis: *A seventeen-year-old schoolgirl, Laura Palmer, is found murdered on the river bank of a small community in NW USA. FBI Special Agent, Dale Cooper, links the girl's death to previous killings elsewhere and his investigations uncover realms of narcotics, prostitution and perversity otherwise incongruous with the town's tranquil appearance. Through a series of revelations and visions Laura Palmer's murderer is revealed to be a deranged psychopath, 'Bob', an evil spirit who has consumed Laura's father, Leland. Leland later murders Laura's look-alike cousin, Madeleine, but when he dies 'Bob's' spirit lives on. Cooper enters an other-world dimension in order to confront this evil, only to be consumed by it himself.*

'Created by Mark Frost and David Lynch,' claims the series credit. *Twin Peaks* has been so conspicuously singled out as pertaining to the David Lynch oeuvre, its omission from this book would be tantamount to neglect. Mark Frost, with his background as a television scriptwriter, has provided a story line and characterisations which allow Lynch to exercise the full reign of his visual prowess. The paradox is that *Twin Peaks* is both the work of an *auteur* (a term customarily reserved for the cinema) and peak-hour commercial television drama. A television drama, however, with distinctive tonal variations.

   Of the thirty episodes, David Lynch has a director's credit on six, including the first and last episodes, and his credit as co-writer extends to the first three episodes, **Joan Chen** and the first episode of the second season. Lynch is a 'choirmaster' to a group of collaborators which make up some of the more engaging talents working within American film and television. Among the fourteen directors are Tim Hunter, who directed *River's Edge* (1986), a film which begins with a high-school girl being drowned in a river in a small American town (see *Blue Velvet*); Diane Keaton, whose directorial style in *Twin Peaks* was evident in her highly original feature film debut, *Heaven* (1989); Tina Rathborne, who directed Lynch and Isabella Rossellini in *Zelly and Me* (1987), Stephen Gyllendaal who directed *Paris Trout* (1991) with Dennis Hopper in the title role, and *Waterland* (1992), and Duwayne Dunham, Lynch's editor on *Blue Velvet* and *Wild at Heart*.

Mark Frost's writer's credit extends to ten episodes; the other regular contributors (among a total of nine writers) include Robert Engels (co-writer of *Twin Peaks: Fire Walk With Me*) and Harley Peyton. Under Lynch's direction and inspired by his predilection for the bizarre, they created a series which revitalised the ailing medium of the American television serial drama. Serials which had dominated audience ratings up until the late 1980s had folded: *Dallas*, *Falcon Crest* and *Dynasty* were all entrenched in the television drama style of the 1970s.

Whereas the feature film, *Twin Peaks: Fire Walk With Me*, seems like television made for the cinema, the *Twin Peaks* television series is cinema made for television. (In the UK and some other European countries, viewers were unhindered by the fade-outs to commercial breaks prevalent in US television drama, enhancing the cinematic tone of the series.) Although the interiors are recorded in the modest Los Angeles City Studios, *Twin Peaks* features a generous proportion of exterior location shooting (Snoqualmie, near Seattle, in Washington State), and is shot on 35mm film. Principal cinematographer, Ron Garcia, avoids the usual flat television lighting in favour of soft hues and suggestive chiaroscuro. Picture composition refrains from television's favoured 'talking heads' shots and three-camera set-ups. In *Twin Peaks* the homes have ceilings, as if to scorn the standard three loose wall studio set of television drama and situation comedy.

Angelo Badalamenti's haunting theme weaves through the narrative with the resonance of a feature film soundtrack. The song as *leitmotif*, which Lynch employs in his feature films, is equally effective in *Twin Peaks*, in contrast to the slapdash, vulgar plundering of hit parade successes in the formula Michael Mann style of television production: *Miami Vice, The FBI Story,* and others.

Twin Peaks, however, is not just superior television drama with the production values of film. It succeeds because it encompasses *all* television: soap opera, melodrama, murder mystery, situation comedy, high-school romance – *Twin Peaks* is the unabridged collection of television clichés. It's *Peyton Place, Gibbsville, Days of Our Lives, The Andy Griffith Show, The Blackboard Jungle, Columbo, The Prisoner,* and much more besides. '*Casablanca* became a cult movie because it is not one movie... it is "movies",' suggests Umberto Eco. *Twin Peaks* is 'cult television' for the same reason.[1] Eco maintains that using just a few of the formula 'from a repertoire that had stood the test of time... the result is simply kitsch.' *Casablanca* is the accolade of the Hollywood system because its authors have 'used wholesale' the 'repertoire of stock formulas.'[2]

Twin Peaks does not use the entire repertoire of television formula, no one programme could, and it is shamelessly kitsch. Television is ephemeral and the cinema endures. *Casablanca* resonates as soundly now as upon its release fifty years ago. If *Twin Peaks* does not simply disappear into television's depository of ephemera it may well be due to the programme having gone beyond television cliché to extract chunks of film history as well.

It is 'the murder mystery', with Holmes and Watson (Cooper and Truman) in pursuit of an archfiend, Moriarty (Windom Earle). There are elements of 'black comedy': Bobby and Shelley openly conducting their previously clandestine love-affair in front of the incapacitated and salivating Leo Johnson; Dick Chamberlayne and Andy Brennan's responsibility for a six-year-old boy, whom they are convinced is a murderer; Nadine's preoccupation with the silent curtain runner; Lucy Moran's doughnut fixation.

It is 'the romantic drama': there are doomed love affairs between James Hurley and Donna Hayward, between Ed Hurley and Norma Jennings, between Audrey Horne and her millionaire boyfriend, John Wheeler, between Harry Truman and Jocelyn Packard, between Dale Cooper and Annie Blackburn.

Twin Peaks is also *film noir,* screwball comedy, melodrama and Gothic romanticism. It is *It's a Wonderful Life, Frankenstein, Sunset Boulevard* and *Blue Velvet.* It is also 'surrealistic'; 'the imaginary tends to become real,'[3] transgressing the established modes of television narrative. Measured against US television's interminable output of mediocre television drama, *Twin Peaks* is decidedly unusual.

The bizarre

The first indication of the bizarre in *Twin Peaks* occurs a few minutes after the opening, when Pete Martell telephones Sheriff Truman to tell him he's found a body washed up on the river bank. The switchboard operator, Lucy, connects the call. In prolonged and agonising detail she describes to the sheriff which telephone not to use, by way of indicating which telephone, should, in fact, be used. Lucy is as eccentric a character as ever graced that most American of film genres, the screwball comedy. Soon afterwards her boyfriend, Deputy Andy Brennan, breaks down tearfully while photographing the body of the drowned Laura Palmer. He is another of *Twin Peaks*' odd characters. 'Is this going to happen every time?' Sheriff Truman admonishes the grief-stricken deputy.

The bizarre is convincing in *Twin Peaks*, especially in the first series of eight episodes, because it is a sparsely-used contrast to the normal. (In the second season, bizarreness is considerably less sparse.) Of the twenty-two plot-bearing characters presented in the first twenty-five minutes of Episode One, only Lucy and Andy, and the eye-patched, curtain-obsessed Nadine, are distinctly odd.

Howard Hawks, discussing his film *Bringing Up Baby* (1938), maintained: 'The picture had a great fault... there were no normal people in it. Everyone you met was a screwball...'[4] In *Twin Peaks* the odd is juxtaposed with the normal, the eccentric against the conventional.

Some of the initially normal characters later become odd (Leland Palmer, Major Briggs, Benjamin Horne), while other decidedly odd characters are introduced as the plot develops (Dr Jacoby, Laura's analyst, Margaret, the 'log lady', FBI forensic scientist, Albert Rosenfield, supervisor Gordon Cole, 'the man from another place', the giant – and as many others as the series progresses). But the majority of characters are identifiable from any number of American television dramas. Sheriff Truman could be straight from *The Andy Griffith Show*, Dr Hayward from *General Hospital*, the high-school students from *Blackboard Jungle*, and so on.

The 'tragic' characters of the series (James Hurley, Josie Packard, etc) are contrasted against 'malevolent' characters – Leo Johnson, Jean and Jacques Renault, Windom Earle, and others.

But the unifying character is FBI Special Agent, Dale Cooper, and the 'psychomachia' of the series concerns Cooper and 'Bob'; as purely white and purely black as any two opposing characters are likely to be.

Cooper is, paradoxically, the most straightforward character and the most complex. He represents the Lynch 'whole body', without blemish either physically or morally. As an outsider he has no dark secrets; indeed his function is to cast light on the 'darkness' of others.

That believable characters are matched against 'unbelievable' characters is an ironic subversion of what decades of television drama has established as 'believable'. Is Sheriff Truman more believable than Andy Brennan, or simply more recognisable?

The bizarre in *Twin Peaks* relates to situations as much as characterisations. Normal procedures are imbued with strangeness which is explained in tangibles. In the first episode Cooper and Truman visit the bank where Laura kept a deposit box. A deer's head lies across the table, its open glass eyes staring upwards. It fell down off the wall, explains the bank manager's assistant, and there was nowhere else to put it. When Cooper and Truman examine Laura's body at the morgue, the flickering light casts eerie shadows across the room. The hospital porter apologises for the faulty lighting.

Visual disturbances at Cooper's breakfasts at the Great Northern Hotel are provided by singing and boisterous Icelanders, uniformed majorettes and visiting Scotsmen. In its second series, *Twin Peaks*' 'oddness' becomes more pronounced, more outré. In the episode directed by Diane Keaton (II.15) Donna arranges to meet James at a roadside bar in a town outside Twin Peaks – the bar is lined with soldiers in what appear to be German uniforms of the Second World War. They sit, stand, drink and sing German songs in unison, in a pastiche of a musical parade number.

The bizarre in *Twin Peaks* extends to the 'soap within the soap', the programme entitled 'Invitation to Love', which several of the characters watch on television. In Episode Three Lucy recapitulates plot points of Twin Peaks' favourite soap opera, and excerpts are screened till the end of the first season. 'Invitation to Love' is the same sinister shadow to *Twin Peaks* as Mrs Beaumont's television set is to *Blue Velvet*'s Lumberton. Safe on the sofa of her suburban home, Mrs Beaumont sips coffee watching TV: a figure bearing a gun ascends a staircase. This televisual 'shadow' becomes a reality for her son Jeffrey at the end of the film, when he hides in a wardrobe, as Frank Booth ascends the staircase outside, gun in hand, seeking him out.

Episodes of 'Invitation to Love' begin with the facial close-ups and interminable dialogue of daytime soap opera, as played out by the programme's four principal characters: Jade, Chet, Montana and Jared. It becomes more macabre, more sinister as it develops, correlating to the escalating violence in *Twin Peaks*. In the penultimate episode of the first series (I.7), as the Johnson household's television screens Chet shooting Jade, Shelley shoots Leo, who flees wounded into the forest.

No-one watches television in *Dallas*. *Twin Peaks* embraces the tube as fearlessly as it embraces television's narrative forms.

'Seventy little stories'

Twin Peaks begins where *Blue Velvet* ends, with a robin on the branch of a tree. We see a waterfall, a timberyard, the forest and a river. An Asian woman paints her face before a mirror – her gaze is solemn, her countenance ethereal. A middle-aged man in a logging jacket picks up his fishing tackle and mutters to himself: 'Gone fishing.' He walks down to the river and at the edge of the flowing stream he notices some plastic wrapping. Closer examination reveals the body of a girl shrouded in the plastic.

The hunt for a killer becomes an excuse to visit small-town America with its idiosyncratic characters, and sub-surface perversities. The heightened absurdity of specific plot and character contrivances periodically reduce the validity of the 'place' to parody and pastiche. Consequently, the series is imbued with the dynamic of the unexpected: it is television in which the viewer can be abruptly thrust into the unknown (for instance in the dream sequences, and the 'lodge' sequences) in the midst of a television drama with enough of the appearance of normality to seem familiar.

The polarising of opposites prevails throughout the series, and the development of key characters provides examples of Lynchian 'conversions' (enantiodromia). Nearly thirty plot-bearing characters are presented in the first episode, most of whom undergo a conversion from one extreme to another. These transformations provide sub-plots which reflect the essence of the main narrative, and also echo a recurring theme in Lynch's films. As we go beneath the image of the pristine Laura Palmer, we uncover someone else; the person who is Laura Palmer's shadow – promiscuous, predatory, drug-addicted: defiled.

Leland Palmer is the grieving father, 'a highly respected citizen of the community', according to Sheriff Truman (II.4). Leland becomes deranged through grief, his hair turns white and he begins to 'dance out' his madness. He is transformed into a 'vengeful' murderer, and suffocates the injured Jacques Renault, the man suspected of Laura's murder, in his hospital bed. Finally, he is the 'psychopathic' murderer, as he kills his niece, Madeleine, by beating her to death, and throwing her in the river as he did Laura. The conversion is complete: the *persona* ('mask') of his personality is stripped away to reveal the face of 'Bob', the embodiment of evil.

'Bob's' identity is not revealed until the second series (II.6) yet those who describe his appearance many episodes earlier, are Leland himself, his mediumistic wife, Sara, and Laura's cousin, Madeleine. 'Bob' remains within the family, until Leland has destroyed himself in a fit of rage, locked in a prison cell, beating his head against the stone wall.

Sheriff Harry S. Truman, as stalwart a character as one could hope to encounter in the pantheon of American television drama, is, at the end of Episode One, revealed to be passionately involved with Jocelyn Packard, the beautiful Chinese widow of the sawmill owner, Andrew Packard. It is this entanglement with Jocelyn that leads to his undoing. He blindly ignores the evidence of Jocelyn's duplicity – her attempted murder of Cooper, and successful murders of underworld figures in Seattle, and her implication in her husband's attempted murder. Truman is finally a witness to another of Jocelyn's successful ploys as she shoots her former 'owner', Thomas Eckhardt, then, mesmerised by an unknown fear, dies before him (II.16). Truman, until now as upright and steadfast as the president from whom he takes his name, retreats into hiding, incommunicado and drinking copious quantities of alcohol. Only an attempted murder by one of Eckhardt's envoys, the seductress Amanda, jolts him back to reality (II.18).

Truman's ordeal – the initiatory journey through a hell shaped by desire – is Lynch's more favoured narrative structure. It's the ordeal of Henry Spencer in *Eraserhead*, of Jeffrey in *Blue Velvet*, it recurs in one form or another in other films, and elsewhere in *Twin Peaks*. The unsullied souls of Lucy Moran and Andy

Brennan, Ed and Nadine Hurley, Eileen and Will Hayward, even Donna and James, make their respective descents into passion's darkness.

Lucy and Andy, well-intentioned innocents, and as likely a pair of twin souls as any to be encountered in *Twin Peaks*, drift apart after communication failures concerning Lucy's pregnancy, and Andy's poor sperm count. Lucy's brief liaison with Richard Chamberlayne (!) leaves her uncertain as to who is the father of her expected child. There are dark moments for Andy and Lucy both, but finally she chooses Andy regardless (II.22) and the couple are reunited.

Ed and Nadine Hurley's relationship makes a similar cyclic return to its uneasy status quo, portrayed in Episode One. Ed's clandestine affair with Norma, the owner of the Double R Diner, comes out into the open following Nadine's concussion, where she regresses into a seventeen-year-old high-school girl (II.1). She embarks on a high-school romance with Donna's former boyfriend, Mike, whose 'conversion' is as drastic as Benjamin Horne's. From an unruly brawling delinquent (I.1), under the powerful ministrations of Nadine, he transforms into a well-dressed, quietly-spoken young man, with brylcreemed hair and open-eyed awe over Nadine's sexual prowess (II.20). After a second blow on the head, however, Nadine reverts to her 'true self', and reclaims her hold on Ed (II.22). Ed and Norma's marriage plans are abandoned.

Father–daughter relationships constitute a particular complication in *Twin Peaks*, not least the incestuous relationship between Laura Palmer and her father. Audrey Horne, whose sexual precocity sabotages her father's business deal (I.1), decides to investigate Laura's death herself, and secures a job at One Eyed Jack's, one of father's more clandestine business ventures, by tying a cocktail cherry stalk into a pretzel with her tongue. Her first client turns out to be none other than the establishment's 'patron', a prospective encounter which teasingly ends the series' first season.

As the second series develops the antagonism between Audrey and her father is displaced by clan loyalty, and following Benjamin's 'conversion' ('I just want to be good': II.16), they collaborate to do humanitarian 'good deeds': saving the pine weasel and saving Ghostwood from redevelopment. Meanwhile, Audrey embarks on a brief romance with a young millionaire colleague of her father's; John Justice Wheeler, who, at her request, plunders her of her virginity in his private jet, just minutes before he takes off for South America (II.20).

Her now unhindered alliance to her father results in her chaining herself to the vault doors of the local bank (in protest against the bank's involvement with the Ghostwood project: II.22), on the same day Andrew Packard, together with Pete Martell, comes to check the contents of a bank box left by arch-rival, Thomas Eckhardt. The bomb that kills all three is one of a number of barbed 'practical jokes' which make up the final episode.

Another is the departure of Donna from the Hayward household, when she discovers her biological father is none other than Benjamin Horne (thus making her Audrey's half-sister). Benjamin's new found urge 'to be honest' leads him to disclose this jumbo-sized skeleton in the Hayward closet, so that Dr Will, too, undergoes the 'enantiodromia', from peaceful loving 'good father', to enraged and violent 'non-father'. 'We're so happy to have a daughter like you,' Dr Hayward tells Donna in the closing minutes of the first episode. In the final episode Donna stands weeping on the doorstep, about to leave for destinations undisclosed.

The victim of the most savage 'practical joke' – and most drastic 'conversion' – is Leo Johnson. Leo Johnson is introduced by his vehicle (I.1) – a murderous truck lifted from the storyboard of Steven Spielberg's film *Duel* (1971). When Bobby Briggs and Leo's wife Shelley drive to Shelley's place to pursue their amorous diversions, the sight of Leo's truck outside the house is enough to cool their ardour promptly, Bobby's hand quickly shifts the gear stick into reverse.

Leo passes his time by terrorising Shelley, and running drug deals across the border. He is involved with a catalogue of illegal activities – and for all his jealous rages against Shelley, his own sexual entanglements are many. As we will later discover, Laura Palmer's last night was spent with Leo.

Leo's shotgun wounds, on the eve of the sawmill burning down (fired by Norma's husband, Hank: I.8) leave him mentally and physically handicapped – a drooling vegetable and a mute witness to Shelley and Bobby's ongoing affair (II.1). His sudden recovery scarcely enables him to wreak his vengeance on the defenceless Shelley (II.13), and he flees wounded into the night, only to become a victim again himself in the malevolent hands of a psychotic even more demented than himself, Windom Earle (II.14). He becomes the tortured and demeaned house slave he previously made of Shelley, at the sadistic whim of Windom Earle. The fate of Leo Johnson (ultimately undisclosed) and the completed conversion from persecutor to victim, sees him the hapless dupe to Windom Earle's elaborately fiendish practical joke – he attaches a wire to Leo's teeth which is connected to an explosive device, set to ensure Leo's rapid demise with so much as an ill-timed twitch.

Lynch fulfils the obligations of narrative drama's formal closure with parodic brutality.

'The beautiful girl across the hall'

... was the credit for the seductress in Henry Spencer's tenement block, who lured Henry to his own bed and drowned him. This was one of Henry's many bouts of paranoia in the prolonged nightmare of *Eraserhead*, and the 'beautiful woman' is one of the many deadly females that inhabit the Lynch film.

The first image of the series shows Jocelyn Packard before a mirror painting her lips. The same evocative image recurs in her final episode (II.16), as she prepares for her meeting with Thomas Eckhardt at a room of the Great Northern Hotel.

The face of the seductress reflected in a mirror is a favoured icon of the *film noir femme fatale*, suggesting both duplicity and narcissism. Jocelyn Packard is a woman 'in two minds' – quite literally in doubt about her identity. 'You don't know me,' she tells Harry (II.6). 'I was what you wanted me to be.' Harry was one victim among many, who included Thomas Eckhardt, 'the man who saved her from the slums of Hong Kong'. In *A Study in Scarlet* (Edwin Marin, 1933) Sherlock Holmes suspects the beautiful Chinese widow of the supposedly murdered Captain Pyke to be harbouring 'dark secrets'. She has the sad doe-eyed face of Joan Chen's 'Josie'. Holmes reveals that Captain Pyke's 'murder' was a hoax, just as the suspicious demise of Josie's husband, Andrew Packard, was a hoax. Andrew returns and Jocelyn has met her lethal match. As Cooper watches her in her death throes, he observes the manic face of 'Bob' behind her – the spirit from the 'evil place in the woods' claims one more victim.

Jocelyn's ruin was masterminded by a more subtle, more devious *femme fatale*, Andrew's sister, Catherine. From the first episode, as Catherine observes Truman and Josie embrace, and makes a mysterious telephone call (to the supposedly deceased Andrew, it transpires), it is apparent she is conspiring in sinister deeds. Her motive is to take over the sawmill for the Ghostwood

Project, a narrative element second only in significance to the murder of Laura Palmer in the full sweep of the *Twin Peaks* saga.

Catherine Martell plots an insurance fraud (I.7), echoing the Barbara Stanwyck role of Phyllis Dethfelsen in *Double Indemnity* (Billy Wilder, 1944). Like Mrs Dethfelsen, Catherine conspires to deceive her husband, Pete, with the aid of an insurance salesman, Walter Neff (Fred MacMurray's role in *Double Idemnity*) in an elaborate scheme of fraud and duplicity. In this instance, however, Catherine fakes her death in the sawmill fire (I.8), only to re-emerge in the guise of a Japanese businessman and swindle the project's initiator, her former lover, Benjamin Horne (II.8).

Even Julee Cruise as the road-house singer owes much to an Ida Lupino role as the pert blonde singer in the film *Road House* (Jean Negulesco, 1948). In the film, Ida Lupino sings 'Again' and a series of wistful ballads in a road house in the north-west USA, 'fifteen miles from the Canadian border', complete with stuffed deer heads and a psychopathic Richard Widmark.

Confused and love-torn, James Hurley rides out of Twin Peaks on his Harley Davison to encounter the most beguiling *femme fatale* of the series. He meets Evelyn Marsh at a highway bar in another town. She persuades him to fix her husband's car; the husband is 'out of town'. She insists he stay, a guest in a large gothic residence, well hidden from the main road. 'There's a room on top of the garage,' she tells him, as James Hurley assumes the Joe Gillis (William Holden) role to Evelyn Marsh's Norma Desmond (Gloria Swanson). This line, from the pages of the *Sunset Boulevard* screenplay (Billy Wilder, 1950), has its origins in the Jean Cocteau film, *Orphée* (1949). Orpheus is the underlying myth to the *Twin Peaks* narrative.

In *Sunset Boulevard*, Gloria Swanson plays the alluring spider woman who ensnares Joe Gillis in her web of subterfuge, and ultimately devours him. In *Orphée*, Herbeteuse, the servant of death, lives in 'a room on top of the garage'. He works as a chauffeur. Death is a beautiful seductress dressed in black. 'How do you expect Death to look?' she asks Orphée. Herbeteuse is an extant suicide with a transitory respite upon the earthly plane to act as 'courier' for his black-dressed mistress, the ultimate *femme fatale*. She ensnares Orphée just as Gillis is the poor fool rushing towards his own death at the hand of *femme fatale*, Norma Desmond.

James Hurley, the '*noir* male' so preoccupied with his

past that there is little question of a future, having left the protective limitations of Twin Peaks, unwittingly offers himself to one more Lynchian *femme fatale*. Having drifted pitifully from one love-torn situation to another, he tells Evelyn Marsh (II.13): 'I loved a girl who died. Her name was Laura. I thought I knew her but I guess I didn't.'

Under Ghostwood

Dylan Thomas's *Under Milk Wood* is a lyrical portrayal of the inhabitants of a Welsh fishing village, Llaregyb. It was made into a film, directed by Andrew Sinclair in 1973, who pieced together 'seventy little stories...into one visual whole,' featuring the memorable characters of the blind Captain Cat (Peter O'Toole), Rosie Probert (Elizabeth Taylor) and the 'visitor', Richard Burton, whose voice narrates Dylan Thomas's verse.

According to Sinclair the main problem in bringing *Under Milk Wood* to the screen was to 'give a unity to the film, a visual reason for all the marvellous speeches of the Voices...'[5]

Mark Frost, David Lynch's co-author on *Twin Peaks*, describes a similar undertaking in the formative stages of the television series. It was 'not until a body washed up on the shore that we had a starting point for the story... The two detectives provide an access into everyone's lives – who all have secrets.'[6]

Sinclair in *Under Milk Wood* created two characters (inspired by Thomas's voices) who go back to Llaregyb to visit Norma Jane Jenkins, a girl whom both men had met during the war. At the end of the film Norma Jane walks away into the graveyard and we realise that she has been dead many years, and the two men who come to visit her are 'two visible spirits from the sea and the dark wood who have come back to relive their life in the timeless town and resurrect their lost love.'[7]

This 'Gothic' element pervades Twin Peaks – 'a timeless town', embracing the decades between 1950 and 1990. Just as the two 'spirits' enter into the lives of the townsfolk of Llaregyb as they search for a 'lost love', Cooper and Truman search for the community's 'lost love' – the real person behind the portrait of Laura Palmer.

Milk Wood is the mysterious place whence spirits emerge and into which they disappear; Ghostwood, outside Twin Peaks, is a mysterious part of the forest where spirits and people alike, disappear and reappear, from Major Briggs to the husband of the 'log lady', Margaret, twenty years earlier.

The forest is the foundation of the Twin Peaks community; its timber is the town's lifeblood, yet as the story opens, the sawmill is running at a loss and Benjamin Horne and Catherine Martell attempt to hasten its bankruptcy in order to implement their redevelopment scheme. The scheme would mean the end of Ghostwood as a forest. Following Benjamin's 'conversion' (II.16) he determines to 'save' Ghostwood, at the same time protecting the local pine weasel.

More sinister powers are at work, regardless of Benjamin's and Catherine's schemes; Ghostwood is the 'unknown' and the 'unknowable' – the realm beyond the enclaves of civilisation. Ghostwood is 'nature' to Twin Peaks' 'culture'. Shots linking scenes consist of trees blowing in the wind – the forest; or traffic lights swaying over an empty road – the town.

Ghostwood is linked to an arcane past – Hawk, the Native American deputy, describes a 'white lodge' and a 'black lodge' housed within the woods; 'the dweller on the threshold where you face your shadow', he says (II.11). Following Major Brigg's disappearance (II.10), Cooper concludes 'there's a powerful force that exists in those woods,' (II.11).

The outdoors, especially by night, is a fearful place for Lynch and he admits there were prolonged periods in his childhood when he dared not venture outdoors.[8] In *The Grandmother* the boy loses his companion in the film's only exterior scenes; once John Merrick in *The Elephant Man* leaves the security of his hospital chambers, the fury of the fates are unleashed upon him; in *Wild at Heart,* beyond the road, in the middle of nowhere and in the middle of the night, young people career off the highway and bleed to death. A casual stroll through a field uncovers a severed ear (*Blue Velvet*), and body parts dangle mid-air from the unseen boundary of the 'black lodge' in the middle of Ghostwood (*Twin Peaks* II.20), as though 'a little opening could exist and we could go somewhere else.'

David Lynch directs

The six episodes directed by David Lynch are the most violent and the most shamelessly sentimental. The Lynch episodes take the limitations of television to the boundaries of the cinema's possibilities. In a *Variety* interview, Mark Frost says that in spite of cautioning the director about the barriers and frustrations to be encountered, 'David was enthusiastic about the challenge of TV, about writing micro-films within commercial restraints.'

Lynch claims that the differences between working for television and film were minimal. 'We were shooting the whole series on film, editing it on film and mixing it just like on a film, so the differences were not so great.'[9]

According to Lynch, he and Mark Frost wrote the script to the pilot episode in eight or nine days, and after twenty-one days of filming, 'it was hard to realise that I had successfully directed a film ninety-three minutes long in such a short time....'[10]

'Laura'

Episode One, First Season. Written by Mark Frost and David Lynch. Directed by David Lynch. 1989. 90 minutes
Pete Martell drinks his coffee, picks up his fishing tackle, and sets off for the river.

Jocelyn Packard stares vacantly at her own reflection – regarding her own face yet looking faraway, somewhere else. She is waylaid by her own internal reflections, arrested in time, lost in an ethereal 'other' world, with the red brush that colours her lips hanging limply from her hand. The image is unexplained – it makes no contribution to plot, but it does establish a narrative style to the series which alternates between dramatic and epic forms from start to finish.

The next close-up, another face of an attractive young woman 'lost' in another world, is Laura Palmer, her features shrouded in an opaque plastic frame. Even in death she is a portrait, but where the gold frame of her high-school photograph accentuated her blonde hair, the pale blue of the plastic wrapping matches the hue of her lips.

News reaches Sheriff Truman that 'the Pulaski girl has been found', and the camera gazes upward towards the iron girders of a railway bridge. A girl in a tattered slip, severed ropes around her bare wrists and ankles, staggers across the line, staring blankly before her. An old man fixing his car on the other side of the bridge, looks up and sees her. The continuity makes little sense (this is her first appearance, yet Truman's just been told she's been found), but the image is arresting – the girl's tiny frame is dwarfed by the imposing steel girders. Her staring eyes, her half naked body, and the severed cords, owe more to 1950s' B-films (*Them!* for example) than television drama.

The gyrating fan above the staircase of the Palmer residence, accompanied by the ominous low hum of its rotation, is the sound and image of a recurring motif, in the series, and in the feature film, casting uneasy premonitions of doom over the household.

Laura's death is disclosed to her schoolfriends during the day's first class. Donna, Laura's best friend, watches with mounting anxiety as a policeman speaks in a hushed voice with the teacher, cutting to exchanged looks between classmates, Laura's empty chair, and the teacher's nervous glances. Donna's realisation is matched to a shot of a girl outside the classroom window, running through the courtyard screaming. The scene's thirty-three separate shots, with a minimum of dialogue and a maximum of point/counterpoint cutting, resemble more a sequence of suspense cinema montage than the two-shot close-up of prime-time television drama.

1. Close-up Audrey's red shoes – tilt up to her face. The teacher's voice-over reads out the roll call.
2. Mid-Shot Teacher at the desk, a young attractive woman calling out the students' names. 'Donna Hayward'
3. CU Donna; a raise of the hand and a compliant smile
4. CU Audrey; nonchalant, impudent: 'in inverted commas' hand gesture
5. CU James Hurley: 'Yoh!'
6. MS teacher – she smiles benignly
7. MS A policeman at the door; looking for Bobby Briggs
8. MS Teacher
9. MS Policeman
10. CU Donna – looks up, something's up
11. MS Teacher
12. CU Donna
13. MS Police 'Can I talk with you...'
14. MS Teacher – camera follows as she joins policeman in doorway.
    Conversation inaudible; 2-shot beneath American flag and picture of Abraham Lincoln
15. CU Donna – looks worried OFF: scream. Donna turns

16. Point-of-view through window – a girl runs across the courtyard, screaming
17. CU Donna – looks to policeman
18. MS 2-shot; policeman and teacher whisper; a second policeman arrives
19. CU James Hurley – he looks up
20. MS 2-shot teacher, policeman
21. CU Teacher – she 'smiles' nervously
22. CU Donna – she looks across
23. POV An empty chair
24. CU Donna – she looks across the room
25. POV Long shot James Hurley – returns gaze
26. CU Donna; bites her lip and holds her shoulders
27. CU James Hurley
28. CU Donna – she looks down and whispers: 'Laura!' She begins to cry.
29. CU James – looking at Donna
30. MS Teacher, nervous; 'There'll be an announcement...'
31. CU James
32. CU Donna; crying uncontrollably
33. CU Audrey nonchalant

The scene begins and ends with Audrey Horne's overt display of nonchalance, resentful, it is later disclosed, of the relationship between Laura Palmer and her father. The sequence continues through to Bobby's interrogation by Truman, the principal's announcement of Laura's death, when Badalamenti's theme fades in over the principal dismissing classes, concluding with a close-up of Laura's photograph in the high-school prize cabinet.

Juxtaposed against this persuasive and emotional sequence, FBI agent Cooper is introduced in a single long take as he drives into Washington State talking non-stop to 'Diane', expounding in detail the scenery, his tasks, and the pie and coffee at a roadhouse diner. 'Diane' is further evidence of Cooper's singular and delicate mental state. His obsessive need to record his daily activities becomes an attempt to maintain control and create an artificial order in the face of chaos. 'Diane' herself remains one of the series' open-ended questions. Is she Cooper's assistant? Does she listen to the tapes? Or is 'Diane' the name of the tape recorder itself? Cooper's tapes also suggest a bond with Laura, who keeps a secret diary, from the outset.

At the Twin Peaks hospital he introduces himself to Sheriff Truman with a taunting cliché concerning FBI authority, representative of the genre. In contrast to the accustomed well-worn scenario, Truman welcomes Cooper's presence, and Cooper waxes lyrical over the Douglas spruce. At the sheriff's office, he and Sheriff Truman conduct their enquiries in accord with police drama conventions. Cooper examines a video-tape recording of Laura and Donna, her diary, and a plastic bag therein bearing traces of cocaine. The scene's ending, however, quickly dispels the illusion of television drama conventionality. Says Cooper: 'Diane, I'm holding in my hand a small box of chocolate bunnies.' Truman's deputy, Andy, at the railway site of the murder, weeps into the telephone, 'Tell Harry I didn't cry.'

The town-hall meeting, a narrative convention to introduce complementary and opposing elements of the community, where Truman describes to Cooper the various personalities, concludes with:

> COOPER: Who's the lady with the log?
> TRUMAN: We call her 'the log lady'.

At night, when the town's restless youth gather at the local roadhouse, the unlikely evening's entertainment is a doll-faced Julee Cruise, singing a Lynch/Badalamenti ballad spotlighted against a billowing red velvet curtain. Cooper and Truman wait outside while inside Julee Cruise sings 'Then I saw your smile...' as Ed (interrupting a clandestine rendezvous with Norma Jennings) attempts to break up a brawl initiated by Bobby and Mike.

Donna meets James Hurley in the woods. 'Bobby had killed this guy...' says James, and provides detailed continuity from the film based on Laura Palmer's last seven days, released some three years after the Twin Peaks pilot. 'It all makes some kind of terrible sense that she died,' concludes James.

A desperate love scene follows, as amidst their anxiety they 'find' each other. Later, a more discreet scene of passion between Sheriff Truman and Jocelyn Packard is observed by Catherine, as we realise that James and Donna had also been observed. The episode ends with the clairvoyant vision of Laura's mother, Sara. A gloved hand picks up a half-heart locket from a mound of earth James and Donna buried in the woods. The locket belonged to Laura. Her scream echoes over the end credits.

The first episode established a form for the series, whereby television drama conventions alternate with parody. As we attempt to orientate ourselves in the 'whodunit' aspects of a television murder mystery, we are set adrift amid irrationalities and television genre burlesque. By the final episode even the Norwegians' involvement in the Ghostwood redevelopment project is imbued with a logic peculiar to the narrative style of *Twin Peaks*.

'The man from another place'

Episode Three, First Season. Written by Mark Frost and David Lynch. Directed by David Lynch. 1990. 45 minutes
The credit sequence portrays the four members of the Horne family dining in opulent splendour before an open fire in cold silence. Benjamin's brother Jerry arrives from France with baguettes and brie fromage. Audrey and wife Sylvia are abandoned in the dining hall as the two brothers set off downstream in pursuit of further sensual indulgence – a new girl at Benjamin's luxury bordello.

Benjamin's excesses are contrasted with the middle-class sobriety of the Hayward family – James and Donna partake of after-dinner coffee as Donna's parents discreetly retire. A ticking clock and a carpeted staircase are icons of domestic insularity. At midnight Donna and James whisper clandestine love as if in earshot of the dead Laura.

Shelley Johnson watches television: 'Each day brings a new beginning and every hour holds the promise of... an invitation to love,' claims the programme announcer. 'Yeh, right,' says Shelley, and a final episode of 'Invitation to Love' (I.7) mirrors Shelley coming full circle in her domestic situation. As she shoots Leo, the programme shows a close-up of a handgun despatching one of the soap opera's leading characters. Shelley's life and the 'Invitation to Love' television serial both begin as soap opera drama and end as *film noir*.

Leo Johnson is one of many suspects in the investigation of Laura's murder who had been introduced in the first two episodes. The television serial convention requires a recapitulation of plot and characters in order to refamiliarise viewers, usually an interior dialogue scene – the breakfast table at Southfork, the law-firm board room in *LA Law*. Cooper's Tibetan deduction technique is a further example of Lynch's transgressive approach to television drama – an exterior sequence involving a blackboard, a map of

164

Tibet, a glass bottle and a bucket full of stones. Cooper provides the assembled cast with a background lecture on the political oppression of Tibet and claims that 'following a dream three years ago' he had 'subconsciously gained knowledge of a deductive technique involving mind body co-ordination operating hand in hand with the deepest level of intuition'.

He lists the names of the suspects on the blackboard and casts stones at the glass bottle as each name is called out. A broken bottle will single out a key figure in the mystery, perhaps even the culprit.

> TRUMAN: Coop. The idea for all of this really came from a dream?
> COOPER: Yes. It did.

Truman slaps him on the shoulder, smiles and nods, in a gesture of indulgence primarily for the benefit of the viewer, while tentatively indicating Cooper's fragile grip on reality.

The Lynch episodes ruthlessly exploit *Twin Peaks'* intertextuality – Julee Cruise singing a Lynch ballad in the pilot episode, Audrey dancing to the Angelo Badalamenti theme on the juke-box at the Double R Diner. 'Isn't this music just too dreamy?' she asks Donna. Yet the purpose of their encounter is to underline Audrey's estrangement from her father and explain her hostility towards Laura. 'Did Laura know my father?' asks Audrey, before succumbing to the music in slow sensual movements emphasising the sexual jealousy on which her enquiry is based.

Likewise Leland Palmer's preoccupation with dance and music serves both as a sexual metaphor and unsettling element of transgressing the television mode: Leland, grieving, plays big band-music ' Pennsylvania Six Five Thousand' and dances clutching a portrait of Laura. When Sara enters, he grabs her and insists, 'We have to dance for Laura.'

Leland's dancing creates uneasy scenes of Dionysian excess combined with a macabre humour, which later culminates in the murder of Madeleine (II.7). In this sequence he breaks the portrait glass, cuts his hand and smears blood on her image which he then presses to his face. Leland's 'dance of grief' which inspired an entire dance floor at the Great Northern Hotel in the previous episode, leaves the viewer intrigued and disorientated. Leland's wound portrays him as an example of the Lynch 'open body' indicating his involvement in Laura's death.

Nowhere is Lynch's directorial presence more pronounced than in the dream sequences. In Cooper's dream one-armed 'Mike' describes his involvement with a man 'touched by the devil himself', 'Bob'.

> 'In the darkness of future past
> The magician longs to see
> One chance ours between two worlds
> Fire walk with me.'

Bob appears in a ring of twelve burning candles; 'I promise I will kill again,' he declares.

Cooper finds himself in the red chamber – shadows fleet by on the velvet curtain of a set inspired by the paintings of Edward Hopper. Cooper meets 'the man from another place'. 'Twenty-five years later' proclaims the subtitle in the European pilot version, and a grey-haired Cooper sits in an armchair, surrounded by drapes of red velvet. 'Where we're from the birds sing a pretty song and there's always music in the air,' the dwarf tells Cooper, in the backwards language of the dream world in which Cooper is a passive observer. 'We had someone reading the lines offstage frontwards and I would translate them backwards and we would film that backwards. Then, when we showed it forwards, two positives make a negative.'[11] Flickering strobe lights inspire 'the man' into movement. 'Let's rock,' says the dwarf, and he dances to the chords of an up-tempo Badalamenti instrumental piece. Laura leans over to Cooper and whispers something we cannot hear in his ear: the name of her murderer. Cooper awakens in his room at the Great Northern Hotel, and telephones to Sheriff Truman. 'Harry, I know who killed Laura Palmer,' he says. By the next episode he has forgotten. But the Laura Palmer mystery pales against the more intriguing mystery of Twin Peaks – where do all these amazing stories come from? A dwarf? A giant? Norwegians and Icelanders? A pattern begins to emerge.

The end credits appear over the dancing dwarf, a sequence reminiscent of a scene featuring a singular deformed dwarf-like woman dancing on a stage before a velvet curtain filmed nearly twenty years earlier, in *Eraserhead*.

'Bob'

Episode One, Second Season. Story by Mark Frost and David Lynch. Teleplay by Mark Frost. Directed by David Lynch. 1990. 90 minutes
'Damned good coffee,' exclaims Cooper in his

introductory monologue to Episode One. The psychopathic 'Bob' is not a coffee-drinker. That the coffee is literally 'damned' becomes more apparent as the series progresses. The first Lynch episode begins with Pete Martell finishing his coffee before going fishing; later he finds a fish in the percolator (I.2). Lynch's next episode (I.3) begins with the Horne family's dinner being interrupted by Jerry's arrival with his 'discovery' of baguettes and Brie, and the first episode of the second season begins with Cooper taking delivery of a glass of warm milk, provided by an antiquated waiter in the Great Northern Hotel. The remaining three Lynch episodes begin with Cooper's morning ritual of coffee-drinking.

The first season concluded with Cooper being shot in the chest by an unknown assassin. The opening of the feature-film-length first episode of the second season begins with Cooper, wounded in the chest, and incapacitated upon the floor. While the ancient room-service waiter agonises over the delivery of Cooper's glass of warm milk, the giant appears to Cooper and 'tells him three things', including that 'the owls are not what they seem.' Also something is forgotten – a note to Cooper it transpires, concealed beneath Cooper's bed.

The giant takes Cooper's ring telling him he will return it when Cooper discloses the 'three things'. Rather than fragments of a 'sick and twisted dream' (as Ben's brother Jerry suggests), this is the stuff of fairy tales – the exchange of rings from the limbo realm of the red chamber into material reality confirms the tie between Laura and Cooper – two innocents pulled into an underworld by an incomprehensible evil.

Meanwhile Laura's incestuous fate awaits Audrey, who, in the guise of a hooker, is about to become a free sample to her father's unscrupulous desires. Concealed behind the mask of a cat, and the name of 'Prudence', her subterfuge is about to be uncovered by her father when he is called away on an errand. 'I like you,' says Ben, as he leaves. 'You know how to interest a man.'

Audrey's tale about helping Cooper find Laura's murderer is further subterfuge concealing her jealousy over her father's interest in Laura. Audrey's suspicions have estranged them – she is resolved to become her father's mistress, without 'the bite of the serpent' that poisoned Laura.

Meanwhile Madeleine is unwittingly attendant prey to the serpent lurking within the Palmer household. 'I had a strange dream', she tells her Aunt Sara, but never gets a chance to describe it. Leland appears, his hair turned white, chanting like a man possessed. 'Mares eat oats and does eat oats...' he sings, while Madeleine sees the face of Bob emerge in the carpet upon which she will be slain six episodes hence.

Leland dances into the office of Ben and Jerry – the Dionysian trance continues – they all dance together. 'I'm back,' says Leland. 'Back and ready.'

The second season suggests a tendency towards extremes of eccentricity which were moderate in the first. Self-parodic elements are advanced – the cry of an anonymous guest, 'Goddamn that pie is good,' introduces us to the Double R Diner. Madeleine gives Donna Laura's sunglasses and a note suggesting she investigate Laura's Meals on Wheels round.

Her investigations will ignite the desire of the wayward Harold Smith. Adolescent sexuality is the disruptive force which daunts the Twin Peaks' community. James Hurley tells Truman Laura's words as she continued her spiral descent shortly before her death: 'Would you like to play with fire, little boy? Would you like to play with fire?'

The representation of unbridled sexual energy as fire is a motif Lynch used to effect in *Blue Velvet* and *Wild at Heart*. In *Twin Peaks*, 'fire walk with me' is the metaphor of uncontained sexuality, the most forceful of threats among the myriad insecurities in the Lynchian world.

Cooper questions Jacoby in hospital and the doctor concludes 'maybe [Laura] allowed herself to be killed', and the image of an open-eyed Jacoby dissolves to that of a closed-eyed Laura Palmer.

Laura's parents, dinner guests of the Haywards, listen to Donna's sister Harriet read a poem about Laura, and younger sister Gersten plays Mendelssohn's Rondo Capriccioso opus 14. 'God, I feel like singing,' says Leland. After two verses of 'Get Happy' he faints.

Cooper retires at the Great Northern Hotel, Audrey is trapped at One-Eyed Jack's and sends a prayer. The giant appears to him and provides a clue as to the identity of the third man present on the night that Laura was killed. At the hospital Ronette Pulaski awakens from a nightmare featuring Bob, who bays like a wolf, with blood dripping from his mouth over Laura's dead body, and a series of images now familiar from the feature film.

Bob is the wild primitive force – an antithesis of Cooper. Long-haired, unshaven, slovenly dressed, mad with uncontrolled and irrational sexual appetite. Cooper is the clean shaven, immaculately groomed and obsessively controlled celibate. The dichotomy between the two characters recalls Orpheus and Dionysus, Baldur and Loki, Jeffrey Beaumont and Frank Booth; they are personifications of the 'perfect' and 'imperfect' body.

'Donna'

Episode Two, Second Season. Written by Harley Peyton. Directed by David Lynch. 1990. 45 minutes

The credit sequence coffee ritual shows Cooper and Albert Rosenfield having breakfast at the Great Northern Hotel with a barber shop quartet humming in the background. Cooper relates the mystic prophecies of an ancient Tibetan king. Albert tells Cooper that ex-colleague Windom Earle has escaped from the lunatic asylum. Earle will be the serpent that poisons Cooper's Eurydice (Annie Blackburn) and will abduct her to the underworld.

Donna takes over Laura's Meals on Wheels round and meets Mrs Tremond and her precocious grandson – a duo familiar from *Twin Peaks: Fire Walk With Me* (under the name of Chalfont), and from *The Grandmother*. The boy is played by Lynch's son Austin and the family resemblance is conspicuous. He is dressed in a dark suit and black bow tie as he sits in an armchair conjuring with the food Donna has brought. 'My grandson is studying magic,' says Mrs Tremond. She tells Donna that Laura was a close friend of 'Mr Smith next door', and Donna leaves a note on his door as she leaves.

Margaret the log lady tells Major Briggs to 'deliver the message', and Benjamin Horne informs Cooper that Audrey is missing. Leland recognises Bob from a sketch and decides to tell the sheriff. Benjamin's brother, Jerry asks: 'Is this for real, Ben? Or some strange and twisted dream?' Major Briggs' message to Cooper tends to suggest the latter.

Briggs' classified work involves monitoring deep space, producing computer printouts of radio waves. Early Friday, at the time Cooper was shot, the printout, amongst reams of gibberish, revealed a message: 'The owls are not what they seem,' followed by Cooper's name.

In the Palmer living room James, Madeleine and Donna deliberate teenage angst through a microphone and electric guitar – James' falsetto voice sings 'Just you and I' while alternating glances between Laura look-alike Madeleine, and his new found love, Donna. The two girls sing the backing vocals.

The song becomes a coda for the pain of youthful

love through several episodes. As he sings Donna looks at him, then at Madeleine, and senses James' passion rekindling before the girl who resembles Laura. The scene employs the same shot/countershot editing as the first episode's sequence in the classroom, when Donna realised that Laura was dead. Despite continuity problems with Donna's red lipstick (lipstick in close-up, no lipstick in medium and long shots), the scene is another of Lynch's sentimental excesses. Donna breaks down tearfully but cannot divulge her jealous misgivings.

Donna receives a telephone call from Harold Smith and Maddie sees 'Bob' crawl over the sofa towards her like a predatory beast, a forewarning of her grisly fate in Lynch's next episode. At the same time Ronette Pulaski is once more attacked in a nightmare montage of shots featuring Bob which recur in the final minutes of the feature-film version.

The giant tells Cooper 'the owls are not what they seem,' and Bob's face transforms to that of an owl. Sara Palmer descends the stairs, the gyrating fan hovering above her head, and Bob laughs madly.

Bob's 'presence' in the Palmer household is fatal to both Laura and Madeleine. Father-daughter relationships provide the foundation of the story-lines in the series: Laura sacrifices herself to the 'demon' within her father; Audrey, having narrowly avoided sexual relations with her father, becomes his platonic 'mistress' instead (also resulting in her death), leaving only Donna apparently protected by the sanctity of 'normal' family relations. Alas, Donna too falls victim to Lynch's perverse renditions of father-daughter relationships which began in the nightmare world of *Eraserhead*, and culminates with Donna being shattered by the discovery that the man she thought was her father is not.

Laura, Audrey and Donna each identify with their fathers (mother roles in *Twin Peaks* are low-key to say the least, with tragic consequences). Poor Madeleine seeks to identify with her look-alike cousin, with equally tragic results.

'Madeleine'

Episode Seven, Second Season. Written by Mark Frost. Directed by David Lynch. 1990. 45 minutes

Hawk, Gordon Cole, Cooper, Mike the one-armed man, Andy and Sheriff Truman, stand in line at the Sheriff's office reception, coffee mugs in hand. Hawk is assigned to visit Harold Smith. 'As soon as I finish my coffee,' he says. Cooper regards Hawk with sympathy, and grips his own coffee mug – his final, tenuous grasp on reality. David Lynch, as the hard-of-hearing Gordon Cole, makes his farewells and leaves for Oregon, going out through the door on the cue of the director's credit coming up on screen.

Mike, who under drugs claimed he could recognise 'Bob' (he was revealed as Leland Palmer at the end of the previous episode), accompanies Cooper and Truman to the Great Northern Hotel where 'Bob' is supposedly present. A background tapping is revealed to be a group of sailors bouncing rubber balls on the wooden floor of the hotel foyer.

Hawk finds Harold Smith hanged in his orchid greenhouse. Meanwhile at the Palmer residence the record player plays Louis Armstrong's 'What a Wonderful World'. Madeleine sits between Sara and Leland on the sofa; they drink coffee as she announces her plans to return home (to Missoula, Montana – Lynch's home town). The camera tracks past portraits of Laura and the playing record in the foreground. 'It's not like Missoula is the far end of the universe,' says Madeleine. Leland squeezes her knee. 'We're going to miss you very much,' he says. The scene dissolves to the police photographing the dead body of Harold Smith.

'What a Wonderful World' continues to play in the background, a perverse juxtaposition against the lonely character's suicide. Camera flash bulbs illuminate the room: his note reads *'J'ai une ame solitaire'* – 'I have a lonely soul'. The police find another of Laura's diaries.

Audrey confronts her father, demanding to know the extent of his involvement with Laura.

> AUDREY: Did you sleep with her?
> BEN: Yes (CU of Laura portrait on desk)
> AUDREY: Did you kill her?
> BEN: (CU portrait) I loved her.

Soon afterwards Truman, Cooper, Hawk and Andy take Ben away for questioning. Meanwhile at the Palmer household Sara crawls down the stairs struggling for breath as the gyrating fan thumps ominously in the background. She crawls on the floor, sees a white horse in the living room, and faints.

Leland, revealed as the human form housing the psychopathic 'Bob', is alone in the house with the unsuspecting Madeleine, and Sara, who is unconscious on the floor. The ensuing murder of Madeleine, possibly the most brutal sequence ever made for American prime-time television, is cross-cut with a static scene in a roadhouse where James and Donna grieve over the death of Harold Smith. Julee Cruise sings two Lynch/Badalamenti numbers ('The World Spins' and 'Rockin Back Inside My Heart') as the sheriff, Cooper and Margaret 'the log lady' sit at a table and watch. Margaret has already assured Cooper that 'something is happening.' Light descends on Cooper and the giant appears. 'It is happening again,' he says.

Leland transforms into Bob before the mirror and puts on a pair of white gloves. He holds Madeleine and punches her with clenched fist, then picks up her limp semi-conscious form as if to dance. 'Laura... my baby,' he mutters. 'You're going back to Missoula, Montana,' he shouts as he pushes her head into a framed painting of what appears to be a Montana landscape. A predatory bird lurks in the foreground.

The scene is cross-cut with Leland's transformation into Bob, and intensified with a roaming spotlight and hand-held camera. Bob's roars evoke a bestial hunting scene.

Cooper is lost in his trance at the Twin Peaks roadhouse, and the giant shakes his head and disappears. An elderly waiter approaches Cooper and tells him: 'I'm so sorry.'

Julee Cruise continues her melancholic ballad, and the atmosphere of loss and inevitability affects Donna and James, who sit holding hands in a nearby booth. Donna weeps. The ambivalent contrast of sentiment and cynicism, of psychopathic violence and mawkish humour, is more unsettling than the extreme violence of the murder itself. The scene is reminiscent of Frank Booth's assault on Dorothy in *Blue Velvet* in the perversity of the violence, yet ambiguous as, during the course of the *Twin Peaks* narrative we recognise both Leland and Madeleine as victims. Madeleine's 'crime', like Laura's, is not having an identity.

'Cooper'

Episode Twenty-two, Second Season. Written by Mark Frost, Harley Peyton and Robert Engels. Directed by David Lynch. 1991. 50 minutes

Over morning coffee, Lucy and Andy are consoled in the pre-credit sequence – Andy is to be the father of Lucy's child and the couple declare their love for each other. Once David Lynch's director's credit appears on the screen the remaining narrative courses veer towards the despondent.

Cooper unravels the mystery of the Ghostwood map, which contains oblique references to the giant and the dwarf of the red chamber. Windom Earle forces Annie through a secret opening in the forest, and leads her into the Black Lodge. The idea 'that a little opening could exist and we could go somewhere else,' says Lynch, 'excites me.'[12] Cooper follows them, while Truman waits outside.

Meanwhile Mike, once an unruly delinquent, now a well-groomed and quietly spoken young man, declares his love for Nadine. A blow to the head, however, has brought to an end Nadine's spell of regressed youth, and with it, the chance of Ed and Norma finally realising the lost opportunity of their formative years: Nadine embraces Ed, Ed and Norma regard each other with wistful resignation.

Donna, discovering Benjamin Horne is her biological father, prepares to leave home. Ben explains that, in setting the family record straight, he only 'wanted to do good' when Dr Hayward returns home and knocks Ben to the ground. Ben strikes his head against the stone fireplace and falls lifeless to the floor. The reasonable and stoic Will Hayward falls to his knees and rages in despair.

Audrey, now her father's closest ally, chains herself to the vault of the local bank in a protest action against the bank's involvement in the Ghostwood redevelopment scheme. Pete Martell and Andrew Packard unlock a bank box with a key left by Thomas Eckhardt, and all three perish in the explosion.

At the Double R Diner Heidi, the giggling German waitress, appears for the first time since Episode One and Bobby proposes to Shelley. This time he proposes marriage rather than a drive to her cabin. Their union, together with Lucy and Andy's reconciliation, is the nearest *Twin Peaks* approaches to the restoration of a moral order and a conventional formal closure. Shelley's teasing about being still married to Leo is succinctly answered in the following shot of Leo whose teeth are connected to an explosive device ensuring his imminent demise and the release of Shelley from any conjugal obligations.

The final episode portrays a series of transformations as characters become their psychological opposites, the most drastic of which occurs in Cooper himself. At the Double R, Cooper, using Sara Palmer as a medium, tells Major Briggs, 'I am in the Black Lodge with Windom Earle.'

Cooper 'loses himself', both literally and

metaphorically in the labyrinth of red velvet. A character reminiscent of Ben from *Blue Velvet* sings 'Under the Sycamore Tree', and Cooper is seated in an armchair. 'Some of your friends are here,' the dwarf tells him. Laura appears. 'I'll see you again in twenty-five years,' she says, then disappears. The giant appears, sits next to the dwarf and explains to Cooper that he and the dwarf are 'one and the same'.

Cooper's showdown, first with Windom Earle, then Bob, culminates in a deal that, for Cooper's soul, Annie is allowed to live. Cooper and Annie are found in the forest. Later at the hotel, in a bathroom mirror, Cooper is revealed as Bob's latest incarnation. Cooper, the Lynchian 'whole body', has lost touch with reality and succumbed to his unconscious 'dark' side, his unholy counterpart, 'Bob'.

As with other Lynch protagonists (Henry Spencer, Jeffrey Beaumont), Cooper's 'closed and perfect body' conceals an uneasy, obsessive mind. He is poet, psychic and psychotic. His tenuous hold on reality is represented throughout by one of his few physical pleasures: drinking coffee. Cherry pie might be next on the list, but sex was not on the list at all, making Cooper an easy target for the sexual destructiveness which 'Bob' represents. In the final scene, Cooper's coffee has solidified into a plastic lump and he has completely lost his grip on reality. 'How's Annie?' he says gloatingly to his transformed reflection, relishing the prospect of releasing 'Bob' on the next unsuspecting victim. Cooper's days of celibacy, self-control and rationality are at an end. The final credits appear over the surface of Cooper's solidified coffee. The portrait of Laura Palmer emerges against the black background.

With forms and styles extracted from both film and television, *Twin Peaks* plunders narrative elements from fairy tales, Greek myths, Nordic sagas and the popular mythologies of the twentieth century from *Lord of the Rings* to DC Comics, Native American folklore and popular astrology. Norwegians and Icelanders vie for the opportunity to develop Ghostwood, a sacred place like the Mirkwood of their own Scandinavian folktales, inhabited by the characters of Nordic legend, including the dwarf and the giant. Cooper could be Baldur, the refined poet of Nordic myth, pursued by Loki, his heinous assassin, or Orpheus journeying into the underworld to claim Eurydice (Annie), poisoned by the bite of a serpent (Earle, her abductor).

Cooper and Bob are also part of a post-modern quasi-mythology which has grown up around *Twin*

Peaks and has generated records, T-shirts, pulp fiction (*The Secret Diary of Laura Palmer, The Autobiography of FBI Special Agent Dale Cooper, An Access Guide to Twin Peaks*), and charter trips to Snoqualmie for Japanese tourists who are served Dale Cooper coffee and slices of cherry pie, and are photographed wrapped up in plastic on the banks of the Columbia River.

In *Twin Peaks: Fire Walk With Me*, Annie appears in Laura's bed and tells her that the 'good Dale' is stuck in the Black Lodge. In *Blue Velvet*, Jeffrey Beaumont survived his journey into the underworld; Henry Spencer's fate in *Eraserhead* is open-ended. Cooper's destiny is like that of Baldur: he must remain in the underworld until all creatures weep for his release. The opportunity for Cooper to wage war with the dark soul within himself in a *Twin Peaks II* is seemingly lost in the face of the public and critical failure of *Twin Peaks: Fire Walk With Me*. According to Lynch, '*Twin Peaks* on television is gone. The jury is out on whether or not we will ever be able to go in there again.'[13]

Conclusion

With half a dozen feature films and an internationally successful television series, what David Lynch's career lacks in profusion is compensated for by its diversity. His work virtually runs the gamut of visual expression available to the contemporary artist. He has made the transition from painter to animator, from working with the smallest of budgets to the largest, from experimental films to mass-market television productions, with a panache unequalled in contemporary film history. From an eclectic viewing public consisting mostly of a moon-bleached, urban, midnight art-house clientele, to the television audiences of the world, the story of David Lynch's career is as beguiling and as multi-layered as his films. His benign demeanour and public 'persona' reveal little, if anything, of the psychological processes at work in his films. As in the Magritte painting (see p. 5), Lynch's reflection shows nothing of his face, only the well-trimmed cut of his suit.

Eraserhead and *Blue Velvet* are virtuoso cinematic performances, imbued with Lynch's sinister, dark romanticism. *The Elephant Man* may be Lynch's most conventional picture, but remains one of the most unconventional Gothic romances of the commercial cinema. *Dune* now finds its 'cult' audience of enthusiasts who applaud the film's imagery and the very excesses that led to its initial harsh critical response. Lynch's intended four-hour long *Dune* 'mood poem', alas, seems destined to remain amongst the surfeit of material that never left the cutting room.

Wild at Heart remains the late 1980s' state of the cinematic art, as Jean-Luc Godard's *Pierrot le Fou* (1965) was 'state-of-the-art' cinema twenty-five years earlier. Little wonder that the cineastes at the 1990 Cannes Film Festival found it the most 'cinematic' of the festival's screenings, combined with Lynchian ingredients of perverse sexuality, decadence and abjection.

'I felt *Eraserhead*, I didn't think it,' says Lynch. Both

Eraserhead and *Blue Velvet* are the two Lynch films cast out from the darker realms of his psyche and most infused with his personal anxieties. By comparison *Twin Peaks: Fire Walk With Me* is a speculative excursion into the well-worn territory of *Twin Peaks* mythology, diminished by the marketing demands of the television medium.

Yet since *Blue Velvet* and *Wild at Heart*, Lynch has immersed himself in television, and television production. His television series, *On the Air* (1992), takes him deep into his much-favoured epoch, the mid-1950s – a meta-television programme about a television programme. In 1957, the Zoblotnik Broadcasting Company launches 'The Lester Guy Show' – 'retro-kitsch', proclaims the publicity material. Or the final word in post-modernist despondency, as Lynch delves into the trivia of collective popular culture, leaving self-analysis firmly in his own past. Three of the seven thirty-minute episodes of *On the Air* were broadcast in 1992 before the US ABC network took the programme off the air, due to low ratings and critical indifference, they claimed. Lynch's former partner, Mark Frost, attributes the series' poor performance to bad scheduling and the American viewing public's inability to grasp bizarre humour.

'Anything different on television is a potential success or just the opposite – a catastrophe. And for the most part it's a catastrophe,' Lynch told a French film journal following the success of the first season of *Twin Peaks*. For Lynch, television's preoccupation with surfaces and wariness of anything deeper that may be concealed beneath them, is both alluring and inhibiting.

In *Wild at Heart*, Sailor and Lula dare not delve below the surface of their own vulnerable relationship, or look beyond superficial America viewed from the inside of their open-topped car. The relationship Lynch describes as 'a modern romance' concerns as much the post-modern flirtation with image for its own sake as the relationship between hungry youth. Lynch toys with a transient iconography for a coterie of cineastes, when his talent is for delving beneath surfaces.

The Gothic mood of David Lynch's films is an ominous shadow of an imaginary past. The achievement of *The Elephant Man* is the credibility of the world that Lynch has made his own, just as *Eraserhead* was his adopted world. They are places filled with 'dark secrets' and unresolved mystery. The tone in Lynch's films suggests a return to times gone by, and a return to the values of a past which is both undefined and idealised. He is an old-fashioned wolf in post-modernist sheep's clothing – strip away the wool and Lynch emerges as a staunch conservative ill at ease in a loosely structured modern world.

The forced smiles of the archetypal 1950s US family, beaming from magazine advertisements and television screens, are as much a lure for Lynch as they are a subject to malign. The family unit represents structure, order, and stability; authority and respect for authority. There are no Democrat voicings of dissent or social critique in the Lynch world. Sheriff Truman is as true to his name as to the values of the president he was named after. Not even under the jurisdiction of J. Edgar Hoover himself has the FBI been so lovingly portrayed as before the camera of David Lynch. The threat is infiltration from outside: a 'false' Canadian mountie investigates FBI internal affairs in an attempt to discredit Cooper (*Twin Peaks* II.10); a colleague turns psychotic and goes over to the opposition, as in the case of Windom Earle (*Twin Peaks* II.2).

Twin Peaks is a homage to 1950s' values and lifestyle, where the unity of the family supercedes the will of the individual. It is a hidden enclave of safe untarnished America, locked up in a time-warp of black coffee and cherry pie, roadhouse diners and high-school proms. The threat lies in the present, the post-1950s 'dis-ease' with its narcotics and corruption, promiscuity and degeneracy, which lure vulnerable schoolgirls to their death.

Post-modernism breaks down structures, not consciously, but surreptitiously. It is the era when the imagination goes high-street shopping for relics of the past and fragments of the present. The essence of post-modernism is irreverence for history, what art historian Arnold Toynbee describes as 'the breakdown and disintegration' for us, 'the children of a post-Christian world'. This is Lynch's quandary, that he is both 'out of time', yet of the times – a romantic and a melodramatist in an age that shuns both.

Cliché and parody are the means at hand by which an 'old-fashioned country boy' expresses his anxieties and his yearning for the stability and structure of times gone by. The 'shock' of Lynch's 'new' is not so much the incursion into virgin territory, but that it integrates old and new, the surreal and the everyday, narrative and non-narrative, sentiment and cynicism.

The 'whole-body' Lynch protagonist is threatened by chaos because he is incapable of internalising the chaos of his own disordered spirit. Henry Spencer loses his frail grip on reality and disappears through a fissure of the material world and into another place, where a deformed smiling lady dances on a stage full of umbilical cords. Jeffrey Beaumont's adolescent restlessness leads him into a netherworld of violent assailants. Dale Cooper clutches his coffee cup and his tape recorder as his remaining tokens of normality. He has failed to identify a murderer before another victim is claimed, and he fails to protect a woman he loves from the hands of a psychopath: for all his visions, psychic premonitions and advanced deduction techniques, he fails utterly, as Jeffrey fails to contend with violence without becoming violent himself, as Henry Spencer fails to deal with reality without succumbing to the nightmare of his psychosis.

The 'whole body' is a 'closed body' and the Lynch protagonists' 'closure' conceals a narrow conservatism which underlies an inability to contend with reality. Recurring themes of blighted romance and perverse desire reveal a film-maker daring in his vision, yet conservative in conviction. Lynch gives us traditional moral tales in post-modern apparel.

Notes

Introduction

1. David Breskin: 'The Rolling Stone Interview with David Lynch', *Rolling Stone*, 6 September 1990.
2. Actor Jack Nance, quoted in 'Moving Pictures', BBC 2, UK; John Powers on David Lynch. Transmitted 20 October 1990.
3. *Rolling Stone*, 6 September 1990.
4. Attributed to the French actor and surrealist, Antonin Artaud, quoted in Wexman: *Roman Polanski*, Columbus Books (London) 1987, p. 18.
5. *Cinefantastique*, September, 1984.
6. Jonathan Ross Presents For One Week Only: David Lynch. Channel Four, UK. Transmitted 19 October 1990.
7. *Cinefantastique*, September 1984.
8. Attributed to Paul Eluard and paraphrased in Balakian: *Surrealism – The Road to the Absolute*, George Allen and Unwin (London), 1972, p.125.
9. David Lynch Presents: 'Ruth, Roses and Revolver', Arena, BBC 2, UK, 1987.
10. *Rolling Stone*, 6 September 1990.
11. For a comparison between the work of Magritte and Poe, *see* Peter Cornell's article: 'Magritte med Poe som guide', *Expressen* (Stockholm), 18 August 1992.
12. As outlined in David Pirie: *A Heritage of Horror – The English Gothic Cinema 1946 – 1972*, Gordon Fraser (London), 1973.
13. Pirie, p.11
14. Martin Bickman: *American Romantic Psychology*, Spring Publications (Dallas), 1988, p. 59.
15. John Weir Perry: *The Self in Psychotic Process*, revised edition, Spring Publications (Dallas), 1987, p. 59.

16. Umberto Eco: *Travels in Hyperreality*, Picador (London), 1987, p. 209.
17. Ibid, p. 209.
18. Richard Kearney: *The Wake of the Imagination*, Hutchinson (London), 1988, p. 330.
19. Gilles Deleuze: *Cinema 1 – The Movement-Image*, Athlone Press (London), 1986, p. 281.
20. Ann Persson: 'Mr Lynch balanserar på gränsen', *Dagens Nyheter* (Stockholm), 29 October 1990.
21. *Rolling Stone*, 6 September 1990.
22. As defined by Bordwell and Thompson in *Film Art*, third edition, McGraw Hill (New York), 1989.
23. *Rolling Stone*, 6 September 1990.
24. Ibid.
25. Carl Jung: *Collected Works*, Vol. 9, Part I, p. 82.
26. Deleuze, p. 210.
27. David Bartholemew in *Cinefantastique* and Danny Peary in *Cult Movies*, Dell Publishing (New York), 1981.
28. Quoted in Jane Root: 'Everyone a Voyeur' in *Monthly Film Bulletin*, April 1987.
29. This aspect of Lynch's cinema is covered fully in Anne Jerslev: *David Lynch i vore ojne*, Forlaget Frydenlund (Copenhagen), 1992.
30. Julia Kristeva: *Powers of Horror,* Columbia University Press, 1982, p. 26.
31. Ibid, p. 15.
32. *Rolling Stone*, 6 September 1990.
33. Ibid.
34. Kristeva is summarized in Elizabeth Grosz: *Sexual Subversions*, Allen and Unwin Australia (Sydney), 1989, pp. 70-78.
35. *Rolling Stone*, 6 September 1990.
36. Ibid.
37. Richard M. Gollin: *A Viewer's Guide to Film,* McGraw Hill Inc (New York), 1992, pp. 105 ff.
38. *Rolling Stone*, 6 September 1990.
39. Carl Jung: *Collected Works*, Vol. 6 p. 426.
40. Carl Jung: *Collected Works*, Vol. 5 p. 375.
41. Clas von Sydow, 'David Lynch', *Scanorama*, March 1991.
42. Janey Place: 'Women in Film Noir', in Kaplan (ed): *Women in Film Noir*, British Film Institute (London), 1980, p. 46.

43. Dyer: 'Resistance through charisma', in Kaplan (ed): *Women in Film Noir*, p 92.
44. *Rolling Stone*, 6 September 1990.
45. Ibid.

The Alphabet/The Grandmother

1. *Rolling Stone*, 6 September 1990.
2. *Monthly Film Bulletin*, April 1987.
3. *Rolling Stone*, 6 September 1990.

Eraserhead

1. In some scenes Lynch used actual umbilical cords fetched from the maternity ward of the local hospital. Noted in Anne Jerslev: *David Lynch i vore ojne*.
2. Sean French: 'The Heart of the Cavern', *Sight and Sound*, Spring 1987.
3. Jonathan Ross Presents For One Week Only: David Lynch, Channel Four, UK. Transmitted 19 October 1990.
4. Ibid.
5. Ibid.
6. Ibid.
7. David Lynch Presents: 'Ruth, Roses and Revolver,' Arena, BBC 2, UK, 1987.
8. Jonathan Ross Presents For One Week Only: David Lynch.
9. *Rolling Stone*, 6 September 1990.
10. Elias Canetti: *Kafka's Other Trial,* Penguin (London), 1982, p. 48.
11. Quoted in Canetti, p. 50.
12. Jonathan Ross Presents For One Week Only: David Lynch.
13. Canetti, p. 48.
14. Canetti, p. 48.
15. Omnibus: 'The Dream Factory', BBC 2, UK, 1987.
16. Robert Grinell: *Alchemy in a Modern Woman*, Spring Publications (Dallas), 1973, p. 78.
17. Ingmar Bergman: *Bilder*, Norstedts (Stockholm), 1990, p. 55.

The Elephant Man

1. Act 1, Scene iv.
2. Sir Frederick Treves: *The Elephant Man*. Reissued as Appendix Three to Howell and Ford: *The True Story of the Elephant Man*, revised and illustrated edition, Allison and Busby (London), 1983.
3. Ibid.
4. Ibid, p. 239.
5. Ibid, p. 175.
6. Ibid, p. 221.
7. Ibid, p. 213.
8. Ibid, p. 236.
9. Ibid, p. 238.
10. Ibid, p. 242.
11. Ibid, p. 242.
12. 'In an age of horror movies this is a film which takes the material of horror and translates it into loving kindness.' Dilys Powell, *Punch*, 1980. Quoted in *Halliwell's Film Guide*, Seventh Edition.
13. Howell and Ford, p. 160.
14. Ibid, p. 245.
15. Derek Winnert: 'Great Outsider', in *Radio Times*, 13 October 1990.
16. Noel Cobb: *Prospero's Island,* Coventure (London), p. 122ff—explores the archetypal relationship between Prospero and Caliban.
17. Howell and Ford, p. 221.
18. Ibid, p. 236.
19. *Rolling Stone*, 6 September 1990.
20. Lynch designed special make-up and costume for the character, which was later taken over by production make-up designers.
21. According to Treves, Merrick had learned to read and write at about the age of ten during his first hospital visit, recovering from an early operation.

Dune

1. Jonathan Ross Presents For One Week Only: David Lynch.
2. Jonathan Ross Presents For One Week Only: Alejandro Jodorowski.
3. Production and pre-production details from Ed

Naha: *The Making of Dune*, W H Allen (London), 1984.

4. Sean French: 'The Heart of the Cavern', *Sight and Sound*, Spring 1987.

5. Jonathan Ross Presents For One Week Only: David Lynch.

6. Leonard Maltin: *Movie and Video Guide 1991*, New American Library (New York), 1991.

7. Frank Herbert: *Dune*, Chilton Book Company (Radnor), 1965, p. 474.

8. Ibid, p. 46.

9. Antony Easthope: *What a Man's Gotta Do – The Masculine Myth in Popular Culture*, Paladin (London), 1986, pp 166f.

10. Derek Longhurst: 'Science Fiction – The Dreams of Men', in Longhurst (ed): *Gender, Genre and Narrative Pleasure,* Unwin Hyman (London), 1989, p. 207.

11. Ibid, p. 198.

12. Joseph Campbell: *The Masks of God – Primitive Mythology*, revised edition, The Viking Press (New York), 1969, p. 73ff.

13. 'The hero represents the positive favourable action of the unconscious, while the dragon is its negative and unfavourable action.' Carl Jung: *Collected Works*, Vol. 5, p. 374.

14. Leslie Halliwell: *Halliwell's Film Guide*, Seventh Edition, Paladin (London), 1989.

Blue Velvet

1. David Lynch Presents: 'Ruth, Roses and Revolver', Arena, BBC 2, UK, 1987.

2. Jane Root: 'Everyone a Voyeur', *Monthly Film Bulletin*, April 1987.

3. Quoted in Gerard Lenne: 'Resa till hjärnans medelpunkt', *Montage* 24-25 (Stockholm), 1990, originally published in *La Revue du Cinema*.

4. Ibid.

5. Ibid.

6. From the shooting script. Quoted in Bret Wood: 'Bluer Velvet', *Video Watchdog*, No. 4, 1991.

7. Bret Wood: 'Bluer Velvet'

8. Michel Ciment and Hubert Niogret: 'Conversation with David Lynch', published in *Positif* (Paris) and

Montage 24-25 (Stockholm), 1990.

9. Arthur Hough: 'Trials and Tribulations – Thirty Years of Sitcom', in Richard Adler (ed.): *Understanding Television*, Praeger (New York), 1983, pp. 204-207.

10. Jonathan Ross Presents For One Week Only: David Lynch.

11. Bret Wood: 'Bluer Velvet'.

Wild at Heart

1. Gifford: *Wild at Heart*, Paladin (London), 1990, p.159.

2. *Rolling Stone*, 6 September 1990.

3. William Boyd: *Brazzaville Beach,* Penguin (London), 1990, p. 87.

4. Jonathan Ross Presents For One Week Only: David Lynch.

5. Philip Kaplan: *The Best, Worst and Most Unusual Hollywood Musicals*, Publications International (Illinois), 1983, pp. 74-75.

6. Salman Rushdie: *The Wizard of Oz*, British Film Institute (London), 1992; in their series of 'books to honour the great films of world cinema'.

7. Humphrey Carpenter and Mary Prichard: *The Oxford Companion to Children's Literature*, Oxford University Press (Oxford), 1984.

8. *Rolling Stone*, 6 September 1990.

9. *Sight and Sound*, Autumn 1990.

10. Gavin Lambert, *Sight and Sound*, Summer 1955.

11. *Rolling Stone*, 6 September 1990.

Twin Peaks: Fire Walk With Me

1. David Lynch interviewed at Cannes Film Festival, May 1992.

2. Janey Place: 'Women in Film Noir', in Kaplan (ed.): *Women in Film Noir*, British Film Institute (London), 1978, p. 43.

3. The director's name is used as a means of identification, rather than authorship. Rouben Mamoulian began directing the picture, and some of his scenes remain in the final print – including the characteristic Mamoulian opening. Three writers are credited to the screenplay, based on Vera Caspray's novel.

4. Place: 'Women in Film Noir', p. 50.
5. Jonathan Ross Presents For One Week Only: David Lynch.
6. Claire Douglas: *The Woman in the Mirror – Analytical Psychology and the Feminine,* Sigo Press (Boston), 1990, p. 173.
7. Jean Cocteau: *Diary of a Film,* Dover (New York), 1965.
8. David Lynch Presents; 'Ruth, Roses and Revolver', Arena, BBC 2, UK, 1987.
9. See Joseph Henderson: 'Ancient Myths and Modern Man', in Jung (ed): *Man and his Symbols,* Aldus Books (London), 1964, pp. 137-140.
10. Kevin Jackson (ed.): *Schrader on Schrader,* Faber (London), 1990, p. 189.
11. Stephen Pizello: 'Twin Peaks: Fire Walk With Me', in *American Cinematographer*, September 1992.
12. 'David Lynch's *Twin Peaks: Fire Walk With Me* – The Press Conference', from the transcript published in *Cinema Papers* (Melbourne), August 1992.
13. Ibid.
14. Ibid.

Twin Peaks

1. Umberto Eco: *Travels in Hyperreality*, p. 208.
2. Ibid, p. 202.
3. André Breton: *Discours sur le Peu de Realite*, quoted in Anna Balakian: *Surrealism – The Road to the Absolute*, George Allen and Unwin (London), 1959, p. 13.
4. Quoted in Brian Henderson: 'Romantic Comedy Today – Semi-Tough or Impossible', in Barry Grant (ed): *Film Genre Reader,* University of Texas Press, 1986, p. 311.
5. Andrew Sinclair: *Under Milk Wood – A Screenplay,* Lorrimar (London) 1973, p. 6.
6. Mark Frost interviewed in Jonathan Ross Presents For One Week Only: David Lynch.
7. Sinclair: *Under Milk Wood – A Screenplay*, p. 6.
8. *Rolling Stone*, 6 September 1990.
9. 'David Lynch's *Twin Peaks: Fire Walk With Me* – The Press Conference', *Cinema Papers* (Melbourne), August 1992.

10. Michael Ciment and Hubert Niogret: Samtal med David Lynch, *Montage* 24-25 (Stockholm), 1990.
11. 'David Lynch's *Twin Peaks: Fire Walk With Me* – The Press Conference', *Cinema Papers* (Melbourne), August 1992.
12. Ibid.
13. Ibid.

Chronology

1946 b. Missoula, Montana, 20 January.

1961 Family moves from Pacific Northwest.

1964 Corcoran School of Art, Washington DC, and Boston Museum School.

1965 Begins studies at Pennsylvania Academy of Fine Arts, Philadelphia.

1967 Graduates art school – completes first animated film.

1968 *The Alphabet*

1970 *The Grandmother*. Daughter Jennifer born. Moves to Los Angeles with wife and daughter.

1971 Begins work on *Eraserhead* script – intermittent years, various jobs, including delivering papers, building garages and plumbing.

1972 May – filming of *Eraserhead* begins.

1976 *Eraserhead* completed.

1977 *Eraserhead*'s official premiere.

1978 Signs contract with Mel Brooks and Brooksfilms to direct *The Elephant Man*.

1979 Working in London with mainly British crew on *The Elephant Man*.

1980 *The Elephant Man*.

1981 Begins work on script of *Dune*.

1983 Principal photography on *Dune* begins in Mexico.

1984 *Dune* released.

1985 Signs contract with de Laurentiis Entertainment Group for a 'low-budget' film, with final cut. Begins contributing 'The Angriest Dog in the World' for the *LA Reader*.

1986 *Blue Velvet* released.

1987 Several feature filmscript projects underway, including two comedies; *Ronnie Rocket* and *One Saliva Bubble*. Later shelved.

1989 *Twin Peaks* pilot completed.

1990 *Wild at Heart* released, awarded Palme d'Or, Cannes Film Festival in May 1990. Lynch/Frost Productions of *Twin Peaks* screened on US television and in sixty other countries.

1991 Lynch/Frost Productions: final episodes of *Twin Peaks*, second season. Also the release of *American Chronicles*.

1992 *Twin Peaks: Fire Walk With Me* released. Premiere Cannes Film Festival in a blaze of publicity – flops. Lynch/Frost Productions television situation comedy series: 'On the Air' – dropped by ABC network after three of seven thirty-minute episodes are transmitted. Lynch/Frost Productions dissolved. Lynch signs three picture contract with the French company CIBY 2000 (Deux Mille).
Lynch reveals plans to film Kafka's *Metamorphosis*. He signs a contract with television company HBO for a TV anthology entitled *The Hotel*. Each half-hour episode takes place in the same hotel room, in different historical periods, beginning in 1900.
Jennifer Lynch, aged 22, directs her first film, *Boxing Helena*, in which Sherilyn Fenn plays a woman without arms or legs, locked inside a box by a love-smitten doctor (Julian Sands).

Filmography

Six Figures get Sick (1967) Animation loop.
Running time: c. 30 seconds

The Alphabet (1968) Live action/animated. Written, animated and directed by David Lynch. Produced by H. Barton Wasserman.
Running time: 4 minutes

The Grandmother (1970) Live action/animated. Written, photographed, animated and directed by David Lynch.
Sound – Alan Splet. Produced by David Lynch with financial assistance from the American Film Institute.
Leading players: Richard White (Boy), Dorothy McGinnis (Grandmother), Virginia Maitland (Mother), Robert Chadwick (Father)
Running time: 34 minutes

Eraserhead (1976) Written, directed, produced and edited by David Lynch. Financed by the American Film Institute. Photographer – Frederick Elmes. Camera lighting – Frederick Elmes, Herbert Cardwell. Sound – Alan Splet. Production design – David Lynch. Director's assistant – Catherine Coulson.
Leading players: John Nance (Henry Spencer), Charlotte Stewart (Mary X), Allen Joseph (Mr X), Jeanne Bates (Mrs X), Judith Ann Roberts (Beautiful Girl Across the Hall), Laurel Near (Lady in the Radiator), Jack Fisk (Man in the Planet), Darwin Jaston (Paul), Neil Moran (The Boss), Hal Landon Jr. (Pencil Machine Operator), Jennifer Lynch (little girl), Peggy Lynch and Doddie Keeler (people digging in the alley), V. Phipps Wilson ('Mr Roundheels', Landlady)
Running time: 89 minutes (Original running time: 110 minutes)

The Elephant Man (1980) Directed by David Lynch.

Written by Christopher de Vore, Eric Bergren and David Lynch. Based on accounts of the life of Joseph Merrick including Sir Frederick Treves: The Elephant Man and Other Reminiscences' and Ashley Montagu: 'The Elephant Man – A Study in Human Dignity'. Produced by Jonathan Sanger and Stuart Cornfield for Brooksfilms. Photographer – Freddie Francis. Sound – Alan Splet and David Lynch. Production Design – Stuart Craig. Editing – Anne V. Coates. Music – John Morris.
Leading players: Anthony Hopkins (Frederick Treves), John Hurt (John Merrick), John Gielgud (Mr Carr Gomm), Freddie Jones (Bytes), Anne Bancroft (Mrs Kendal), Michael Elphick (Night Porter), Wendy Hiller (Mrs Mothershead), Hannah Gordon (Anne Treves)
Running time: 124 minutes

Dune (1984) Written and directed by David Lynch. Based on the novel 'Dune' by Frank Herbert. Photography – Freddie Francis. Sound – Alan Splet. Editor – Antony Gibbs. Production design – Anthony Masters. Music – Toto, Brian Eno. Produced by Rafaella de Laurentiis. Creatures created by Carlo Rambaldi.
Leading players: Kyle MacLachlan (Paul Atreides), Francesca Annis (Lady Jessica), Jose Ferrer (Padisha Emperor Shaddam IV), Linda Hunt (Shadout Mapes), Freddie Jones (Thufir Howat), Richard Jordan (Idaho), Brad Dourif (Harkonnen's Doctor), Virginia Madsen (Princess Irulan), Silvana Mangano (Reverend Mother Ramallo), Kenneth McMillan (Baron Vladimir Harkonnen), Jack Nance (Nefud), Sian Phillips (Reverend Mother Gaius Helen Mohiam), Dean Stockwell (Dr Wellington Yueh), Jurgen Prochnow (Duke Leto Atreides), Sting (Feyd Rautha), Max von Sydow (Dr Kynes), Sean Young (Chani).
Running time: 140 minutes

Blue Velvet (1986) Written and directed by David Lynch. Photography – Frederick Elmes. Sound – Alan Splet. Editor – Duwayne Dunham. Music – Angelo Badalamenti. Production Design – Patricia Norris. Produced by de Laurentiis Entertainment Group, Richard Roth.
Leading players: Kyle MacLachlan (Jeffrey Beaumont), Isabella Rossellini (Dorothy Vallens), Laura Dern (Sandy Williams), Dennis Hopper (Frank Booth), Hope Lange (Mrs Williams), Dean Stockwell (Ben), George Dickerson (Detective Williams)
Running time: 120 minutes

Wild at Heart (1990) Written and directed by David
Lynch. Based on the novel 'Wild at Heart' by Barry
Gifford. Photography – Frederick Elmes. Sound – Alan
Splet. Editor – Duwayne Dunham. Music – Angelo
Badalamenti. Produced by Propaganda Films; Monty
Montgomery, Steve Golin, Sigurjon Sighvatsson.
Leading players: Nicolas Cage (Sailor Ripley), Laura
Dern (Lula Pace Fortune), Diane Ladd (Marietta Pace),
Harry Dean Stanton (Johnnie Farragut), Willem Dafoe
(Bobby Peru), Isabella Rossellini (Perdita Durango)
Grace Zabriskie (Juana), J. E. Freeman (Marcello
Santos), Crispin Glover (Dell)
Running time: 124 minutes

Twin Peaks: Fire Walk With Me (1992) Written by
David Lynch and Robert Engels. Directed by David
Lynch. Photography – Ron Garcia. Sound design –
David Lynch. Editor – Mary Sweeney. Music – Angelo
Badalamenti. Scenography and costumes – Patricia
Norris. Produced by Mark Frost and David Lynch/CIBY
Pictures.
Leading players: Sheryl Lee (Laura Palmer), Ray Wise
(Leland Palmer), Chris Isaak (Chester Desmond), Kiefer
Sutherland (Sam Stanley), David Lynch (Gordon Cole),
Kyle MacLachlan (Dale Cooper), David Bowie (Phillip
Jeffries), Harry Dean Stanton (Carl Rodd), Moira Kelly
(Donna Hayward), Mädchen Amick (Shelley Johnson),
Dana Ashbrook (Bobby Briggs), James Marshall (James
Hurley), Pamela Gidley (Teresa Banks)
Running Time: 134 minutes

For television

Twin Peaks (1989/1991) Created by Mark Frost and
David Lynch. Music – Angelo Badalamenti.
Leading players: Kyle MacLachlan (FBI Special Agent
Dale Cooper), Michael Ointkean (Sheriff Harry S.
Truman), Richard Beymer (Benjamin Horne), Sherilyn
Fenn (Audrey Horne), Sheryl Lee (Laura Palmer/
Madeleine Ferguson), Ray Wise (Leland Palmer), Grace
Zabriskie (Sara Palmer), David Lynch (Gordon Cole),
Lara Flynn Boyle (Donna Hayward), Warren Frost (Dr
William Hayward), Mädchen Amick (Shelley Johnson),
Eric Da Re (Leo Johnson), Dana Ashbrook (Bobby
Briggs), James Marshall (James Hurley), Jack Nance
(Pete Martell), Piper Laurie (Catherine Martell), Joan
Chen (Jocelyn Packard), Catherine Coulson (Log Lady),

Russ Tamblyn (Lawrence Jacoby), Everett McGill (Ed Hurley), Wendy Robie (Nadine Hurley), Peggy Lipton (Norma Jennings), Chris Mulkey (Hank Jennings), Miguel Ferrer (Albert Rosenfield)

First season

Episode 1. Written by Mark Frost and David Lynch. Directed by David Lynch. 1989. 90 minutes.

Episode 2. Written by Mark Frost and David Lynch. Directed by Duwayne Dunham. 1990. 45 minutes.

Episode 3. Written by Mark Frost and David Lynch. Directed by David Lynch. 1990. 45 minutes.

Episode 4. Written by Harley Peyton. Directed by Tina Rathborne. 1990. 45 minutes.

Episode 5. Written by Robert Engels. Directed by Tim Hunter. 1990. 45 minutes.

Episode 6. Written by Mark Frost. Directed by Lesli Linka Glatter. 1990. 45 minutes.

Episode 7. Written by Harley Peyton. Directed by Caleb Deschanel. 1990. 45 minutes.

Episode 8. Written and directed by Mark Frost. 1990. 45 minutes.

Second season

Episode 1. Story by Mark Frost and David Lynch. Teleplay by Mark Frost. Directed by David Lynch. 1990. 90 minutes.

Episode 2. Written by Harley Peyton. Directed by David Lynch. 1990. 45 minutes.

Episode 3. Written by Robert Engels. Directed by Lesli Linka Glatter. 1990. 45 minutes.

Episode 4. Written by Jerry Stahl with Mark Frost, Harley Peyton and Robert Engels. Directed by Todd Holland. 1990. 45 minutes.

Episode 5. Written by Barry Pullman. Directed by Graeme Clifford. 1990. 45 minutes.

Episode 6. Written by Harley Peyton and Robert Engels. Directed by Lesli Linka Glatter. 1990. 45 minutes.

Episode 7. Written by Mark Frost. Directed by David Lynch. 1990. 45 minutes.

Episode 8. Written by Scott Frost. Directed by Caleb Deschanel. 1990. 45 minutes.

Episode 9. Written by Mark Frost, Harley Peyton and

Robert Engels. Directed by Tim Hunter. 1990.
45 minutes.

Episode 10. Written by Tricia Brock. Directed by Tina Rathborne. 1990. 45 minutes.

Episode 11. Written by Barry Pullman. Directed by Duwayne Dunham. 1990. 45 minutes.

Episode 12. Written by Harley Peyton and Robert Engels. Directed by Caleb Deschanel. 1990. 45 minutes.

Episode 13. Written by Harley Peyton. Directed by Todd Holland. 1990. 45 minutes.

Episode 14. Written by Scott Frost. Directed by Uli Edel. 1990. 45 minutes.

Episode 15. Written by Harley Peyton and Robert Engels. Directed by Diane Keaton. 1990. 45 minutes.

Episode 16. Written by Tricia Brock. Directed by Lesli Linka Glatter. 1990. 45 minutes.

Episode 17. Written by Barry Pullman. Directed by James Foley. 1991. 45 minutes.

Episode 18. Written by Harley Peyton and Robert Engels. Directed by Duwayne Durham. 1991. 45 minutes.

Episode 19. Written by Mark Frost and Harley Peyton. Directed by Jonathan Sanger. 1991. 45 minutes.

Episode 20. Written by Harley Peyton and Robert Engels. Directed by Stephen Gyllenhaal. 1991. 45 minutes.

Episode 21. Written by Barry Pullman. Directed by Tim Hunter. 1991. 45 minutes.

Episode 22. Written by Mark Frost, Harley Peyton and Robert Engels. Directed by David Lynch. 1991. 45 minutes.

Also

Twin Peaks, European version. Issued on video 1989, 110 minutes.
Consists of Twin Peaks Episode One, the dancing dwarf dream sequence from Episode three, and fifteen minutes' new material written and directed by Lynch in which Cooper and Truman trace 'Bob' to a hospital basement and shoot him.

Industrial Symphony Number One – The Dream of the Brokenhearted (Julee Cruise in concert). 1990. Directed by David Lynch. 50 minutes.

The Cowboy and the Frenchman. (An episode from 'Les Francais vus par...), 1989. Written and directed by David Lynch. 23 minutes.

On the Air, (7 x 25 minutes). 1992.

Wicked Game, 1990. Music video with Chris Isaak.

We Care About New York, 1990. Information film for New York City.

Opium, 1990. Advertisement for Yves Saint Laurent.

Obsession, 1990. Advertisement for Calvin Klein.

As actor:

Zelly and Me. (1988). With Isabella Rossellini.

As presenter:

Ruth, Roses and Revolver. (1987). Directed by Helen Gallagher.

In 1987 David Lynch made a documentary programme for BBC television's Arena entitled *David Lynch Presents: 'Ruth, Roses and Revolver'*. (Named after a film by Man Ray.) In the programme he presents extracts from what he considers films and filmmakers most significant to his own work. These include:

Dreams That Money Can Buy (Hans Richter, 1946)
'Films should have a surface story but underneath things should happen – things should resonate.'

Entr'acte (Rene Claire and Francis Picabia, 1924)
Man Ray and Marcel Duchamp play chess on a Parisian rooftop accompanied by the music of Erik Satie. This twenty-minute long film produced by the Ballet Suedoise was made to be shown between acts of a Dadaist ballet. 'The greatest influence on my work is the city of Philadelphia. Man Ray was born in Philadelphia...'

Emak-Bakia (Man Ray, 1926)

Subtitled 'Cinepoeme', the title means 'leave me alone' in Hungarian. The film combines animated sequences with live-action footage – eyes are painted on eye-lids.

The Girl with the Prefabricated Heart (Ferdinand Leger – from *Dreams That Money Can Buy* – Hans Richter, 1946)
Lynch compares the film with a contemporary music video. Singer Libby Holman accompanies images of dress mannequins – dressed and animated into a sequence of courtship. 'Anything that looks human but isn't is frightening,' says Lynch.

Vormittagspuk (Hans Richter, 1928)

'Ghosts in the Morning' concerns four hats in search of

four heads, which they finally locate seated at a table for morning tea. A trance-like rhythmic music accompanies images of the swirling hats, guns and clocks.

'Things beneath the surface,' says Lynch. 'Strange feelings of death, or opposites, or time... How exciting it must have been to have been a filmmaker in the early days of the cinema, because not only was it so magical to see paintings begin to move, but they could start altering time...'

Man with a Movie Camera (Dziga Vertov, 1929)

Lynch quotes Sergei Eisenstein's view of Vertov – 'a visual hooligan!'

Discs (Marcel Duchamp, based on his own painting *Nude Descending a Staircase* accompanied by the music of John Cage. Included in *Dreams That Money Can Buy* – Hans Richter, 1946)

Blood of a Poet (Le Sang d'un Poete – Jean Cocteau, 1930)

'Cocteau is the heavyweight of surrealism.' The first episode, 'The Wounded Hand', concerns an artist who acquires a second mouth on the palm of his hand.

Desire (Max Ernst – from *Dreams That Money Can Buy* – Hans Richter, 1946)

'I'm very happy to be a fellow traveller with any one of these guys...'

References

Books

Adler, Richard: *Understanding Television*, Praeger (New York), 1983.

Allen, Robert: *Channels of Discourse, Reassembled*, Routledge (London), 1992.

Andrew, Geoff: *The Film Handbook*, Longman (London), 1989.

Balakian, Anna: *Surrealism – The Road to the Absolute*, George Allen and Unwin (London), 1972.

Bergman, Ingmar: *Bilder*, Norstedts (Stockholm), 1990.

Bickman, Martin: *American Romantic Psychology*, Spring Publications (Dallas), 1980.

Bordwell, David and Thompson, Kristen: *Film Art*, third edition, McGraw Hill (New York), 1989.

Canetti, Elias: *Kafka's Other Trial*, Penguin (London), 1982.

Carpenter, Humphrey and Prichard, Mary: *The Oxford Companion to Children's Literature*, Oxford University Press (Oxford), 1984.

Cobb, Noel: *Prospero's Island*, Coventure (London), 1984.

Cocteau, Jean: *Diary of a Film*, Dover (New York), 1965.

Deleuze, Gilles: *Cinema 1 – The Movement-Image*, Athlone Press (London), 1986.

Douglas, Claire: *The Woman in the Mirror – Analytical Psychology and the Feminine*, Sigo Press (Boston), 1990.

Easthope, Antony: *What a Man's Gotta Do – The Masculine Myth in Popular Culture*, Paladin (London), 1986.

Eco, Umberto: *Travels in Hyperreality*, Picador (London), 1987.

Frost, Scott: *The Autobiography of FBI Special Agent Dale Cooper – My Life, My Tapes*, Penguin Books (London), 1991.

Gifford, Barry: *Wild at Heart*, Paladin (London), 1990.

Gollin: *A Viewer's Guide to Film*, McGraw Hill (New York), 1992.

Grant, Barry (ed): *Film Genre Reader*, University of Texas Press, 1986.

Grinell, Robert: *Alchemy in a Modern Woman*, Spring Publications (Dallas), 1973.

Grosz, Elizabeth: *Sexual Subversions*, Allen and Unwin Australia (Sydney), 1989.

Herbert, Frank: *Dune*, Granada (London), 1967.

Howell, Michael and Ford, Peter: *The True History of the Elephant Man*, revised and illustrated edition, Allison and Busby (London), 1983.

Jackson, Kevin (ed): *Schrader on Schrader*, Faber (London), 1990.

Jencks, Charles: *Post Modernism – The New Classicism in Art and Architecture*, Academy Editions (London), 1987.

Jerslev, Anne: *David Lynch i vore ojne*, Frydenlund (Copenhagen), 1991.

Jung, Carl (ed): *Man and his Symbols*, Aldus Books (London), 1964.

Kaplan, E. Ann (ed): *Women In Film Noir*, British Film Institute (London), 1980.

Kaplan, Phillip: *The Best, Worst and Most Unusual Hollywood Musicals*, Publications International (Illinois), 1983.

Kearney, Richard: *The Wake of the Imagination*, Hutchinson (London), 1988.

Kristeva, Julia: *Powers of Horror*, Columbia University Press, 1983.

Leonard, Linda: *The Wounded Woman – Healing the Father-Daughter Relationship*, Shambhala Publications (Boston), 1982.

Longhurst, Derek: *Gender, Genre and Narrative Pleasure*, Unwin Hyman (London), 1987.

Lynch, Jennifer: *The Secret Diary of Laura Palmer*, Penguin Books (London), 1990.

Naha, Ed: *The Making of Dune*, W. H. Allen (London), 1984.

Peary, Danny: *Cult Movies*, Dell Publishing (New York), 1981.

Perry, J. W.: *The Self in Psychotic Process*, Spring Publications (Dallas), 1987.

Pirie, David: *A Heritage of Horror – The English Gothic Cinema 1946 – 1972*, Gordon Fraser (London), 1973.

Rushdie, Salman: *The Wizard of Oz*, British Film Institute (London), 1992.

Sinclair, Andrew: *Under Milk Wood – A Screenplay*, Lorrimar (London), 1973.

Twin Peaks Access Guide to the Town, Pocket Books, 1991.
Wexman, V. W.: *Roman Polanski*, Columbus Books, (London), 1987.

Articles

Berthelius, Marie: 'En outsider och gentleman' (*Chaplin*, Stockholm, September 1990)
Björkman, Stig: 'Bakom hjärnridån' (*Chaplin*, Stockholm, September 1990)
Breskin, David: 'The Rolling Stone Interview with David Lynch' (*Rolling Stone*, 6 September 1990)
Ciment, Michel and Niogret: 'Samtal med David Lynch' (*Montage* 24 -25, Stockholm 1990) Originally published in *Positif.*
Combs, Richard: 'Crude Thoughts and Fierce Forces' (*Monthly Film Bulletin*, April 1987)
Combs, Richard: 'Wild at Heart' (*Monthly Film Bulletin*, September 1990)
Cornell, Peter: 'Magritte med Poe som guide' (*Expressen*, Stockholm, 18 August 1992)
David Lynch's Twin Peaks: Fire Walk With Me - The Press Conference. (*Cinema Papers*, Melbourne, August, 1992)
French, Sean: 'The Heart of the Cavern' (*Sight and Sound*, Spring 1987)
Fuchs, Cynthia: '"I Looked For You In My Closet Tonight"' – Voyeurs and Victims in *Blue Velvet*' (*Spring 49 – A Journal of Archetype and Culture*, Spring Publications, Dallas, 1989)
Jenkins, Steve: 'Blue Velvet' (*Monthly Film Bulletin*, April 1987)
Julich, Solveig: 'Lynch-ståmningar' (*Montage* 26 - 27, Stockholm, 1991)
Lenne, Gerard: 'Resa till hjårnans medelpunkt' (*Montage* 24 - 25, Stockholm, 1990) Originally published in *La Revue du Cinema.*
Persson, Ann: 'Mr Lynch balanserar pågränsen' (*Dagens Nyheter*, Stockholm, 29 October 1990)
Rafferty, Terence: 'Out of the Blue' (*Sight and Sound*, Winter 1986)
Root, Jane: 'Everyone a Voyeur' (*Monthly Film Bulletin*, April 1987)
Rosenbaum, Jonathan: 'Wild at Heart' (*Sight and Sound*, Autumn 1990)
Strick, Philip: 'The Alphabet' (*Monthly Film Bulletin*, April 1987)

Strick, Philip: 'The Grandmother' (*Monthly Film Bulletin*, April 1987)
von Sydow, Clas: 'David Lynch' (*Scanorama*, March 1991)
Wood, Bret: 'Bluer Velvet' (*Video Watchdog* 4, 1991)

Television programmes

"Ruth, Roses and Revolver": David Lynch and Surrealism.' Presented by David Lynch, *Arena*, BBC Television, UK, 1987.
'David Lynch' *Jonathan Ross Presents For One Week Only*, Channel Four, UK, 1990.
'Alejandro Jodorowski' *Jonathan Ross Presents For One Week Only*, Channel Four, UK, 1991.
'David Lynch' John Powers on *Moving Pictures*, BBC Television, UK, 1990.
'The Dream Factory' *Omnibus*, BBC Television, UK, 1987.

Index